Success
Intelligence

❖ ❖ ❖

Also by Robert Holden, Ph.D.

BOOKS
Be Happy*
Happiness NOW!*
Shift Happens!*
Balancing Work & Life (with Ben Renshaw)
Every Day is a Gift (with Marika Borg) Burton)

CD PROGRAMMES
Be Happy*
Happiness NOW!*
Success Intelligence*

FLIP CALENDAR
Happiness NOW!*
Success NOW!*

❖ ❖ ❖

*Available from Hay House

Please visit Hay House USA: **www.hayhouse.com**®
Hay House Australia: **www.hayhouse.com.au**
Hay House UK: **www.hayhouse.co.uk**
Hay House South Africa: **www.hayhouse.co.za**
Hay House India: **www.hayhouse.co.in**

Success
Intelligence

Essential Lessons and Practices
from the World's Leading Coaching
Programme on Authentic Success

Robert Holden PhD

HAY HOUSE

Australia • Canada • Hong Kong • India
South Africa • United Kingdom • United States

Published and distributed in the United Kingdom by:
Hay House UK Ltd, 292B Kensal Rd, London W10 5BE.
Tel.: (44) 20 8962 1230; Fax: (44) 20 8962 1239. www.hayhouse.co.uk

Published and distributed in the United States of America by:
Hay House, Inc., PO Box 5100, Carlsbad, CA 92018-5100. Tel.: (1) 760 431 7695
or
(800) 654 5126; Fax: (1) 760 431 6948 or (800) 650 5115. www.hayhouse.com

Published and distributed in Australia by:
Hay House Australia Ltd, 18/36 Ralph St, Alexandria NSW 2015.
Tel.: (61) 2 9669 4299; Fax: (61) 2 9669 4144. www.hayhouse.com.au

Published and distributed in the Republic of South Africa by:
Hay House SA (Pty), Ltd, PO Box 990, Witkoppen 2068.
Tel./Fax: (27) 11 467 8904. www.hayhouse.co.za

Published and distributed in India by:
Hay House Publishers India, Muskaan Complex, Plot No.3, B-2, Vasant Kunj,
New Delhi – 110 070. Tel.: (91) 11 4176 1620; Fax: (91) 11 4176 1630.
www.hayhouse.co.in

Distributed in Canada by:
Raincoast, 9050 Shaughnessy St, Vancouver, BC V6P 6E5.
Tel.: (1) 604 323 7100; Fax: (1) 604 323 2600

Originally published in Great Britain in 2005 by Hodder & Stoughton,
a division of Hodder Headline

'More': words and music by Stephen Sondheim • © 1990 Touchstone Pictures
Music and Rilting Music Inc. USA • (12.5%) Warner/Chappell Artemis Music,
London W6 8BS • (92.5%) Warner/Chappell North America, London W6 8BS •
Reproduced by permission of International Music Publications Ltd • All rights
reserved

A catalogue record for this book is available from the British Library.

ISBN 978-1-8485-0167-6

Printed and bound in Great Britain by CPI William Clowes, Beccles, NR34 7TL.

Note: Every case history in this book appears with the consent of those
involved. Names have been altered where requested.

To my father

There are two kinds of intelligence: one acquired,
as a child in school memorises facts and concepts
from books and from what the teacher says,
collecting information from the traditional
sciences as well as from the new sciences.

With such intelligence you rise in the world.
You get ranked ahead or behind others
in regard to your competence in retaining
information. You stroll with this intelligence
in and out of fields of knowledge, getting always
more marks on your preserving tablets.

There is another kind of tablet, one
already completed and preserved inside you.
A spring overflowing its springbox. A freshness
in the centre of the chest. This other intelligence
does not turn yellow or stagnate. It's fluid,
and it doesn't move from outside to inside
through the conduits of plumbing-learning.

This second knowing is a fountainhead
from within you moving out.

    – **Rumi**[1]

Contents

Prologue

From the unreal lead me to the real.
– Ancient Hindu prayer[2]

Life is full of moments. One moment after another. Some moments pass by with you barely noticing. Other moments stay with you forever. They change the way you think, you see, you live.

I had a life-changing moment when I was 16 years old. It was a Saturday afternoon, and I was half-walking and half-running down a very busy street in Winchester – the city I grew up in. I was late and was on my way to meet friends outside a record shop. At 4 o'clock. As I hurried along, I noticed a man lying facedown on the pavement. He could have been dead or dying. Everyone saw him. He was in plain view. We all pretended not to see him.

I was going to pass him by. I was late. I was only 16. But something made me stop. I moved cautiously towards him. He was wearing an old, dishevelled coat. His glasses lay next to his head. Tortoiseshell frames. The lenses were smashed. His hair was long and wild. He stank of alcohol. I guessed he was homeless. I pulled at his arm and turned him over. His face was a mass of cuts and bruises. He was barely conscious. He smiled at me.

'Hello, Dad,' I said.

My dad suffered from alcoholism. Which he denied, of course. He had hidden his drinking for years. We didn't see it. One psychiatrist showed us some brain scans. 'Your father has been an alcoholic for most of his adult life,' he said. With hindsight, I remember Dad liked to drink. I also remember he was often very tired. Sometimes he would suddenly look very old. But we were happy, or so I thought. Mum; Dad; my brother, David; and I – 'the Holdens' – all loved each other. Everyone knew that. But none of us knew that Dad was in so much pain. Silent pain.

My dad's alcoholism became obvious just before my 16th birthday. We started to find empty vodka bottles everywhere – under the car seat, in his sock drawer, and behind the garage. His drinking accelerated and his denial increased. Mum tried to get through to Dad. We all did, but we were on the outside and could not get in. Confrontations, ultimatums, and more denials followed. Eventually Dad moved out. For the last nine years of his life he lived homeless. He slept on park benches, under bridges, in cemeteries, and in low-budget accommodation.

The pain I felt was beyond words. I woke up every day for ten years with a sharp, stabbing ache in my belly. I was having a midlife crisis inside a teenager's body. Most weekends my brother David and I would meet up with Dad. He would phone us on a Thursday or Friday to arrange a time and place. Sometimes he looked dishevelled and beaten up. At other times he was clean-shaven and sharply dressed. Amazingly, even as Dad's alcoholism worsened, he still held senior management positions for investment banks and stock-market companies. The drinking never stopped, though.

My dad's fast demise shocked everyone. Alex Holden was a successful man in most people's eyes. He had enjoyed a rich and varied career with multinational companies such as Hertz and TWA. He had held executive posts in Canada, Africa, Europe, and Britain. He had a family who loved him. He lived in a beautiful village in Hampshire in England. Certainly there had been difficult times, too. He made money and he lost money. He got promoted and he got fired, several times. Some ventures grew and some folded. But he was always well respected and held in high esteem.

So what had happened to my dad? The doctors said it was all due to alcoholism. I think it was something worse than that. The more time I spent with Dad – and also with his new homeless and alcoholic friends who shared their stories with me – the more I understood that he was not ill; he was lost. Somewhere along the road to success he had got lost. He had lost sight of what is real. He had also lost sight of himself. And then the meaninglessness and valuelessness set in, slowly killing him. It can happen to anyone. It happens.

What happened to Dad felt so unreal. It somersaulted me forward into an intense search and enquiry. I still kicked footballs, played guitars, and kissed girls (I tried, at least), but I was mostly preoccupied. I had questions, big questions like 'What is life for?' 'What is success?' and 'What is happiness?' I soon realised that these questions scared the shit out of most people. They did me, too. No wonder we keep so busy. I couldn't find anyone who was prepared to talk honestly with me. All I really wanted to know was: 'What's real?' No bullshit, just the truth.

One day shortly after finding my dad on the pavement, something strange happened at school. Without any warning we were given a one-hour session of career advice. There was a lot of talk about banking and catering, nursing and journalism, and also training to be a teacher. We soon realised we had been strong-armed into choosing a career – in under one hour. The truth was, I didn't want a career. My dad had had a career, and look what had happened to him. *Surely there is more to life than just having a career,* I thought.

So at the grand old age of 16 I became a philosopher. Very uncool. But I couldn't ignore what was happening to my dad. I don't know if you have ever tried to be a philosopher, but in my experience you don't get much encouragement. Especially if you're a shy, confused teenager. My big questions about the purpose of life had no place in a school curriculum stuffed with algebra and chemistry. My questioning probably seemed precocious, but it was sincere. My one refuge was English literature classes, where people like Harold Pinter, George Orwell, and J.D. Salinger were asking the same questions.

For the next nine years, I prayed each night that my dad was safe and sleeping under a roof. My dad's pain taught me that in a world full of front-page news, fast-tracked careers, designer clothing, and tragic sports results, you have to remember what is real. Success is about seeing the truth in all things. It is about living wisely and knowing what you love. It is being able to discern between true values and neurotic cravings. Most goals that we pursue so feverishly lose all value and meaning when, for example, we are diagnosed with cancer or we experience the break-up of a relationship.

My dad's pain, and my own, motivated me to take a highly personal curriculum of learning in psychology and philosophy. I have met so many wonderful teachers along the way. I have received many gifts. This rich journey continues to unfold; it inspires the work I do today in psychology, coaching, and education. I can't help but feel I owe it all to my dad. In this book, I will share with you some of the most relevant parts of this journey and also the most important lessons I have learned about success.

Introducing Success Intelligence

Success Intelligence is, in essence, a collection of stories, insights, and conclusions from my work over the last 20 years. I am probably best known as the director of The Happiness Project, which has pioneered the use of positive psychology in work and life. The Project is based on a model that teaches people how to use their innate intelligence to be more happy and successful. My work on Success Intelligence grew out of my corporate work with The Happiness Project, and it is now a project in its own right.

I've spent thousands of hours coaching people on the psychology of success. As a coach, I often work with business leaders, passionate entrepreneurs, writers and artists, sports professionals, and talented people from all walks of life. These people like to think deeply about success. They are visionaries who want to realise their potential and contribute fully to life. Without breaking any confidences, I will share some of the experience and techniques I use to coach success with these people.

I gave my first talk on Success Intelligence in 1996, which was five years after my father's death. Since then, I have given master classes on Success Intelligence at conferences all over the world. I have also taught Success Intelligence workshops to businesses, governments, schools, hospitals, and charities. Some of my major clients include the BBC, BT, Dove, Marriott Hotels, Sony Corporation, The Body Shop, Unilever, Virgin Media, and London's Royal National Theatre. In this book I will present the key principles and exercises I teach in my Success Intelligence presentations.

What is Success Intelligence? Simply put, it is about applying wisdom to success. When I first started to study success, I was struck by what I called the 'insanity of success'. I witnessed so many apparently intelligent people chasing after success in the most foolhardy and bird-brained manner. They seemed willing to pay for their cockeyed success with peptic ulcers, broken marriages, and crazy lifestyles. They were manic, hyper, and busy – to the point of distraction. They might have gotten A's for effort, but not for intelligence.

We live in a 'Success Culture', Many people pursue success as a primary goal in life and are often obsessed with it. They judge their entire lives on whether or not they're a success. They secretly attack themselves for not being successful *enough*. But how much success is enough? People crave success because they hope it will deliver salvation from the ego's self-attack. They hope that being able to say 'I've made it' will silence the inner taunts. William James, a modern father of psychology, once referred to 'the moral flabbiness of the bitch-goddess success'. He described the egocentric craving for success as a 'national disease'.[3]

I decided to use the name 'Success Intelligence' to emphasize the need to think wisely about success. I also chose the name because I wanted to contribute to the important dialogue on intelligence currently taking place in our society. In 1995, Daniel Goleman wrote *Emotional Intelligence,* in which he collated research on a new model of intelligence that included logic and emotions, thoughts and feelings. In 2000, Danah Zohar and Ian Marshall wrote *Spiritual Intelligence,* in which they explored the importance of vision and meaning.

The major challenges we face today require not more effort, but more wisdom. More than ever, we have to rethink the way we work. In business, the new economy is called a 'knowledge economy'. Books like *Intelligent Leadership* by Alan Hooper and John Potter call for more vision and inspiration. We're also being called to rethink how we relate to each other. Richard Panzer, author of *Relationship Intelligence,* asserts that your 'RQ' influences your success and happiness much more than your IQ. Overall, there is a call for greater wisdom and intelligence.

Success Intelligence challenges you to apply your best thinking to success. The book is divided into seven parts. Part I is called 'Vision' and it asks the question 'What is success?' Common definitions of success include achieving goals, making money, finding love, knowing God, and being happy. What do you say? Part I examines four major blocks to success, which are: the lack of vision in our Manic Society, the chronic busyness of the Busy Generation, the over-efforting in the Hyperactive Workplace, and the inner poverty of our Joyless Economy.

Part II is called 'Potential' and it addresses the psychology of success. Here I explore how self-knowledge can help you discover your strengths, liberate your talent, and enable authentic success. In the chapter entitled 'The Success Contract', I introduce a unique model for releasing inner blocks to success.

Part III is entitled 'Wisdom' and it concentrates on the goals of success. Here I introduce an 'Intelligent Goals System,' which clarifies and strengthens your spiritual and material goals in life. I focus on the power of goals, your criteria for success, the wisdom of happiness, the psychology of money, and the purpose of love.

Part IV is 'Relationships' and it examines the heart of success. Too often our most important relationships are sacrificed in the manic dash for success. In a chapter called 'The Broken Community', I count the cost of the rapid rise of excessive individualism in recent decades. I also unravel four blocks to success: dysfunctional independence, the competition block, thin conversations, and a poor work/life balance.

Part V is entitled 'Courage' and it explores the shadow of success. Here I cover key themes of emotional intelligence, such as handling the fear of failure, recovering from mistakes, and responding positively to setbacks. Success Intelligence challenges us to translate the so-called negative experiences of life into lessons for greater success.

Part VI is called 'Grace' and it focuses on the spirit of success. Here I introduce the idea of universal intelligence and the ability to be inspired. I examine more blocks to success, such as Destination Addiction, psychological absenteeism, chronic impatience, and personal burnout.

Part VII is called 'Renaissance' and it addresses the purpose of success. For me, the true purpose of success is not to gain advantage over others; it is to serve and inspire people. I examine here the spirit of leadership and the challenge 'to be the difference'. I also introduce FOSI – the Fear of Success Indicator – which explores the most hidden block to success. In the chapter called "A Ph.D. in Happiness', I highlight the difference between the pursuit of happiness and following your joy. I finish the book on the power of commitment and knowing what to say "Yes" to in life.

I have written *Success Intelligence* in the hope that it will help you be more successful and happy. I've met many so-called successful people who have not learned how to enjoy their success. True success should not have to cost you your joy, your health, or your relationships. On the contrary, true success is about enjoying these things. I'm also convinced that practising Success Intelligence helps to make any true personal success into a valuable gift for others. May your success inspire and help us all.

– **Robert Holden, Ph.D.**

PART I

Vision

● ● ● ● ●

Where there is no vision, people perish.

– **Proverbs 29:18**

The Manic Society

The Busy Generation

The Hyperactive Workplace

The Joyless Economy

I was born at the Princess Elizabeth Hospital in Nairobi, Kenya. The midwife told my mother it was the fastest birth she'd ever seen. There was virtually no labour, and I arrived in record time. Apparently I couldn't wait to get the umbilical cord cut. My mother says she immediately recognized in me a sense of purpose and urgency. She tells me that I had a look on my face that said, 'I have things to do, places to go, and people to see.'

I was born with fast genes. I had what a family friend once described as 'an aggressive urge for progress'. Nearly all the photographs of me as a young child depict a very earnest and thoughtful little old man. When I was three years old, my mother found me outside one night looking up at the stars.

'What are you doing?' she asked.

'I'm thinking about life,' I said.

One day when I was four years old, my mother asked me why I looked so worried. I told her, 'I'm thinking about how to get a mortgage.'

From the beginning, I was eager to make my mark on the world and do something important with my life. 'I want a brief-case for my birthday,' I told Dad when I was six years old.

'What for?' he asked.

'For something important,' I said.

When I was eight years old, I opened my first shop in my front yard. I bought penny candy from the local store and sold it at half price. I did a booming business, but I soon ran out of pennies. As a teenager, I turned my attention to sports, and later to music. The band I played in met regularly to practise signing autographs.

Like most teenagers, I was ambitious for success, but I didn't really know what success was. After my father's downfall, my ambition for success intensified. I was a hugely driven young man, determined to make a success of myself. Looking back now, I think I hoped that my success would help to heal the pain I felt about my dad. In rapid-fire succession, during my 20s, I pioneered two health-care clinics, authored five books, lectured internationally, gave over 1,000 media interviews, and was financially set up. I never stopped, for there was always more to do.

My list of achievements looked impressive, but there was also something frantic about it. I had sprinted through my life without much pause or stopping. I was so impatient for my life to happen. Of course, after 21 you hit 30 too soon, and then 40 even faster. 'We imagine that we can turn the pages slowly, one by one, pausing at each paragraph,' wrote Sir Harold Nicolson, the historian and biographer. 'But it is not like that, believe me. The pages are caught by a gust of wind, a hurricane, and they flutter and rush through our fingers.'

Looking back, I realise that I was in too much of a hurry for success to know what I was looking for. I was chasing *after* success, but I had no real vision of what it really was. The more successes I achieved, the more I began to wonder about the nature of true success. Over time, I learned that success is not a race; it is a journey. I also learned that success is not an achievement; it is a discovery. The primary task, then, is to create a vision for success – one that engages your whole being. Vision is what helps you discover the truth about success. Vision is the first key to Success Intelligence.

The Manic Society

Dear God, help me to slow down and
notrushpasteverythingthatisimportanttodayamen.

Have you ever seen the Monty Python comedy sketch about the 100-yard dash for people with no sense of direction? It is featured in a 'best of' compilation called *Parrot Sketch Not Included*. Picture the scene:

> It is the Silly Olympics. The stadium is full. There is a blue sky overhead. There is a sense of great anticipation as the main event is about to begin. Assembled at the starting line are the finalists – an elite band of runners who have absolutely no sense of direction.
>
> The runners are clearly agitated. They are itching to get on with the race. The starting gun fires and the runners are off. Very quickly they all leave the track – sprinting forward, sprinting backward, sprinting sideways, sprinting in circles. They are all running extremely fast. Maximum haste. Great effort. Fantastic speed. Very athletic. But there is no track, no direction, no finish line, and, ultimately, no purpose to the running.

This comedy sketch is a favourite of mine. It offers an excellent metaphor for our sped-up world, full of people chasing success and pursuing happiness. There is no doubt we are living in a 'Fast Society.'[1] The pace of life and work is accelerating beyond all previous measures. We are rapidly becoming a generation of fast-laners[2] who are testing the limits of fast living and fast business. More of us are also questioning the wisdom of it.

In the Fast Society, we find ways to do everything faster than ever before. It is an ASAP way of life. Fast is exciting. Fast offers us the possibility of success sooner, happiness sooner, love sooner, everything sooner. Every morning we wake early to the sound of our alarm clocks. We rise immediately. The 'Snooze' button is for losers. But we are winners, or at least we hope to be. We hit the shower. Speed-dry our hair. Switch on our fast-boil coffeemaker. Drink caffeine to lift our spirits. Scan the headlines. Take our breakfast with us to the car. And aim to beat the rush hour.

In the Fast Society, convenience is essential if we are to manage the pace. Fast companies, such as Federal Express, Fresh Direct, and Travelocity, understand that we can't afford to take our foot off the accelerator. They serenade us with 'speed-speak', like 'no waiting', 'no queues', 'express lane', 'priority club', and 'to go'. They understand we need our quick-fix meals, our overnight services, our instant remedies, and our all-in-one products, because without them we fear we won't go fast enough.

The convenience economy is booming as we attempt to go faster, or rather, as we attempt to keep up. I was in a supermarket recently (real fast-laners use Internet home delivery), and I noticed a new kind of teabag for sale – the quick-releasing flavour kind, with the added extra of powdered skimmed milk already inserted inside each teabag. Imagine how much time this new product could save you! Could this really be the difference between success and failure? As I read the product packaging I wondered, *Is this clever or sad? Is this genius or madness?*

The Fast Society has had such a short history and has delivered much that is good, and yet its time is almost up already. Isn't it true that the Fast Society has now become a Manic Society? The pace of life for many of us has accelerated past fast to manic. The word *manic* is derived from 'mania', which is a psychology term for an absence of intelligence, a type of madness, 'a mood disorder characterised by a variety of symptoms including extreme motor activity, impulsiveness, obsessiveness, and excessively rapid thought and speech'.[3]

In the Manic Society, we speed ahead, on fast-forward, and the danger is that we leave ourselves behind, we leave behind what is precious, and we leave behind the truth. In my Success Intelligence seminars, I often share a saying by Sir Winston Churchill that I think is more relevant today than ever. He said:

Men stumble over the truth from time to time,
but most pick themselves up and hurry off
as if nothing happened.

In the Manic Society, we propel ourselves so fast that we often exceed the speed limit of intelligence and common sense. Speed certainly can be a criterion for success, but it's not the only one. In my work with some of the world's biggest companies, I've often witnessed how the obsessive need to be first to market (a 'first move' in corporate-speak) has almost bankrupted them. I have also worked with many ambitious entrepreneurs whose obsession with quick profits and fast results has cost them their health, their money, and their happiness.

Of particular concern is how our relationships suffer in the Manic Society. Our frantic schedules cause us to skim across the surface of each other's lives without ever really connecting. The mad rush demands so much of our time and energy that we have to resort to 'quality time', date nights, text messages, and speed dating to connect with anyone. We excel at shorthand relationships in which we get each other's abridged headline news, but miss out on any intimate heart-to-heart exchanges. The pressure to work harder is relentless, and we often end up emotionally unavailable and socially isolated.

Personally, as someone who often lives life fast, I find I have to be constantly mindful about giving my relationships my best attention. In my heart of hearts, I know that my relationships are more important to me than more money, more business, book deals, and television studios. And yet, periodically, I let my relationships lapse into a shorthand form of communication in which I barely manage to 'catch up' with those I love. I find it helpful, and necessary, to continually reset my intention to put my relationships first. Whenever I do so, it enriches my life and my work.

Instant Success

The Manic Society peddles the myth that everyone can be an 'instant winner' and an 'overnight success' if we would just go faster. I remember attending a prestigious book award ceremony at the Dorchester Hotel in London. One award presented that evening was for Best Newcomer. The winning author collected his trophy, said his thanks, and was about to exit the stage when he stopped and said with a wry smile, 'Just for the record, I am a newcomer who has been writing for more than ten years now.' With that, he left the stage. For some reason he received the longest applause of the night.

So preoccupied are we with finding shortcuts to success that intelligence often gives way to expediency, and all we end up doing is going faster and faster. Our personal mission statement simply reads 'FASTER', which is catchy and easy to remember, but the fact is we're often lost in a chaotic sea of impatience, fear, and neurosis. More speed is not the answer. True success is about speed and time for reflecting, about pace and patience, about action and inspiration, about now and tomorrow. As the psychologist Robert J. Sternberg says:

> *If anything the essence of intelligence would seem to be in knowing when to think and act quickly, and knowing when to think and act slowly.*

In the Manic Society, our nonstop speed ethic can easily blur our vision. We are living faster and working faster, but what for? What is the vision? Without vision, we can so easily confuse speed with progress, adrenaline with purpose, and urgency with importance. Without vision, we may simply be attempting to win prizes that aren't worth winning. We may be 'getting there' faster, but we may also be missing what is 'here, now,' within us and before us. As Mahatma Gandhi said, 'There is more to life than increasing its speed.'

© 1998 Randy Glasbergen.
www.glasbergen.com

FASTER!

GLASBERGEN

"That's our new mission statement."

In the Manic Society, we are changing faster, succeeding faster, and failing faster. The challenge is to make sure we do not blur the vision, blur the goals, blur what is important. Graham was a finance director of a computer company whom I coached for six months. He was 38 years old; managed offices in Chicago, London, and Paris; and was so financially rich he could retire tomorrow. Other than making money, Graham had no clear vision. When I asked him about his vision, he told me he had once written a 'mission statement' in a training course four years before. 'Would you like me to try to find it?' he asked.

Graham arrived for one session carrying a gift for his four-year-old daughter, Claire. I asked what the gift was, and he told me he had just purchased a copy of *One-Minute Bedtime Stories*. This is a book of traditional children's stories that have been condensed to save busy parents 'valuable time'.

'What the hell are you doing?' I asked.

Graham said, 'My time is tight and my company really needs me.'

I said, 'Graham, you are the richest man I know. If you can't afford more than 60 seconds with your daughter, what hope is there for the rest of us?'

Like so many people in the Manic Society, Graham had allowed his addiction to speed to blur his vision and perspective.

He no longer had any idea what success is, other than to do more of the same and faster. 'We all pay for our mad rush, our blind push, our hurried lives,' wrote Jonathon Lazear, author of *Meditations for Men Who Do Too Much,* a must-read bible for citizens of the Manic Society. Vision must always lead the pace, otherwise we are simply fast-forwarding to nowhere in particular.

Inner Direction

Where there is no vision in the Manic Society, our direction must also falter. Think for a moment . . . how often do you catch yourself participating in the 100-yard dash for people with a poor sense of direction? Each morning when your alarm clock goes off and you get up and go, where are you going and why? In other words, what direction are we taking? As the writer James Thurber commented:

> *All men should strive to learn before they die,*
> *what they are running from, and to, and why?*

The word *direction* has two broad meanings. It can mean 'route', as in the direction of a journey. It can also mean 'guidance', as in receiving inspiration, heeding advice, and being wise. The most successful and happy people I know are good at making time for reflection and inspiration. They stop regularly to go deeper, to gain perspective, to hold a vision, and to receive direction.

How often do you make time in your day for inspiration, meditation, and reflection? Or does time pass too quickly? How often do you make time for vision and strategy? Or is there not enough time? How often do you communicate with the people who are most important to you? Or is your time already taken up? And how often do you stop and acknowledge a success, a joy, or a good moment? Or are you so revved up and so behind already that you can't find the time?

The paradox of the Manic Society is that no matter how fast we go and how many shortcuts we take, there never seems to be enough time. The more we speed up, the faster time passes, too. More haste, less time – so our perception tells us. This is the speed trap. Hence, we are obsessed every day with saving time. But saving time for what? Take this quick test.

In the last seven days, have you:

1.   Gone into work early?
2.   Skipped a meal?
3.   Eaten fast food?
4.   Exceeded the speed limit?
5.   Applied make-up in the car?
6.   Rushed a job?
7.   Used an express service?
8.   Used speed-dial on your mobile phone?
9.   E-mailed or texted instead of phoned?
10. Cancelled a meeting?
11. Gone shopping online?
12. Re-microwaved your coffee?
13. Skimmed a report?
14. Multitasked while on the phone?
15. Had your picture taken – by a speed camera?

Now estimate how much time you saved. How many minutes? How many hours? Then ask yourself, 'What did I do with that extra time I saved?' Our number one goal today seems to be to save as much time as possible, yet we still habitually run late. Our manic behaviour seems to chew up more time than it saves. Maybe the key is to stop trying to save time and start spending the time we have more wisely.

Pit Stops

Shortly before my 36th birthday, I woke one morning with acute pain in my lower back. At first the pain felt like an angry bee sting, but it soon worsened into a sharp, stabbing sensation. I should have stopped everything and visited my doctor. Instead, I elected to press on with my busy schedule of seminars, master classes, and coaching sessions, which I wanted to honour. Over the next few days, the pain became so intense that my body was in a constant sweat. Still I didn't stop. I gave several presentations wearing an ice pack and standing on one leg. Then one day the pain became so horrible I passed out. I finally got the hint that it was time to stop.

No longer able to override the pain, my life came to a grinding halt for about eight weeks. The pain was so intense that no painkiller had any positive effect. Not even morphine injections worked. Every day I would periodically pass out because of the extreme pain. My wife nursed me full-time and arranged visits to doctors, surgeons, and other health specialists. It was a frightening time, and I was eventually diagnosed with a prolapsed disc. It was also – at least initially – a hugely frustrating time as I fell further and further behind with my work schedule.

I returned to work early, as any fast-laner would. That said, I had to take each day slowly. I couldn't walk without the aid of my walking stick for the first three months. Therefore, instead of six appointments a day, I did two. And instead of doing 20 things on my to-do list, I did what was necessary. My change of pace forced me to become more discerning, more strategic, and ultimately, I believe, more effective. I ran around less, but I got through more of what was really important. This was a real eye-opener, to say the least. I had finally slowed down, and I was doing better than before.

Several specialists recommended I have immediate surgery, but instead I chose a holistic programme of treatment that included chiropractic, massage, acupuncture, and healing. I made a full and quick recovery, mostly because I really slowed down. I was surprised and delighted by how slowing down – and stopping – had radically helped improve the quality of my life and work. With more intelligent pacing, I became more present and more effective. Also, I found more time to have important conversations I would previously have missed. Mentally, I felt centred and more peaceful all through the day.

In the Manic Society, we increasingly display what psychologists call 'Type H' behaviour.[4] The 'H' stands for hurried, hostile, and humourless. We are so hurried that we have no time to be present. We are so hostile for fear of losing speed that we end up feeling isolated. And we are so humourless that we forget to enjoy this moment or, indeed, any moment. We have run out of short-cuts and are completely lost. And all we can think to do is to go faster. The psychologist Rollo May wrote:

> *It is an old ironic habit of human beings to*
> *run faster when we have lost our way.*

In the Manic Society, we live our lives fast, but we do not always live them well. Perpetual motion. Internal combustion. Permanently busy. There is no stillness. There is no stopping. We are afraid to stop because we're afraid of losing time and falling behind. We suffer from an appalling sense of inner poverty and lack. When we don't stop, we forget – we forget what is important, we forget who we are, we forget that there are other options, and we forget what life is really for.

Cultivating the regular habit of stopping is an essential skill for being successful and staying sane in the Manic Society. If we never stop, we end up skimming the surface of life; our time disappears and we miss the richness, depth, and texture of each occasion. Stopping, if only for a few minutes a day, is a way to connect again to your vision, your wisdom, and your purpose. As a coach, one of my chief functions is to help people stop for a while.

I illustrate the crucial importance of stopping to my clients by using an example from Formula One motor racing, the fastest sport in the world. Central to the strategy of winning a Formula One race is the pit stop. No driver, no matter how fast he or she drives, can win a race without taking a pit stop. In the pit stop the drivers get refreshment, receive instructions, have engine repairs, fill the petrol tank, and set off on fresh tyres. A Formula One race is all about speed and strategy – and it is in the timing and management of the pit stop that the race is often won.

In life, a pit stop can take many forms. A coaching session can be a pit stop. Meditation can be a pit stop. Prayer can be a pit stop. A Sabbath can be a pit stop. So too can a lunch break, an inspiring book, a game of golf, a regular yoga class, and time with friends. Stopping can help us remember our vision, connect more deeply to our wisdom, and make us more open and available to inspiration. Stopping can save us so much time, so many mistakes, and so many heartaches.

SUCCESS INTELLIGENCE TIP 1 – *VISION*

Pierre Teilhard de Chardin, the Jesuit priest and philosopher, famously said, 'The whole of life lies in the verb *seeing*.' Cultivating a strong vision, in which you learn to 'see' not just with your eyes but also with your mind and your heart, is essential for success.

- What is your vision for your life? Describe a life well lived.

- What is your vision for your relationships? Describe the sort of person/friend you want to be.

- What is your vision for your work? Describe the contribution you want to make.

Make time for vision.

The Busy Generation

Busy, busy, busy, busy, busy, busy . . . dead!

Richard is a successful accountant. During one of our coaching sessions he told me, 'Every week I enter the lottery, but I am always too busy to check if I have won or not.' He looked up to the heavens and said wistfully, 'I'm probably sitting on a fortune, and I don't know it.' Richard is a fully paid-up member of what I call "The Busy Generation'. Aren't we all?

Are you aware of the new greeting that has emerged recently in our society? Once upon a time, after 'Hello' we used to say things like 'Nice to see you', 'How are you?' and 'Are you well?' Now, after 'Hello' we say, 'Are you keeping busy?' This is our new greeting for one another. What's more, we expect the reply to be an emphatic 'Yes!' In fact, to say no, as I have done on occasion, arouses grave concern and much awkwardness, as though it were news of bereavement or a disaster.

In my Success Intelligence seminars, I often ask my audiences: 'Is there anyone here who is less busy now compared with ten years ago?' Generous laughter is the usual response. Into every life some occasional busyness must fall. As the Bible says: 'There is a time for everything and a season for every activity under heaven' (Ecclesiastes 3:1). There will always be projects, goals, birthday parties, and deadlines that require extra time and energy. Occasional busyness is fine, but most of us aren't occasionally busy; we're permanently busy.

For the Busy Generation, *busyness has become a way of life.* We're either busy or looking busy. Busyness is our status symbol. Every time we proclaim, 'I am busy', we're saying to the rest of the Busy Generation that we are worth something, that we have value, and that our lives are important. Our mantra is: 'I am busy, therefore I am okay.' Busy is good. Very busy is even better.

From a distance, being busy looks damned impressive and very necessary. It looks like purpose, focus, drive, and huge productivity. Oh, to be busy like that! Up close, however, our busyness often betrays us. Busyness often hides levels of confusion, fear, anxiety, and pain. Busyness is often just noise. It has no real substance to it. This is particularly true for people who suffer from 'permanent busyness.'

Permanent Busyness

Permanent busyness is not intelligent. In fact, it is my experience that permanent busyness is often a major block to success in work, relationships, and life.

The Busy Generation has to learn that *it is not enough to be busy*. A busy life is not necessarily a life well lived. A busy work schedule is not evidence of any great accomplishment. Being busy neither guarantees success nor equates to success. Henry David Thoreau, the American philosopher, who has inspired so many leaders and thinkers, once wrote:

> *It is not enough to be busy; so are the ants.*
> *The question is: What are we busy about?*

Permanent busyness might start with the best of intentions, but along the way we disconnect from what is truly important, sacred, and real. We lose the power to discriminate. We are so busy, so overbooked, and so obsessed with our schedules that we are no longer open and available to the essential truth and beauty of our lives. We are lost, but we are usually too busy to notice. As the popular saying goes: 'Life is what happens when you are busy making other plans.'

The Busy Generation may achieve 'optical success' – in other words, the look of success – but we do not necessarily feel successful. We may achieve a lot, but we are often too busy to enjoy it. We're too busy paying off the mortgage to enjoy any quality time at home. We have lovers to whom we're too tired to make love. We have children who seem to grow up too fast. We have 'really great friends' whom we hardly ever see. We don't take holidays; we prefer long weekends. We are too busy to be happy.

Permanent busyness is usually counterfeit success. The 'buzz' and the 'rush' feel great for a time, but the adrenaline soon runs out. We become exhausted and are forced to get through the day on a diet of caffeine, stimulants, aggression, and other 'uppers'. We stay busy – at all costs. The 'wow' of permanent busyness does not stand up well to closer inspection. We are busy about nothing in particular. We have confused adrenaline with purpose. Our permanent busyness is a façade, and when the busyness finally stops, the house falls down.

Permanent busyness blocks vision. I see this most clearly when I coach leaders of companies and organisations – the visionaries – who struggle every day to overcome permanent busyness. It is my fervent belief that leaders are not meant to be permanently busy. Leaders are the custodians of vision. They are meant to take the time to meditate and to focus on the essential truth of the work. My goal is to help them discipline themselves to make time for the big picture and inspiration. I help them to lead with vision.

To live with vision is an essential talent for lifelong success. We are all called to meditate from time to time on the essential truth of our lives.

Being busy can make you feel important, but is what you are busy about important? This is the sort of 'Intelligent Question' a good coach asks. In my experience, permanently busy people tend to confuse busyness and success, adrenaline and purpose, and effort and effectiveness. Robert J. Shiller, professor of economics at Yale University and author of *Irrational Exuberance,* writes:

> *The ability to focus attention on important things is*
> *a defining characteristic of intelligence.*

Permanent busyness is not only unintelligent, it can sometimes be insane. The most insane example of permanent busyness I have witnessed was when I worked on the New York Stock Exchange. I won't name the Wall Street company because I wouldn't wish to give them cause for huge embarrassment. This company ran an aggressive, macho, long-hours working culture where everyone was expected to adopt a 'start early, finish late' attitude. Working for this company was as much a test of endurance as anything.

One evening I saw one of my colleagues walking out of the office. It was an open-plan office shared by 100 financial analysts. It was 6 P.M., and Terry looked like he was going home for the evening.

'Terry, you forgot your jacket,' I called out.

'I'm coming back,' replied Terry. But Terry didn't come back. The next morning at about 7:45 A.M., I saw Terry arrive at his desk for work. I saw him fold up his old jacket, the one he had left overnight, and put it into his briefcase.

'So, you did forget your jacket, Terry,' I observed.

'Not really,' he replied.

Terry later initiated me, in careful whispers, into a secret ritual that he (and allegedly others) participated in called 'The Double Jacket'. Terry explained that in an effort to beat the boss's blind insistence that workers start early and finish late, he would always leave a jacket on the back of his chair.

'Why?' I asked, somewhat naively.

'To make it look like I'm always here,' whispered Terry. I later learned that 'The Double Jacket' is a very common manoeuvre against the pressure to be permanently busy.

Over the years I have worked for many companies and organisations that reward busyness, not success. Their employees work in 'busy cultures' that are ideal environments for growing new varieties of busyness and ineffectiveness. Everyone works late because it's considered a sign of commitment. Anyone who dares to leave at 5 P.M. expects to receive mindless taunts from peers like 'Part-timer!' and 'It's all right for some.' Permanent busyness may well be evidence of commitment, but it is commitment without imagination. And it does not guarantee success.

Individuals can also suffer from a 'busy ethic' that keeps them permanently occupied. We have to remember that the goal of life is not to be busy, it is to be successful. Each and every member of the Busy Generation – of which I am one – has to be willing to sacrifice busyness for true success. Often it is only when we let go of our busyness that vision returns, inspiration appears, and a new level of true success is possible.

Busyness Audit

> *Now that it's all over, what did you really do*
> *yesterday that was worth mentioning?*
> **– Coleman Cox**

I often begin my Success Intelligence seminars with an exercise called 'Success Review'. I give delegates ten minutes to walk around the room and introduce themselves to one another. With the first person they meet, they share a personal success they've had in the last week. With the next person they meet, they share another personal success from the last week. The goal is to meet at least seven people and to recall at least seven personal successes from the last seven days. Each success must be different.*

Most people's initial response to the Success Review is that they've been given an impossible assignment. Delegates wander around with abject faces, looking lost, desperately trying to remember what happened last week. In the feedback session afterward I ask, 'What did you notice?' Even the most accomplished people say they find this exercise challenging. Some people find it easier to remember successes at home, but not at work, or vice versa. When I ask if it has been a particularly hard week, the usual answer is "No". It was just another normal week.

Many of us live and work in an 'I want it yesterday' world, and we fail consistently to remember what was so important about yesterday. The Success Review asks for just one success per day – in other words, one valuable experience or accomplishment every 24

---

*Before reading on, see if you can recall seven personal successes from the last seven days.

hours. I ask my audiences, 'Were you busy last week?'

'Yes,' they say.

'Did you work long hours?'

'Yes.'

'Did you get a lot done?'

'Yes.'

What makes this exercise difficult for most people is that they rarely stop to review success. At a recent conference a participant said, 'My company specialises in failure analysis; we never talk about success.'

Busyness is not true success. I often use a more in-depth version of the Success Review in my one-to-one coaching sessions with clients. The benefits of doing a regular Success Review include creating a clearer vision of success, using time more wisely, and making better decisions. Sometimes I include what I call a 'Busyness Audit', which helps you to distinguish between mere busyness and true success. A rigorous Busyness Audit can clear away the clutter of permanent busyness and create a path to greater success.

It is my experience that permanent busyness is mainly coMpensation for a lack of clarity about true success. I notice that whenever an individual, a team, or a family becomes clearer about success, they naturally become less busy. Personally, I find that whenever I meditate on the nature of true success, any unnecessary busyness quickly falls away. I also find that a regular Busyness Audit helps me to be better at saying 'Yes' to what is truly important and 'No, thank you' to what is not.

Busyness is not your purpose. I once coached a man named Neil who said, 'For 23 years I went to work without a purpose. I had a reason, which was money. But a reason is not the same thing as a purpose.' Neil had worked for a bank his entire adult life and, although he had had many promotions and pay rises, he still felt unfulfilled. He came to see me to find his purpose. We talked about the difference between busyness and purpose. I told him, 'Busyness is what you give your time to; a purpose is what you give your heart to.' Purpose is about love and wholeheartedness.

Your purpose is not to be busy. In fact, permanent busyness often blocks purpose. When we lose sight of our purpose, we may compensate with another type of busyness called 'competitive busyness'. This occurs when people compete with one another to prove how busy they are. For instance, Tom says to Harry, 'I got 100 e-mails today', and Harry says to Tom, 'I got 150 e-mails today', and then Dick says to Harry and Tom, 'I got 200 e-mails today in both my e-mail accounts.' Then Sally tells them she has six e-mail accounts and that she travelled over 100,000 company miles last year, and then Jane tells everyone that she is owed six months' holiday that she is too busy to take.

Busyness has no implicit value.   A few years ago I saw a cartoon of a man sitting in his own coffin with a computer on his lap, answering e-mails. The caption read: 'Even on your deathbed the inbox will still be full.' The Busy Generation lives as if each moment must be filled with an action or a task. We know how to busy ourselves. We operate in a constant 'doing' mode and only reset when everything is done. But there's no end to the doing and often no real purpose either. Permanent busyness may well be compelling, but that doesn't make it valuable.

Another variety of busyness that blocks success is 'addictive busyness'. People who suffer from addictive busyness become insanely neurotic if they're not do-do-doing something. They feel guilty and valueless without a to-do list. These feelings run deep. Angela, a client of mine, worked for a company where everyone was permanently busy. She said, 'Either I leave work on time and feel guilty, or I get home late and feel guilty.' Angela quit her job and went freelance. Now she was her own boss, yet she was as busy as ever. 'I feel guilty if I'm not doing enough,' she said. The Busy Generation has to learn that *success is not about doing enough; it is about doing what is valuable.*

Busyness is not very productive.   I once went on a six-week sabbatical to the Hawaiian island of Kauai. I was very clear that the purpose of my trip was to 'do nothing' and 'simply be'. Upon arrival, I discovered that my accommodation had no facilities for Internet connection. Despite all my efforts, I was unable to receive any e-mails for my entire visit. When I got back home, I made it a priority to answer my e-mails. There were over 1,000 of them waiting in my in-box (not wishing to sound competitive about it). Here is the interesting thing: not one single person had phoned or e-mailed to ask why I hadn't replied to them. This was an eye-opener for me.

I estimated that to answer each of these e-mails would have taken (at two minutes per e-mail) 40 hours of work. For what, I wonder? Those of us who feel driven to be productive in every waking minute like to think that our hard work is producing some useful results; this is not always the case, however. Permanent busyness is rarely as productive as it feels or looks. In fact, permanent busyness can often be counterproductive in that it invariably leads to exhaustion and feeling overwhelmed. The sigmoid curve for busyness (see Figure 1) shows that permanent busyness takes people up, up, and up until inevitably they suffer a drop in energy and results.

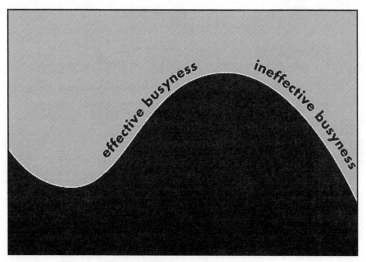

FIGURE 1: Sigmoid Curve for Busyness

Busyness is not people-friendly. I was once invited to speak at an international conference in Venice for a well-known computer company. The Chief Information Officer (CIO) began his talk by saying, 'I welcome this face time we have today." As soon as I heard the phrase 'face time', it sent a shudder down my spine. I realised that we had now invented a new name for the fact that we almost never meet in person. We are so permanently busy that meeting face-to-face is apparently impossible, impractical, or even unnecessary. Face time is a luxury we can ill afford not to have, but we are often too busy to realise this.

Our most important relationships with family, friends, and colleagues often have to compete with our addiction to busyness. The busyness often wins. We're so busy trying to be successful that we end up being too busy to connect, too busy to communicate, too busy to say 'I love you' and 'Thank you'. We forget to keep company with others and also with ourselves. Our daily tasks receive our best energy, and our relationships are left with what remains. We coexist, but we are rarely fully engaged with each other. As a result, our relationships often feel dead and deeply unsatisfying.

Busyness bypasses the heart. Wayne Muller, author of *Legacy of the Heart,* wrote: 'The Chinese word for 'busy' is composed of two characters: "heart" and "killing". When we make ourselves so busy that we are always rushing around trying to get this or that 'done' or 'over with,' we kill something vital in ourselves, and we smother the quiet wisdom of our heart.'[5] When we are mindlessly busy, we become like walking shadows with an empty center and no real point. The essence of who we are is lost.

A major survey by the *Discipleship Journal* – a publication for Christian living – reported that more than two-thirds of those interviewed 'identified being too busy as the greatest obstacle to spiritual growth'. The survey found that 41 per cent of people consider themselves to be "too busy" and therefore do not have enough time or energy to cultivate a rich spiritual life.[6] The fact is that it is very difficult to be permanently busy and truly inspired.

We inevitably experience a fall from grace when over-busy, and then everything feels more difficult and overwhelming.

I am too busy not to pray.
– **Charles Wesley**

Beyond Busyness

I define coaching as *the opportunity to get into important conversations you would otherwise have been too busy to have.* The value of regular coaching is that it creates a space that helps you to punctuate your busyness. Space is good for the soul. It is a restorative that helps people breathe more deeply, clear their minds, connect to their wisdom, remember what is important, and be open to new possibilities. Space is like a womb that gives birth to new insights, inspirations, epiphanies, and eurekas. Space can also be a lifesaver.

Most of my coaching clients do not have enough 'white space' in their schedules. White space refers to thinking time for vision and re-evaluation. White space is the 20 minutes you take each day to make sure you are living and working wisely. White space is an internal phone call you have with your inner intelligence – the inner wisdom we all have. White space is the opportunity to review success and conduct a Busyness Audit. Without these moments, life is just more busyness as usual.

An important key to success is the courage to look at your busyness and identify what it is really about. It is my experience that busyness is often an excuse, a defence, or a resistance to an important challenge. In other words, busyness is a blindfold you wear when you're afraid to face something. Busyness is often just fear. It can also mask a lack of trust. I often challenge my clients to explore how they might be using their busyness to avoid something important, such as intimacy, change, purpose, God, themselves, and even success.

Another important key to success is the willingness to look beyond your busyness in order to find a better way. On the other side of busyness there are all manner of gifts waiting to be discovered, such as new inspiration, creative partnership, increased effectiveness, and a whole new level of success. Here are some key questions I include in a typical Busyness Audit for clients who want to move beyond permanent busyness:

What do I lose when I am permanently busy?

List what goes first whenever you are permanently busy, such as time for self, clarity of vision, inner wellbeing, personal development, relationship joy, daily prayer time, relaxation, and fun.

What would I be doing if I were not this busy?

Is your permanent busyness really about your purpose or your fear of purpose? To be successful, you have to identify the key measures that help you to distinguish between fake busyness and true purpose.

What is my busyness helping me to avoid?

Permanent busyness can be a convincing excuse not to face up to a current challenge or a certain truth. Also, people can use busyness as a behavioural Valium to prevent them from feeling a fear, sadness, anger, or heartbreak.

What is my busyness defending me against?

Permanent busyness is often used as a defence against giving up control, taking a risk, having to trust more, and learning to receive. Sometimes we're busy because we are afraid to give up our independence.

How could I be less busy and more successful?

Permanent busyness is a call for more imagination, more invention, and more creativity. It is a challenge to dig deep, listen to your wisdom, be open to help, and to lead with vision.

What good things could happen if I gave up permanent busyness?

The more time you give to this question, the more valuable answers it will give you. Beyond busyness there are gifts waiting for you.

SUCCESS INTELLIGENCE TIP 2 – *VALUES*

When was the last time you thought deeply about what you really value? Put some white space in your calendar and reflect on these three questions: 'What do I really value about my life?' 'What do I really value about my work?' and 'What do I really value about my relationships?' Write your values down so that you can refer to them regularly for guidance and inspiration. Also, make some white space in your calendar every day to reflect on how you can use your time wisely in work and life and be of more value.

The Hyperactive
Workplace

*Career (verb): to move forward quickly or violently in a
way that can cause a serious or fatal accident.*

I once witnessed a miracle in New York, near 34th Street. It took
place in the subway. I was heading downtown to Wall Street. It
was rush hour – about 7 A.M. – and it was already hot, sticky, and
humid. The subway was heaving with hundreds of people anxious
to board the crowded subway cars. As I made my way to my plat-
form, I could hear a street musician singing.

The man was in his early 30s. He played an acoustic guitar,
and he sang his heart out to the Beatles song 'With a Little Help
from My Friends'. No one paid much attention at first, but soon
he got through to us. He wasn't just busking; he was *live in concert.*
He was brilliant. Then the miracle happened. A train arrived and
nobody got on it. We all delayed our journey to hear him finish.
We stood together listening to a love song. The ovation at the end
was spectacular.

A few weeks later I found the street musician again, this
time on 68th Street and Lexington Avenue. It was rush hour
again, and he was singing his heart out, this time to 'A Hard
Day's Night'. The subway riders loved it. I was so pleased to see
him, as I had regretted not thanking him personally before.
This time we got talking. His name was Michael, he had a young
family – two children – and he described himself as 'a stockbro-
ker in recovery'.

Over coffee, Michael told me cryptically how he used to work
'eight days a week' in the city. At 28 years old he had a high-
six-figure salary and hypertension. Work dominated his life.
I remember him saying, 'Work became an enormous black hole

that chewed up my energy, my dreams, my relationships, my health, everything.' It got to a point where every day Michael would ask himself the same question: 'What am I doing this for?'

Michael said, 'I made great money but at the expense of everything I valued.' His hyperactive career took him to the edge of burnout, and his heart simply wasn't in it any more. I remember something else Michael told me. He said, 'I used to work for a boss called "money", but now I work for love.' Michael rediscovered his love of music. Part of his new life now was serving ex-colleagues by helping them take their hearts to work.

More Heart

The modern world of work is increasingly fraught. We are being asked to work faster and better, to do more with less, to change continuously, and to invent new ways of working. The modern formula for work appears to be: More Success + Greater Speed + Fewer Resources + Constant Uncertainty + Increased Competition. It is important to ask yourself, 'Do I really want to play this game?' It would be so easy to lose your life to a game like this. Many people, like Michael, find something else to do. Others choose to stay and play.

More and more of us are working in what I call the 'Hyperactive Workplace'. Modern work is often dominated by a culture of long hours, permanent busyness, addiction to 'to-do' lists, endless goals, inhumane attitudes, and no 'downtime'. One company to which I was a consultant, a global bank, issued some leadership behaviour guidelines that included: 'Leaders must always adopt a "Can do, will do" attitude' and 'When in the office, leaders must always walk fast'. Mindless.

In the hyperactive world of work, we are constantly 'doing'. In fact, we are doing more than before *and* we are not getting enough done. We have become increasingly hyper in response to corporate downsizing, global markets, and 24/7 technology. We are 'doing' all through the day, 'doing' in our free time, and 'doing' ourselves out of a life. In fact, we are 'doing' to the point of exhaustion. We think insomnia is a chance to get more work done. We are literally 'doing' ourselves to death – killing ourselves for our careers, killing ourselves in the name of success. The Japanese have a name for it – *karoshi* – meaning death by overwork.[7]

Today's leaders have an interesting challenge on their hands – to raise the dead. They have to heal the culture of 'death by overwork' – that is, death of creativity, death of talent, and death of fresh ideas. I recently attended a leadership event for the global communication company BT, which was unveiling a new set of leadership guidelines, strikingly different from the old-school JFDI* command-and-control tactics. They emphasised the need for more visionary leadership, better teamwork, a healthy work/life balance, and also more emotional intelligence. A key word that was mentioned over and again was 'heart'.

Phil Dance, BT's CIO for Technology, gave an impassioned speech on the need for more heart at work. He said, 'We need to stop talking to each other as if reciting from page six of a financial report and start talking more from our heart.' Phil went on to say, 'Above all, we have to remember what is the heart of our business. If we lose that, we lose everything.' Phil didn't ask his team for more effort or more overtime; he asked for more heart. He received an ovation for his speech, not just because he speaks well, but because he leads by example.

I have coached many people who give absolutely everything to their work, except their hearts. They give their time, their energy, their weekends, their health, their lives, but not their hearts. I often ask clients to talk from their hearts about their work. Many cannot do this. I also ask leaders, 'How do you manage the heart of your team?' Many have not thought about it. Many people fear the Hyperactive Workplace is too brutal for the human heart. The heart is wise, however. The heart is strong. The heart is a muscle. Besides, how intelligent is it to expect to feel any success at something you don't give your heart to?

In the Hyperactive Workplace, many people fear complete burnout if they were also to give their hearts. They are already exhausted – they feel drained, having given their pounds of flesh.

However, it is precisely because we do not give our hearts that we live so perilously close to burnout and defeat. We have to give our hearts to something if we are to be truly successful. Whole-heartedness is the antidote to burnout and hyperactivity. The heart engages the whole being; it accesses all your potential; and it opens you up to greater inspiration and success.

More Balance

Clive is a lawyer at a medical insurance company. He is in his late 30s; married to Sarah; and has a young son, Toby, who is three years old. Clive had read a book I co-wrote with Ben Renshaw called *Balancing Work & Life*. He contacted me through the publisher to arrange a series of coaching sessions. Clive had accepted a prestigious promotion nine months previously, had since been working around the clock, and felt there were not enough hours in the day to get everything done.

Clive told me that since his promotion he rarely got home on weekday evenings before Toby was in bed asleep. He also worked most Saturdays at the office in an effort to clear the backlog. Clive made up his mind to contact me when one morning, as he was leaving the house for work, Toby ran up to him, grabbed hold of his legs, and pleaded, 'Daddy, can I come and live with you?' Clive had been spending so little time at home that his son thought he must have another home somewhere else.

'I work full-time; I live part-time,' said Clive. 'I love my work, but I want my life back.' Many people like Clive find that the Hyperactive Workplace chews up too much of their time. Clive had so much to do that he had no time to look at his vision, assess his strategy, meet with people, delegate some work, share best practices, prioritise his goals, or anything else. 'Every day I try to get as much done as possible,' Clive told me.

I explained that this was his major mistake. 'Your goal is not to maximise productivity; it is to be more valuable.'

One of the questions I asked Clive was, 'At the end of a day of

Copyright 2003 by Randy Glasbergen.
www.glasbergen.com

GLASBERGEN

**"Son, we need to spend more quality time together.
Stop by my office and fill out a job application."**

work, do you get on with your life or do you merely recover from work?'

Clive replied, 'I don't have a life.'

I also asked Clive to assess how much of his working day he spent on: (a) tasks, (b) relationships, and (c) vision. He estimated it was 85 per cent on tasks, 14 per cent on relationships, and 1 per cent on vision. I told Clive his first goal was to achieve 2 per cent vision, which meant finding another seven minutes a day to assess his purpose and priorities. His next goal was to achieve 25 per cent relationships, mainly by working more in partnership. Within a month, Clive no longer worked on Saturdays.

A recent 'Quality of Working Life' survey[8] among managers showed the following results:

- 68 per cent reported that their long hours had an adverse impact on their productivity.

- 71 per cent reported that their long hours had an adverse impact on their health.

- 79 per cent reported that their long hours had

---

*JFDI stands for the *Just Fucking Do It!* style of leadership.

an adverse impact on their relationship with
their spouse or partner.

• 86 per cent reported that their long hours had
an adverse impact on their relationship with
their children.

Most troubling, nearly half of the managers who responded
thought they had no choice but to work longer hours. In fact, they
believed longer hours are a necessary sacrifice for success. In other
words, they believed that in order to win at work you have to lose
in life. Is this really true? Is there really not a better way than this?
Have these managers explored all the possibilities, or are they too
hyperactive to stop and think?

A primary goal of my coaching work is to help people be less
hyperactive and more effective. On the surface it looks as if the
hyperactive world of work is asking us to 'do more', but really it is
asking us to think more, imagine more, innovate more, and partner more. In the modern world of work there is no way we can do
everything, so we have to be less hyperactive and more strategic.
Og Mandino, author of *Secrets for Success and Happiness,* writes:

> The great difference between those who succeed and
> those who fail does not consist in the amount of work
> done by each but in the amount of intelligent work.
> Many of those who fail most ignominiously do enough
> to achieve grand success but they labour haphazardly at
> whatever they are assigned, building up with one hand to
> tear down with the other.

More Joy

*The Hyperactive Workplace is a modern tragedy
where people work without vision and joy.*

In the hyperactive world of work, we forget to enjoy ourselves. We

31

forget why we do what we do. We just do it, but with no heart. We just do it, but with no vision. We just do it, but with no soul. I once conducted a 'Joy of Work' survey in which I asked 1,000 professionals to answer a confidential questionnaire. One of the questions was, 'Would you want your son or daughter to work here?' A total of 621 professionals ticked the 'No' box. The 'Comments' section contained the same basic remark over 50 times: 'I want something better for my children.'

An increasing number of people report that they are generally unhappy with their jobs. One recent work survey interviewed 5,000 households and found that job satisfaction has decreased by 10 per cent overall in the last few years. Additionally, fewer than one out of three people said they were happy with the training and education programmes their company offered, and only one out of five people said they were happy with their company's promotion policies and bonus plans.[9] In another survey, three out of four people said they did not trust the CEOs of large companies. Relationships rarely prosper in a hyperactive climate.[10]

The American Medical Association recently issued a grave report entitled 'Physicians Are Working More, Enjoying It Less.'[11] Six out of ten doctors said their enthusiasm for practising medicine had dropped during the last five years. And 87 per cent of the physicians surveyed said that the overall morale of physicians has also significantly decreased in that time. One doctor told me, 'The soul of the workplace is in trouble.' He said, 'We doctors are miserable in our work and we spend all day treating people who are also miserable in their work.'

Joy is often a notable absentee in the Hyperactive Workplace. It seems we are simply too busy to enjoy ourselves. I often witness an extreme dissociation between work and joy in the companies for which I consult. Joy is not a priority in these places; it isn't even on the agenda. And yet, the economics of happiness shows that people who enjoy their work are a great asset. Joy is good for work, good for creativity, and good for success. People who think they can work without joy are fooling themselves. The cost of no joy at work is too high for any enterprise to be truly profitable.

It is a mark of intelligence, no matter what you are doing,
to have a good time doing it.
– Anonymous

Work without joy inevitably ends up as sacrifice. Too many people put up with a 'bad job' situation to earn money for 'good things' in life. This is not wise. This is not necessary. This is not success. In the hyperactive world of work, we end up overworked and overspent, and our lives are over before we know it. If we are not careful, we get so lost in our constant activity that we fail to recognise what the real work of our lives is about.

I once worked for a British company with a rich Quaker heritage, which asked me to run a series of 'Joy at Work' seminars. A recent in-house survey had identified a long-hours work culture that was affecting productivity, absenteeism, and sickness. The managing director took me on a tour of the company headquarters. We passed by a room that looked like an old store cupboard. 'We store computers, printers, and that sort of thing in here,' he said. 'It used to be a prayer room.'

I asked him, "Where do you pray now?"

He gave me a quizzical look. "We don't pray anymore," he said.

In the hyperactive world of work, more computers, more printers, and more photocopiers will not save us. Prayer can. Vision can. And so can courage.

SUCCESS INTELLIGENCE TIP 3 – *PRAYER*

I sometimes ask my coaching clients, whether they are religious or not, to write:

1. 'A Prayer for Life'
2. 'A Prayer for Work'
3. 'A Prayer for Relationships'

A genuine heartfelt prayer is a powerful way to clear the mind and listen to your best thoughts. Prayer inspires vision, strengthens focus, and supports intention. What do you pray for? What is in your heart? Clear a space in your schedule to reflect on what it is you really want to do with your life. Do this soon.

The Joyless Economy

Is it asking too much to be successful and happy?

I have worked closely with very successful people from all walks of life. It has been a great education. It has also prompted some deep questioning about success and happiness. For instance, why do millionaires take Prozac? Why do CEOs have heart attacks? Why do film actors need rehab? Why do rock stars commit suicide? Why do politicians cover up scandals? Why do sports champions self-destruct? Why isn't their success enough?

In 1996, BBC television filmed a 40-minute *QED* documentary on my work, entitled 'How to Be Happy'.[12] It was made by an Emmy Award–winning team at True Vision. The synopsis read:

> Modern science has endowed the human race with just about every gadget under the sun to improve the human lot, but it has cast little light so far on what is of prime importance to us all – how to be happy. Millions of man-hours have been invested in the treatment of depression, yet people remain depressed. We want to conduct an experiment to make people happy.

The BBC began by running 'Who wants to be happy?' ads in the national media seeking volunteers for a 'unique eight-week psychology training in happiness', which was based on a course I had pioneered for the National Health Service (NHS). The public response exceeded all of our expectations. For days we waded through mail bags with thousands of applications. Many people wrote about their 'inner discontent', 'feeling empty', ,something missing', and 'wanting more' out of life. One person described himself as 'one of life's dissatisfied customers'.

Eventually three people were chosen – Dawn, Caroline, and Keith. Five million television viewers tuned in on August 28 at 9:25 P.M. to watch their progress over an eight-week course of group workshops, personal coaching, home learning, and daily exercise. Their happiness training had four major areas of focus: (1) inner happiness, (2) everyday abundance, (3) positive relationships, and (4) true success. The results, as measured by independent scientists, were truly outstanding. Each volunteer made remarkable breakthroughs in his or her life.

The producers chose the three volunteers for their contrasting backgrounds. Keith, in his early 40s, was successful, rich, attractive, healthy, and discontented. He had all the symptoms of what scientists call the 'new depression'.[13] Keith told the producers: 'I thought I had everything I'd ever really wanted: a well-paid job, a girlfriend I was happy with – we'd been seeing each other a while – and a Mark II Jaguar. But there still seemed to be something missing. I wasn't happy about something, but what that something is I don't know.'

Keith's experience was a classic case of what I call 'the failure of success'. He had achieved a lot, he had everything he wanted, and now the only thing missing was the *feeling* of success. In our first coaching session I asked Keith to define success. 'Well, I thought success was having a great job, a beautiful girl, enough money, a nice house, a family one day, good friends, and, of course, my Mark II Jaguar.'

I told Keith that his definition of success sounded like a shopping list. He nodded thoughtfully.

The Golden Era

Economists inform us that the worldwide creation of wealth is currently at a new high. It all began in the 'Golden Era' between 1950 and 1973, when the Gross National Product (GNP) of developed countries grew at an unprecedented rate. Since then income, ownership, and buying have continued to increase. In other words, it is a good time to go shopping. We are richer than before, so therefore we should – with enough skilled shopping – be able to 'have' the happiness we want. In theory.

Since 1974, the World Values Survey[14] has charted the relationship between income, success, and happiness in 60 countries that represent 75 per cent of the world's population. One of its conclusions is that 'among advanced industrial societies, there is practically no relationship between income level and subjective wellbeing.' More specifically, the research finds: 'As we move from low-income societies to high-income societies, there is a steep increase in subjective wellbeing. But the impact of rising income stops when we reach the threshold of $10,000 [about £5,300].'

David Myers, a social psychologist, describes today's society as a 'doubly affluent' society. We are much better off in terms of income, ownership, and accessories than we were 50 years ago. So, therefore, our increased purchasing power has made us feel more successful and happy, right? After all, when people are asked what would improve the quality of their life, they always say, 'More money.' But Myers tells us that 'since 1957, the number of Americans who say they are "very happy" has declined from 35 to 32 per cent.'[15]

As well as working harder and enjoying it less, we are also consuming more and enjoying it less. In his book *The American Paradox: Spiritual Hunger in an Age of Plenty,* David Myers concludes from all his research that:

> We are better paid, better fed, better housed, better educated, and healthier than ever before, and with more human rights, faster communication, and more convenient transportation than we have ever known. Ironically, however, for 30-plus years . . . since 1960 . . . the divorce rate has doubled, the teen suicide rate has tripled, the recorded violent crime rate has quadrupled, the prison population has quintupled . . . [16]

The so-called Golden Era has a shadow. Accompanying the increase in wealth and consumerism, there has also been a significant increase in recorded depression,[17] mental illness,[18] violence,[19] drug abuse,[20] and suicide.[21] The World Bank and World Health Organization have both published reports that show that children of the 'Golden Era' are more likely (as much as ten times so) to suffer severe, life-threatening depression than their parents.[22]

Keith was experiencing his own golden era of success, and he was still miserable. At our second meeting, I suggested to Keith that his depression was a sign that his success was not the genuine article. Keith, to his credit, was willing to reassess his model of success. I recommended a process of self-enquiry to help him think more clearly about success.

Keith's self-enquiry began with me asking a series of questions, the first being 'Who is the most successful person you know?' Keith quickly identified someone who had a great job, a beautiful wife, a dream home, a vintage car, etc. Unfortunately, Keith had made another shopping list.

To help Keith better understand his own story about success, I asked him two key questions: 'What did your father teach you about success?' and 'What did your mother teach you about success?' Keith found both of these questions very challenging.

'We never really talked openly about things like success and happiness,' he said.

I encouraged Keith to reflect on how his father's and mother's attitudes to success might somehow have influenced his own thinking. Keith learned a lot about himself through this process.

Next, I asked Keith to identify five major lessons he had learned in his life about true success. With each major lesson, I asked him to reflect on when it happened, who was involved, what the real lesson was, and, most important, how well he had learned the lesson. This process took Keith two weeks to complete. He described this process as 'a lot of soul-searching'. On one occasion he said, 'I'm a salesman, you know, not a philosopher.' I told him that I believe none of us is short of wisdom; we just need the confidence to use it.

Finally, I invited Keith to write a letter to his son teaching him about the true nature of success.

'What should I write?' he asked.

I encouraged Keith to write about what true success is and is not, what lessons he had learned, and how best to live wisely in this world. When Keith read this letter, it completed a process of self-enquiry that most people never get around to – not least because we are too busy making money and too busy shopping. Keith had begun his course in Success Intelligence.

Being Successful

According to the Lexus ad, 'Whoever said money can't buy happiness isn't spending it right.' In our consumer-driven society, we have developed what philosopher Erich Fromm called a 'having mode' of existence. In this mode we define success, happiness, and love as 'things' apart from us that we must pursue, catch, and own. We speak in terms of 'achieving' success, 'getting the girl', and 'having' a great life. Our creed is 'I have, therefore I am.' And, also, 'The more I have, the more I am.'

Fromm, in his book *To Have or To Be?*, contrasted the 'having mode' with a 'being mode'. He said that 'to be' successful requires an enquiry and education about our identity (*Who am I?*), about our personal values (*What do I want?*), and about our vision (*What is my life for?*). Fromm warned us that if we skip this learning and try only 'to have' success, we risk accumulating more and more 'things' that we don't need or want anyway. We become 'thing junkies' who try to work and spend our way to success, but finish up feeling empty of any true purpose or value.

Economist Tibor Scitovsky wrote a landmark book in the 1970s called *The Joyless Economy*. It is considered by many thinkers to be one of the most important books written in the late 20th century. Tibor argued that the reason why so many people are successful and unhappy is not because there is not enough to accumulate; it is because we have not figured out what we really want. He writes:

> . . . the economist's approach tacitly assumes that con-
> sumers know what they are doing and are doing the best
> they can, so that the economist's only task is to see to it
> that the economy delivers what consumers want.
>
> That approach overlooks the fact that tastes are
> highly variable, easily influenced by example, custom,
> and suggestion, constantly changed by the accumulation
> of experience, and modified by changing prices and the
> availability of some satisfactions and the unavailability
> of others. In short, the economist's standard procedure of
> postulating that each consumer knows best what is good
> for him and trusting the consumer's behaviour to reflect
> that knowledge seems to me unscientific. [23]

In our consumer society, which has so much on offer, it is essential to know what you value and what you really want. Otherwise
the distractions and the disappointments can be endless. Several
research studies show that when people earn more they believe
they need even more to achieve any life satisfaction. For instance,
in one poll, people who earned $30,000 a year said that $50,000
would help them to reach satisfaction, whereas those who earned
$100,000 a year said they would need $250,000 to be satisfied.
And guess what the people who earned $250,000 a year said?[24]

The warning bells over our obsessing with 'having more' have
been ringing on deaf ears. As long ago as 1920, R. H. Tawney, in
his book *The Acquisitive Society,* wrote, 'Unless [society] is to move
with the energetic futility of a squirrel in a revolving cage it must
appeal to some standard more stable than the momentary exigen-
cies of its commerce or industry or social life . . .'

In 1970, Swedish economist Staffan Linder, in his book *The Harried Leisure Class,* warned that as our income increases – and therefore
the value of our time increases – the more rational it seems to devote
all our time to accruing more money. And thus, interest in friendship, beauty, art, literature, and spirituality wane and atrophy.

The truth is, however, that when it comes to feeling successful no amount of money is enough because *money is not enough.*
Hence, the key to feeling successful is not only more stuff,

more money, more credit, or more shops, but also *more wisdom.* Before you ask yourself 'How much more can I get?' you first have to ask 'What do I really want?' This one simple question – 'What do I really want?' – is the key to feeling truly successful. No amount of materialism can provide the answer to this question; only you can do that. You must learn to be wise.

In essence, a new model of success is needed – a model that knows that success is primarily a way of being and not just a shopping list. Keith was willing to have a new conversation about success. In our coaching sessions we often explored the question 'What do I really want?' I encouraged Keith to extend his conversation beyond 'having' to also include 'doing' and 'giving' and "being' and 'learning'. This is reflected in Keith's summary at the end of the television documentary, when he talks about the value of reflection, his new beliefs about success, the importance of relationships, and his renewed determination to enjoy his life.

SUCCESS INTELLIGENCE TIP 4 – *TRUTH*

At my seminars I use a self-inquiry exercise called 'Truth' in which people are given three questions to answer as honestly as possible. The first question is 'What do I want?' Here, you are given ten minutes to speak your mind.

The second question is 'What do I really want?' You now have another ten minutes to share from your heart.

And the third question is 'What do I really, really want?' You now have ten more minutes to bare your soul.

Each question is an invitation to be clearer about true success.

PART II

Potential

• • ● • •

Not in the clamor of the crowded street,
Not in the shouts and plaudits of the throng
But in ourselves are triumph and defeat!

– Henry Wadsworth Longfellow

Authentic Success

The Self Principle

The Success Contract

Inner Dialogue

I was once thrown out of class at school for being 'smart'. It was a maths class, and we had been given another one of those questions: 'If Bob and Bill live 30 miles apart and Bob travels at 20 miles per hour and Bill travels at 40 miles per hour, at what exact minute will they meet?' I dreaded those questions.

'What is your answer, Robert?' snapped the teacher.

I had no idea, so I said, 'It all depends how bad the traffic is. If they are meant to meet, I am sure they will. And if Bob is a few minutes late, Bill will forgive him.'

'Out!' shouted the teacher, pointing to the door. 'Don't get smart with me!'

I didn't do well in school. My academic education was a conversation I never really got the hang of. I studied algebra, but I didn't know what for. I did experiments with magnesium, but the conclusions were vague. I learned about the Factory Act of 1833, which was a long time ago. I gave up French, because I didn't know any French people. I dissected some grasshoppers, and I got a B+. I was always being told that my academic studies were very important, but I never fully understood why.

Many of my schoolteachers told me I had great potential, which I greatly appreciated. *Potential for what?* I wondered. I still have a copy of my final report, which I received in June 1982 when I was 17 years old. It reads:

> Robert has great potential – a most pleasant person whose academic limitations are offset by an excellent character which should recommend him strongly to any place of Higher Education.

My academic education was not bad, just irrelevant. I participated, but I wasn't inspired. My education prepared me to get through school, but not through life. I was taught lots of facts and how to pass a test, but not how to create a vision, discover a purpose, and live a successful life. After my father's illness and his ongoing homelessness, the sense of irrelevance only deepened. Then, at 16 years old, one of my best friends, Adam, was killed in a motorcycle accident. I had so many questions.

In 1983, at 18 years old, I received on the same day two very different offers for higher education. One was a fast-track one-year post-graduate course in journalism at Portsmouth College, which guaranteed a position on a local newspaper. I was told I would be the youngest student in the course by four years. It was a high-speed opportunity to learn a skill, land a job, and start earning a wage. The college dean encouraged me to make up my mind quickly.

The second offer was a three-year course in communications at Birmingham Polytechnic, which offered 'an excellent range of learning modules in psychology, sociology, arts, and media'. Would I choose the express work placement or the slower, more philosophical education? Most of my friends had already given up on education and had walked into the first job they found. Maybe I should do the same? After all, I didn't want to get left behind. My head said 'Portsmouth' and my heart said 'Birmingham'. So I took the slow boat to Birmingham.

In Birmingham, I finally found a curriculum that inspired me. After three years at the Polytechnic, where I graduated with distinction, I completed a further three years of self-directed study with advanced courses in psychology, counselling, psychotherapy, and philosophy. I read the works of political philosophers, Western sociologists, Eastern saints, metaphysical poets, religious mystics, and modern psychologists. My education was rich, broad, deep, thrilling, and challenging. I wasn't just studying, I was growing.

My psychology training taught me a lot about human potential – mostly our unlimited potential for pain, conflict, and disease. In my book *Happiness NOW!*, I recall how my psychology professors delivered a curriculum that covered the A to Z of suffering. Year One was 'Basic Suffering', Year Two was 'Deeper Suffering', Year Three was 'Advanced Suffering', and so on. My philosophy studies were also rather cheerless. 'There is no record in human history of a happy philosopher,' wrote the humorist H.L. Mencken. Almost true.

In the spring of 1990, I wrote my first major thesis, entitled *Psychology of Self*,[1] which explored the human potential for suffering and happiness, failure and success, mistakes and wisdom. My thesis began with an old story told in a modern setting:

One lazy Sunday afternoon a busy businessman was hard at work entertaining a potential client at his home. The businessman had a young son of about six years old called David who kept running in and disturbing the negotiations.

David was bored, and he hoped Daddy and his new friend might want to play. Each time David entered the room, his father gave him something to play with: first a pen, then a calculator, then a book to read.

Finally, David's father found a map of the world, which he tore up into 50 pieces. He gave David a roll of tape and asked him to return only when he had stuck the world back together again.

David returned after only five minutes with the map of the world complete again. His father was astonished. 'How did you do that in so short a time?' he asked.

'Easy,' replied David. 'On the back of the map of the world I had already drawn a big picture of myself, and when

I put myself together the world came together, also.'

In my thesis I asserted that every person is the custodian of a vast potential, the width and breadth of which no scientist has ever been able to measure. This innate potential has two poles – heaven and hell, light and dark, joy and sorrow, oneness and separation, ego and God, truth and illusion. Intelligence, which comes from the Latin *intelligens,* meaning 'choose among', is the ability to keep choosing the potential you most want to foster.

Success Intelligence begins with an awareness of and respect for the vast potential inside us all. William James, author of *The Principles of Psychology,* wrote:

> Most people live, whether physically, intellectually, or morally, in a very restricted circle of their potential being. They make very small use of their possible consciousness and of their soul's resources in general, much like a man who, out of his whole bodily organism, should get into a habit of using and moving only his little finger.

In the Manic Society, we live and work so fast we rarely have time to go deep. Such is the maddening pace of our life that we are often too manic, too busy, and too hyper to really get to know ourselves. Occasionally, we may enjoy some fleeting awareness of our true talent, but these peak experiences are not normal. Mostly, we get by and make do with the little we know about ourselves, and rarely if ever do we dip our toes into the deep pools of vision and creativity and beauty that exist inside us.

Every successful person has been helped by someone who believed in his or her potential. We all need mentors and friends to help us cultivate the 'Golden Seed' that is our true potential and divine natural ability. One of the chief functions of my work is to help people be more aware of their true potential. Realizing our potential, and using it in intelligent ways, is our purpose and our salvation. It is the key to success and happiness, for in ourselves are triumph and defeat.

Authentic Success

Your goal is to find out who you are.
— A Course in Miracles

Peter was a chief scientist for NASA. He was in his mid-40s. We had first met on a three-day leadership seminar. He telephoned me nine months later to request a private one-on-one coaching session. When we eventually met, I began by asking Peter what he wanted from our time together. He said, 'I am here because I have been given a second chance.'

Peter told me how he had survived a heart attack only two months earlier. It happened suddenly, without warning. He was at a conference, in his hotel room dressing for dinner, when, in his words, 'I felt my heart exploded inside me.' A colleague found Peter lying on the bedroom floor. Peter said, 'I was rushed to hospital and operated on immediately. The surgeon said if the hospital had been 15 minutes farther away I probably wouldn't be sitting here talking to you now. I would be dead.'

Peter was visibly shaking as he recounted his near-death experience. He became even more nervous as he told me, 'During the operation to save my life, I had an out-of-body experience. I actually saw the whole thing. I could hear everything they said.' Peter had heard of a department at NASA that researched out-of-body experiences, but he had not believed they really happened. Understandably, he was somewhat surprised.

I told Peter I was familiar with the research, to reassure him that it was okay to talk about it. He continued, 'As I floated over my body, I became aware I was seeing images of my life projected on a shimmering silk screen in front of me. I saw myself growing up, attending school, meeting Deborah [Peter's wife], bringing my son Neil home for the first time, moving to Washington, D.C. – everything.' Peter hadn't even told his wife about his experience, and he was clearly very unsure of himself as he spoke.

What Peter told me next was most remarkable of all. He said, 'As I watched the film of my life, I sensed something was missing. At first I wasn't sure what was missing, but finally I saw that it was me. My life has been about everybody else, not me. It has been about my work, not me. It has been about research, not me. It has been about income, not me. It's like I haven't really been present in my own life.'

I asked Peter, 'How could that be?'

He paused for a moment and then said something I will remember forever. He said, 'I think I just got busy.'

Peter was a knowledgeable man. He had a Ph.D. in astrophysics and had studied celestial mechanics, gravitational fields, the internal structure of planets, and stars. He was conversant in cosmogony, which is the study of the origin and development of the universe, and he was also an expert in the technology that can send astronauts into space. He could write a dictionary of physics, not just read one. As I got to know Peter, it was clear he could speak eloquently on almost any subject except one – himself.

In our Manic Society, it is easy to become strangers to ourselves, just as Peter had. Our rapid, unrelenting schedules demand so much of our energy and awareness. Time flies, and we are so busy with our projects, plans, and Palm Pilots that there is no time for reflection. We attend to what is in front of us, not within us. Our drive for achievement and recognition demands that we override our feelings, our wisdom, and our exhaustion – just to get through another day.

> *Ninety per cent of the world's woe comes from people not knowing themselves, their abilities, their frailties, and even their real virtues. Most of us go almost all the way through life as complete strangers to ourselves.*
> – **Sydney J. Harris**

Reading Ourselves

In the Manic Society, we forge ahead and we forget. We become so habitually hyperactive that we forget how to be still, relax, and tune in to how we really feel. We forget how to 'read' ourselves. We have an endless list of PINs and passwords for various accounts and clubs, but we have no real access or connection to our inner selves. We are so saturated with the increasing demands of our lives that we forget how to be self-aware, inner-directed, and true to ourselves. 'To do my job well I had to become someone I would rather not be,' Peter told me.

Peter had been too busy – for more than 20 years – to make any significant time for himself. He had become so outer-directed that a lot of his decisions were based only on what other people wanted of him. To put it another way, Peter had become less and less self-referent (i.e., referring to his vision and values for his decisions) and more and more object-referent (i.e., using only external cues such as approval, status, and finance). Peter said, 'Somewhere along the line I have forgotten how to distinguish between good goals and authentic goals.'

I shared with Peter my work on the Psychology of Self. In relation to his heart attack, I talked about what the Greek philosopher Pythagoras had said: 'There is no illness, only ignorance.' The 'ignorance' Pythagoras spoke of is a lack of self-awareness. I told Peter that his heart had probably been sending him 'messages' (in the form of physical symptoms) for years, but because he hadn't read the messages they eventually became louder. 'That's probably true,' he said. Most schools of psychology – Freudian, Jungian, Adlerian, and Rogerian – acknowledge that a lack of self-awareness is a common root cause of personal disease and unrest.

To help Peter 'read' himself better, I gave him something called an 'I AM' Self-Rating Scale (see Figure 2). I often use this scale in workshops and coaching sessions as a mirror for self-awareness and a prompt for deeper self-enquiry. The 'I AM' Self-Rating Scale starts by encouraging you to notice your response to each 'I am' statement. For instance, with 'I am happy' you notice how true or not this feels and mark your score accordingly. Next, you investigate your response; for example, 'Why do I feel this way?' 'What is the lesson here?' 'What could I be doing differently?'

'I AM' SELF-RATING SCALE

I am successful	+3 +2 +1 0 -1 -2 -3	I am not successful
I am happy	+3 +2 +1 0 -1 -2 -3	I am not happy
I am on purpose	+3 +2 +1 0 -1 -2 -3	I am not on purpose
I am healthy	+3 +2 +1 0 -1 -2 -3	I am not healthy
I am energised	+3 +2 +1 0 -1 -2 -3	I am not energised
I am centred	+3 +2 +1 0 -1 -2 -3	I am not centred
I am wise	+3 +2 +1 0 -1 -2 -3	I am not wise
I am grateful	+3 +2 +1 0 -1 -2 -3	I am not grateful
I am loved	+3 +2 +1 0 -1 -2 -3	I am not loved
I am optimistic	+3 +2 +1 0 -1 -2 -3	I am not optimistic

Read each 'I am' statement on the left. Notice your response to each statement.

How are you feeling? What are you thinking? Circle your answers.

3 means 'very', 2 means 'often', 1 means 'sometimes', 0 means 'not sure'

Take time to enquire and learn about your responses.

FIGURE 2: 'I AM' Self-Rating Scale

I wanted Peter to get to know himself better, so I asked him to complete the scale once a week. Each time we met we used the scale as a focal point for our discussions. Once I asked Peter for his response to the statement 'I am successful.' Peter told me his score was minus three.

'How long have you felt like that?' I asked.

'I have never felt successful,' Peter replied.

'Why is that?'

Peter realised he had never defined success for himself, and also that he rarely acknowledged his successes. 'I am always chasing the next success,' he said.

On another occasion I asked Peter for his response to the statement 'I am energised.' Peter again gave a minus three score.

'Why is your energy reading so low?' I asked.

'Maybe a lack of vitamin C,' he joked. Peter was unused to this depth of self-enquiry and would often playfully resist. 'Does there have to be a reason?'

I invited Peter to close his eyes and tune in to his tiredness. 'Ask yourself, why are you this tired?'

After a few minutes, Peter opened his eyes and said, 'I'm tired because I don't like my job, and I don't want to do it any more. It's not me.'

Who Am I?

Self-knowledge is a primary key to Success Intelligence. It is far more important than your IQ, your CV, your Ph.D., your MBA, or your last job reference. The better you know yourself – what you value, what inspires you, what you are made of – the more effectively you will live, work, and relate to others. Self-knowledge is the jewel in the crown of success. It enables you to be inner-directed, self-referring, and true to yourself.

Without self-knowledge there can be no authentic success, no authentic happiness, and no authentic living. If you do not know who you are, how can you know what success really is? Without self-knowledge you may end up chasing other people's definitions of success, but not your own. The failure to be true to oneself, to be faithful to core values, and to listen to innate wisdom leaves even the most accomplished person feeling unsuccessful and as if something is missing.

My coaching sessions with Peter were all about re-education. I wanted him to get to know himself again. Like any good coach, I asked Peter a lot of questions. A coach's chief tools are questions, especially the open-ended ones that invite self-enquiry and self-insight. It is the questions we ask ourselves – and those we fail to ask – that shape our lives. Intelligent questions are often the answer to our problems and challenges. They have a way of unlocking awareness, wisdom, and potential that we have hidden from ourselves for ages.

Peter's first major piece of homework was to answer the question 'Who am I?' This question is what every mystic, philosopher, executive, housewife, and child tries to answer. I often ask this question of my clients because I believe the answer leads to authentic success and true happiness. I also ask this question of organisations and companies. Once I asked a board of six regional directors each to write a 1,000-word essay about their company entitled 'Who are we?' The perspective they gained from examining this question enhanced their sense of identity, their clarity of purpose, and their ability to serve.

Peter had never asked himself 'Who am I?' before. I told him that I didn't want a quick answer from him. I also said that he could answer the question however he liked.

'That's not much help,' he jibed.

'It's your question, and therefore it must be your answer,' I said.

When I met Peter a month later, he produced a poem called 'At the Distant Horizon'. It was about a man who had chased success all his life but only arrived at the horizon of success after first journeying into his heart. Peter said, 'I thought I would bring you an essay, a flowchart, or a technical drawing, not a poem. I had no idea I could write a poem.'

Peter's self-enquiry taught him a lot about himself. It unlocked a potential for creative self-expression that had previously been dormant. His self-enquiry also helped him to discover other innate forms of potential, including the potential for inner wisdom, the potential to choose his own life, and the potential to enjoy authentic success. Through self-enquiry, Peter learned he already had the potential within him to enjoy everything he truly wanted.

Peter and I continued to explore the big questions of life together – questions like 'Who is the real me?' 'What is a successful life?' 'Knowing I will die, how shall I live?' and 'Is there a God, and what does She look like?' These big questions have value if the intention in the asking is genuine. Peter was 100 per cent genuine. He wanted a second chance to live a happy and successful life. He discovered that, as the writer James Baldwin said:

> *The questions which one asks oneself begin,*
> *at last, to illuminate the world,*
> *and become one's key to the experience of others.*

SUCCESS INTELLIGENCE TIP 5 – *BIOGRAPHY*

Imagine you received an invitation in the mail today to submit your biography to the next edition of *The International Who's Who*. Before you write your biography, think about your life and about what you really value, what inspires you, and what you love. Then answer these four questions:

1. 'Who is the real me?'
2. 'What have I learned?'
3. 'What have I contributed?'
4. 'What am I committed to?'

Don't edit. Write something authentic. We want to know about the real you. When you have finished, show your biography to a friend and ask for feedback.

The Self
Principle

Knowing others is intelligence; knowing yourself is true wisdom.
– Lao Tzu

Central to all of my work is something I call the 'Self Principle'. This principle has an enormous influence on how every person experiences his or her life. It is an essential key to potential and talent, transformation and growth, success and happiness. The Self Principle (see Figure 3) states unequivocally that: the quality of your relationship with yourself determines the quality of your relationship with success, happiness, love, God, money, time, health, luck, and everything.

How does this work? Self-knowledge is a good starting point. Your self-knowledge is your central reference system for every other type of intelligence and wisdom. The better you know yourself, the better you can live and work with authenticity and authority. Your self-knowledge is what helps you to discern between true purpose and pointless goals. Self-knowledge also teaches you about your inner strengths and true values. The better you know yourself, the better you can trust your wisdom, follow your joy, and liberate your talent.

Equally important is self-acceptance. The more we practice self-acceptance, the easier it is to acknowledge our strengths, appreciate our successes, face up to challenges, be open to feedback, receive offers of help, and so on. Self-acceptance makes everything easier, whereas a lack of self-acceptance creates more struggle and disharmony and requires much more effort. Psychologist Carl Jung emphasised the importance of self-harmony in all of his written works.[2] He wrote:

*Man can meet the demands of outer necessity in an ideal
way if he is also adapted to his own inner world,
that is, if he is in harmony with himself.*

The Self Principle also highlights the importance of self-observation. As we grow up, most of us learn how to judge ourselves but not really how to see ourselves. Our parents, our teachers, our relatives, our friends, and everyone else feed us a diet of judgments that we internalise as 'I am' and 'I am not' and 'I can' and 'I can't'. For example, if your schoolteacher tells you that you sing so badly it gives the whole class a stomach-ache (I was put in the 'nonsinging group' at school), you might easily conclude, 'I am not a singer' and 'I can't sing'. A self-image begins to form.

During my three-year communications course at Birmingham Polytechnic, I did a four-week internship at a BBC radio station. The aim was to gain experience in live radio and explore possible career options. I have always loved radio, and I gave this opportunity my very best. After three weeks the boss called me in because, I hoped, he wanted to give a young man some encouragement. Actually, what he did was tell me in no uncertain terms that I had no voice, no talent, and no future in radio.

The question is: was my boss telling the truth, or was it just his opinion? At first, the way I heard it, I thought he was telling the absolute, unequivocal truth. I was devastated. My heart was on the floor. I had no voice, apparently. And no talent, apparently. And no future, apparently. All of my subsequent soul-searching was essentially about 'What is the truth about me?' 'Who decides if I have talent or not?' and 'Who decides my future anyway?' Five years later I had my own radio phone-in show on a BBC radio station, but I nearly gave up before I had even begun.

A self-image is formed from the judgments you and others make about you. This self-image is your 'Learned Self'. It is fashioned out of information, experiences, feedback, and conclusions you make. It may bear no relation to your 'Unconditioned Self',[3] which houses your original potential and spiritual essence. Indeed, I believe the self-image is at best like a very poor photocopy of the

Unconditioned Self. Rediscovering the Unconditioned Self often requires us to transcend the self-image, let it go, and re-educate ourselves about who we really are.

Figure 4 illustrates the connection between our self-image and our perceptions, our beliefs, our psychology, how we communicate, and how we behave. Your self-image is pivotal to the process of how you live in the world. It is the key to your life story. Nothing has more influence. When you change the way you see yourself, you change your experience of the world. Herein lie enormous possibilities. Let's take a closer look:

1. Self-image and Perception

'We see things not as they are, but as we are,' wrote Immanuel Kant. Your self-image is the lens through which you see the world. If you cannot see yourself being successful at something, you will probably talk yourself out of trying. Or, if you can see you have a talent for something, you may find all sorts of inner strength and external help. All your decisions are based on what you see you are capable of and, also, what you think you deserve.

The new view of modern science is that we live in a participatory universe in which the observer and the observed are inseparable. Werner Heisenberg, the Nobel Prize winner for physics in 1932, changed science forever when he concluded, 'The common division of the world into subject and object, inner and outer world, body and soul is no longer adequate.'[4] Ultimately, then, perception is a projection and the world is a mirror. Thus, if you will see yourself differently, your outlook can change and so can your experience.

2. Self-image and Beliefs

You do not see a world that is objective to you. You see your beliefs. You see your hopes. You see your fears. A cynic and an optimist both believe they see the 'truth', but really they just see what they most identify with. Thus, a cynic sees an 'opportunity' as a prelude to more disappointment, whereas an optimist sees an 'opportunity' as a chance for adventure. Self-belief is really your personal take on what is possible or not. Whenever you change your beliefs, a new world of opportunity appears.

Ralph Waldo Trine begins his book *In Tune with the Infinite* with a prelude, which states:

> The optimist is right. The pessimist is right. The one differs from the other as the light from the dark. Yet both are right. Each is right from his own particular point of view, and this point of view is the determining factor in the life of each. It determines as to whether it is a life of power or of impotence, of peace or of pain, of success or of failure.

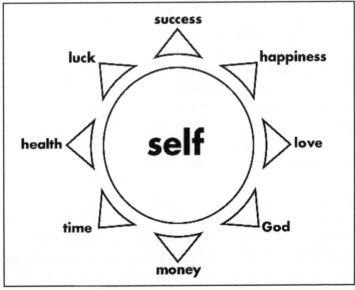

FIGURE 3: The Self Principle

3. Self-image and Thoughts

Psychologist Albert Bandura is a leader in research on self-regard and success. His research shows that 'people who regard themselves as highly efficacious act, think, and feel differently from those who perceive themselves as inefficacious. They produce their own future, rather than simply foretell it.'[5]

Imagine that two people each receive invitations to give a public speech. The person who sees himself as capable and talented will think positively about this opportunity, whereas the person who thinks *I always make a fool of myself in public* will think negatively about this chance to die a public death. Similarly, after a trauma, the person who sees himself only as a victim will think differently from someone who sees himself otherwise.

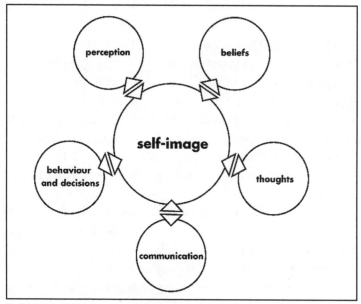

FIGURE 4: Self-Image Connection

4. Self-image and Communication

Your self-image influences greatly the way you relate to and communicate with everyone else. In essence, every relationship you have with others is an extension of your relationship with you. 'Your confidence in people, and your doubt about them, is closely related to your self-confidence and your self-doubt,' wrote Kahlil Gibran, author of *The Prophet*. Again, it is your self-image that influences what you think is possible and what you deserve in relationships.

In my work I find that many relationship conflicts are really, at root, self-image conflicts. For instance, it is so difficult for someone who refuses to see his or her own value to accept the praise, kindness, and love of another. It falls on deaf ears. Poor self-regard can cause unhealthy levels of independence, competition, jealousy, self-editing, people-pleasing, and self-attack. We may say, 'I have nothing to prove to anyone,' but that isn't really how we feel. Conversely, positive self-regard can help promote better intimacy, partnership, generosity, and overall success.

5. Self-image and Behaviour

How you see yourself determines the sorts of roles you take on in your relationships, at work, and in life generally. Your self-image is your 'internal advisor' that counsels you 'to do or not to do'. It assesses every situation and suggests various courses of action or non-action. Naturally, your self-image cannot help but look after its own interests. In other words, we do not always act or behave in a truly authentic way because our self-image is trying to preserve itself.

Maxwell Maltz was a 20th-century facial cosmetic surgeon who learned that no matter how much people alter their appearance (new nose, new lips, new chin, no frown lines), they will not see themselves as 'beautiful enough' if their self-image is still in need of repair. In his best-selling book *Psycho-Cybernetics*, he wrote:

> The most important psychological discovery of this century is the discovery of the 'self image'. Whether we realize it or not, each of us carries about with us a mental blueprint or picture of ourselves. It may be vague and ill-defined to our conscious gaze. In fact, it may not be consciously recognizable at all. But it is there, complete down to the last detail. . . All your actions, feelings, behavior – even your abilities – are consistent with this self-image. In short, you will 'act like' the sort of person you conceive yourself to be.[6]

Liberating Talent

An important aspect of Success Intelligence is knowing how to liberate talent. In my coaching sessions and my major seminars (one is called 'Liberate Talent'), I help people identify their strengths and express their talents. Tom Peters, co-author of *In Search of Excellence,* is someone I collaborated with on a leadership event in Sri Lanka. He says that business leaders should think of themselves as 'connoisseurs of talent'. I like this. I think that parents, teachers, psychologists, doctors, friends, and coaches should all think of themselves as talent connoisseurs.

Many people go through life unaware of their true strengths, talents, and gifts. When I ask people to speak of their talents, they often give me a blank stare, as if I had suddenly spoken in a foreign tongue. Marcus Buckingham, co-author of *Now, Discover Your Strengths,* has conducted some excellent research on this subject. He writes:

> Unfortunately, most of us have little sense of our talents and strengths, much less the ability to build our lives around them. Instead, guided by our teachers, parents, and managers we become experts in our weaknesses and spend our lives trying to repair these flaws, whilst our strengths lie dormant and neglected.[7]

Many people have a habit of dismissing or making light of their talents. Sometimes this is conscious, sometimes not. Media entrepreneur Oprah Winfrey is someone who has dared to express her talent on the world stage. In many ways she has grown up 'live' in front of the world. She is an inspiration to millions of people, *and* she speaks openly about her own personal challenge to her own talents. In *O The Oprah Magazine,* she once wrote:

> One of my defining moments came in the third grade – the day a book report I'd turned in earned my teacher's praise and made my classmates whisper, 'She thinks she's so smart.'
>
> For too many years after that, my biggest fear was that others would see me as arrogant. In some ways, even the extra weight I carried was my apology to the world – a way of saying, 'See, I really don't think I'm better than

you.' The last thing I wanted was for my actions to make me appear conceited. Full of myself.

I now understand that the true measure of womanhood is exactly what I'd avoided for so long – to be filled with all of who I am. Beginning when we are girls, most of us are taught to deflect praise. We apologise for our accomplishments. We try to level the field with our family and friends by downplaying our brilliance.

We settle for the passenger seat when we long to drive. That's why, every week, I find my television studio filled with women who tell me they're so concerned with what others think that they've compromised their dreams and completely lost themselves.[8]

In my Liberate Talent seminars, I ask leaders, 'Is it safe to be talented in your organisation?' Too many people work in climates where innovation and talent are systematically stifled and unrewarded. They work in what I call 'survival cultures', as opposed to 'success cultures', where the working day is all about looking busy, obeying the system, managing insane bureaucracy, practising quiet violent obedience, learning blame avoidance, and forwarding e-mails. People who dare to be original and successful in a survival culture are quickly mocked and ostracised by their colleagues.

Any external culture (be it a work culture, a school culture, or a family culture) can have a major influence on personal development, but most influential of all is a person's internal culture – his or her own self-image, self-beliefs, and self-doubts. It is often said that success is a state of mind. It can also be said that the major blocks to success are states of mind. One of the major internal obstacles to success that I frequently encounter is 'Fraud Guilt' or the 'Imposter Syndrome'[9]. For many people, their Fraud Guilt ruins their experience of success.

In relation to the Self Principle, Fraud Guilt is experienced when people think others' estimation of them is higher than their own. For example, a newly promoted manager should feel successful, but secretly he fears his company has made the biggest mistake in its history. Or an actor receives a standing ovation at the final curtain, but he is full of self-attack because he sees only the technical flaws in his performance. Or a man is engaged to the woman of his dreams and knows he should be happy but he isn't because he can't believe his luck. Fraud Guilt is the shadow of success that can darken our finest moments.

I have coached many people who were afraid that their success was too good to be true or that they didn't really deserve it. People who achieve quick success are especially prone to bouts of Fraud Guilt. So too are people who experience a success that is bigger than anything they dared think possible. John R. O'Neil, in his book *The Paradox of Success,* says that Fraud Guilt occurs when 'the outer [learning] curve of public identity rises faster and peaks sooner than the internal [learning curve] of personal discovery.' Many famous people have shared with me their amazement at how they 'get away with it' and 'cheat the odds'.

Famous people often talk very openly to the media about their Fraud Guilt experiences. Here are a few examples:

> *I still think people will find out that I'm really not very talented. I'm really not very good. It's all been a sham.*
> – **Michelle Pfeiffer**, *People News,* January 18, 2002

> *With every new film, I still go back thinking, 'Oh my gosh. I'm going to get fired.'*
> – **Nicole Kidman**, *People,* April 3, 2003

> *I used to have this dream that somebody was knocking at my door. I'd say 'Who is it?' and they'd answer 'Police.' I'd open the door and they would say to me, 'Pack your bags. We realised you have no talent.'*
> – **Leslie Nielsen**, *Philadelphia City Paper Interactive,* 1999, **cpcn.com**

Sometimes I wake up in the morning before going off to a shoot, and I think, I can't do this. I'm a fraud. They're going to fire me – all these things. I'm fat. I'm ugly.
 – **Kate Winslet,** *Interview* magazine, November 2000

I still think the no-talent police are going to send me to jail.
 – **Mike Myers**

People with Fraud Guilt may appear to accept success, but internally they feel like they are faking it, and their big fear is that they will be 'found out' at any moment. Hence, they fail to own their talents, internalise the appreciation, and enjoy their success. Their successes leave them feeling empty and questioning what happens next. One option is to achieve even more success, but this will only increase the experience of Fraud Guilt. A better option would be to address the self-image and self-attack that prevents them from feeling successful.

When anyone faces a new beginning, addresses a blank page, and starts at zero again, it is likely they will meet their inner fears and doubts. The biggest challenges of our lives often stretch us beyond our self-image to something deeper. Who we think we are won't win this challenge, but who we really are can. The fear that our success quota is already used up may cause havoc with our mind. Yet, each time we stop still and reach inwardly to our Unconditioned Self – which houses our unlimited potential – it becomes more possible to discover strengths, liberate talent, and enjoy success. This is how the Self Principle plays itself out.

Success Intelligence Tip 6 – *Talent*

What do you respect most about yourself? What are your most valuable strengths, talents, and gifts? Answer these three questions. Be honest.

1. 'What am I really talented at in my work?'
2. 'What makes me very good at relationships?'
3. 'What have I mastered about living life well?'

Next, ask three people who know you well to share what they think your best talents are. If you have a block or conflict in your life at present, think about which talent you are not using in this situation.

The Success Contract

What is possible and what is not?
How do you know?

Imagine the following scenario. Put yourself fully in the picture. Notice what you think and feel as you read on.

You are having the time of your life. You believe life has never been better. Work is going really well. No interruptions. No conflicts. No unnecessary meetings. No junk e-mails. No difficult customers. No late nights. Your boss requested a meeting with you this week. He wanted to thank you personally for your excellent contribution. He has never done that before.

You are so in love with your partner. It's like you are having a second honeymoon. Yesterday, your partner bought you flowers.

'What's this for?' you asked.

'No reason,' your partner said.

Your children are happy. They seem to want to go to bed early these days. Their rooms are tidy. They even told you how much they appreciate your wisdom and advice.

You feel healthy. You are at your best weight in ten years. Your double chin is gone. The 'banish cellulite' cream really works. Your doctor gave you a clean bill of health at your last appointment. It occurs to you that you have never needed to use the health insurance you keep paying for.

You recently had an unexpected windfall in the stock market. Some old shares tripled in value due to a merger.

Your sports team is on a record winning streak. On

all your recent car trips the roads are clear and the traffic lights are always green. And the weather has been perfect. Blue sky. Warm. A gentle breeze. And the forecast says it's going to stay that way for . . .

Can life ever be that good for more than a day, a week, a month, a year? What were you thinking while you read how good everything is? Did it feel 'fantastic' or 'peculiar'? Did you notice a heightening sense of gratitude or an increasing sense of fear and disbelief?

What do you believe about life? How good can life be before you think *This is too good to be true*? How long can a winning streak last before you tell yourself *This can't last*? How happy can you be until you begin to question it? How complimentary and admiring can people be to you before it feels wrong? How easy can life get before you feel guilty? How successful can you be before you think 'unbelievable' and start knocking on wood everywhere for fear that your life is about to fall apart?

How much success can you really handle?
You may be cool under pressure,
But are you cool under success?

Imagine that in the back of your mind, beneath a pile of thoughts, there is a document entitled 'Success Contract'. Naturally you would be curious to find such a document. Where does it come from? Who wrote it? What does it say?

I first 'discovered' the Success Contract while coaching people one-on-one on the psychology of success. Much of my work with coaching success concentrates primarily on vision and wisdom, that is, defining success intelligently and adopting smarter strategies. Thereafter, it is about undoing blocks to success, many of which are internal and are written up in a person's Success Contract. By learning how to 'read' and 'rewrite' their Success Contracts, people can experience more happiness in their relationships and more success in their life.

The Success Contract is a metaphor, but its effects are very real. The Success Contract is a personal agreement drawn up by you and your ego (your self-image) that states – in categorical terms – how much success is possible and how much is impossible. The Success Contract is your guide to potential success. It is full of conditions and rules that are, essentially, your beliefs about success. These beliefs are very influential and may determine fully your relationship with success if you let them.

Everyone has a Success Contract. In fact, my work has taught me that we also have other contracts buried in the backs of minds, such as a 'Happiness Contract', a 'Relationships Contract', a 'Money Contract', a 'God Contract', a 'Health Contract', and so on. All of these contracts are authored and added to from a very early age. Contained within each of these contracts are the beliefs that help shape your experience of life.

According to your faith be it unto you.
– **Matthew 9:29**

If I were your coach, we would spend at least three coaching sessions on your Success Contract. Using a form of narrative psychology, I would ask you to tell me how successful you believe you will be in this lifetime. I would help you to uncover your beliefs and projections about how much career success you will enjoy, how much relationship success you will enjoy, how much financial success you will enjoy, and how much inner fulfilment you will enjoy. On one level it is all just make-believe, but it is also true that *what you believe will be how you live.*

Personal Laws

The Success Contract is a legally binding document in the sense that it has many 'laws' to which you consent and that you make real. These laws are your conditions of success. They stipulate what you must do in order to realise your potential for success. So, here is a question for you: *What are your conditions for success?* Think carefully about this. Search your mind for internal laws, rules, and regulations you believe you must comply with if you are to enjoy success.

In my experience most people are not conscious of how compliant they are with these laws. That is why I describe the Success Contract as 'sitting beneath a pile of thoughts at the back of your mind'. Below is a short list with brief descriptions of the more common laws of success. Take what I am saying personally. I recommend that you not just read this next section, but investigate it thoroughly and learn as much as you can about your relationship with success.

1. The Deserving Law

The world is full of talented people searching for a lucky break, full of intelligent people whose genius needs recognition, full of good-hearted people who surely deserve success. What really determines success? No matter how intelligent, talented, or committed you may be, it is your sense of worthiness that ultimately supports or sabotages your success. Ask yourself, then, 'How much success do I deserve?' Check the 'fine print' you have written in your Success Contract because, according to 'personal law', you are bound by it.

Some people have a long list of qualifications they must achieve in order to deserve success. Examples include 'I must really earn my success' and 'I must never slip up', 'I must always go the extra mile' and 'I must win everyone's approval'. Otherwise the success does not feel real or deserved. Ask yourself, 'What do I tell myself I must do in order to deserve success?' Many people who suffer from Fraud Guilt believe they do not deserve their success because they have not passed some internal qualification.

2. The Work Ethic

The Work Ethic is a philosophy that dictates that success is a by-product of blood, sweat, and toil. According to the Work Ethic, success 'must', 'can only', and "only ever does" happen through labour, labour, and more labour. If you are not experiencing success, the Work Ethic would advise more effort and hard work. If that doesn't work, you need to try even harder. The Work Ethic does not believe in natural talent, inspiration, synchronicity, flow, or effortless accomplishment.

People who believe that the Work Ethic is the only way to achieve success agree with statements like 'Success is 99 per cent perspiration and 1 per cent inspiration.' However, I have coached many people whose major block to success is that they are trying too hard. For instance, I have coached executives who work too hard, athletes who train too hard, artists who rehearse too much, and students who revise too much. Also, certain relationships can falter because we are trying too hard to make them work. If only we would relax, it could be so much better.

© 1997 Randy Glasbergen.
www.glasbergen.com

GLASBERGEN

**"Psssst—you should be back at the office!
Vacations are for lazy people!
What have you accomplished today?"**

3. The Pain Permit

Some Success Contracts carry a 'Pain Permit', which dictates that a person can only purchase success with pain tokens. Do you believe in the law 'No pain, no gain'? If so, you may have written pain into your Success Contract. Some people seem to attract a heavy load of struggle, setbacks, and misfortune. Their projects always hit a wall, their relationships are complicated, and their life is never easy. In fact, they often have a blind spot where the easy option lies. They are like Jacob, who wrestles with the angels instead of letting them help him.

Another mantra associated with the Pain Permit is 'Easy come, easy go.' I once knew someone who could not accept a large inheritance of money from a deceased relative because it didn't feel right. All her life this person had achieved success by going to the 'school of hard knocks'. She wasn't about to let some 'easy money' ruin everything she had fought for. Life can be hard at times, but we must be careful not to *believe* that life is hard. If we insist that this is true, we will unwittingly make everything harder than it needs to be.

4. The Hidden Cost

Do you ever find that having deserved, earned, and worked hard for your success, you then get hit with yet another 'bill' to pay? In my coaching sessions, I ask people: (1) 'What is the most success you would like to experience?' and (2) 'What do you believe that amount of success will cost?' Most people I have coached believe that success has a price that must be paid sooner or later. What does your Success Contract have to say about the price of success?

People who believe that success has to have a cost also believe in the law 'There is no such thing as a free lunch.' To them, everything is a negotiation, a deal, a transaction. Nothing just 'is'. There are no unconditional moments. There are no gifts. They find it difficult to accept success, happiness, and love because they believe all good things carry an invoice that has to be paid eventually. They are often afraid to succeed too much because they believe the price will be too high.

5. The Sacrifice Demand

Every day people make sacrifices for their success. This is particularly true in the Manic Society, where people are permanently busy chasing money, doing the deal, and putting in the hours. We routinely sacrifice our relationships, our families, our values, and our health for success. 'Success must entail some sacrifice,' we say. The highest truth about success and sacrifice is that *success requires you to sacrifice what is not important for what is*. If your idea of success leads you to sacrifice what you most value, surely it is not true success.

People are often afraid of the next level of success because they fear that more success demands even more sacrifice. They are afraid to step forward and be swallowed up by exhaustion, over-work, and sacrifice. Is this demand for sacrifice a God-given com-mandment, or is it just another narrow-minded, non-intelligent rule of your ego? Must success always demand sacrifice, or is there a better way? Identify an area of your life where you are in sacrifice at present and be open to a better way, even if you do not know what that is yet.

6. The Perfection Order

Some Success Contracts have a precisely worded 'Perfection Order', which states that a person is entitled to large amounts of success if he or she agrees never to make a mistake, fail, mess up, or come in second at anything. 'Get it right the first time' is the mantra here. According to the Perfection Order, success requires a perfect score or you forfeit your right to it. Apparently, failure is not a learning curve because failure is not an option.

Perfectionism is a double-edged sword: it can inspire great-ness, but it can kill inspiration. Perfectionists' greatest hope is that if they are never satisfied, everything will get better. Unfortunately, they cannot see the flaw in this thinking. Perfectionism is mostly a self-attack that distorts perceptions and causes self-defeating behaviour. I have never met a happy perfectionist. Even when a perfectionist scores a perfect '10', the '1' and the '0' appear not to line up straight. People who experience strong Fraud Guilt often have a lengthy Perfection Order in their Success Contract.

7. The Independence Rule

Do you know any very independent people in your family or at your workplace? How independent are you? If you have an 'Independence Rule' in your Success Contract, you probably don't like to burden other people with your problems. In fact, you prefer to be self-sufficient because you believe that asking for help is illegal. Also, you feel guilty about accepting offers of help because it feels like cheating. Anyway, success only means something to you if you do it all by yourself.

The Independence Rule states that you must reinvent the wheel, build the bike by yourself, and pedal on alone if you are to win prizes that mean anything. Dysfunctional independence is a prevalent block to success in Western first-world nations, where excessive individualism is the dominant trend. People who are too independent always have difficulty in relationships because they are not good at intimacy, receiving, and partnership. The Independence Rule also blocks the big successes that are possible only with cooperation and synergy.

New Beliefs

There are times in life when a person will surpass his own expectations and dreams with a moment of brilliance. Inspiration, grace, destiny – call it what you will – intervenes and takes a person beyond his psychology to a whole new level of success. Technically this person is now 'in breach of contract' because his success was greater, better, easier, and faster than he believed possible. What will this person do with his Success Contract now? Will he reinstate the old laws or rewrite them?

Your Success Contract is your own success agreement. The laws therein are made by you, not God. They are your beliefs, and therefore you can revise and update your Success Contract at a moment's notice. The choice is yours because you are the author of your own contract. My coaching sessions are often about helping people to become aware of their Success Contract and then helping them to reauthor it. When they do this, it can unlock their potential for success, often in immediate and dramatic fashion.

I recently did a one-time coaching session for Cliff Cotton, a young, talented manager at IBM. Cliff told me he had been in an 'acting role' of senior manager for the last six months. Initially, he had been daunted by the extra challenges and responsibility. I told him he was probably 'in breach of contract'.

'Did the move come sooner than you expected?' I asked.

'Yes,' he replied.

Cliff had adapted well. He had got over his self-doubt, found his feet, and performed well. In other words, he had amended his Success Contract with himself.

'The thing is,' he said, 'it's been six months now, and I have had no payrise, no acknowledgment, and no permanent job offer.'

I talked to Cliff about the Self Principle and also the Success Contract.

'Sometimes when we don't get acknowledgment, it's because deep down we are not acknowledging ourselves,' I said. Cliff explored his self-beliefs and self-doubts. I asked him to imagine I was his manager and to give me five good reasons why he was really ready for the job *now*. Cliff left in good spirits. The next day, I received an e-mail from him that read:

> Back into the lion's den today, but a strange thing happened. I had a call from my boss telling me a pay increase had been approved for me. He also gave me an interview date for the permanent position. Spooky!

But it isn't spooky. Not when you understand that if you raise your beliefs you can tap into greater possibilities and something higher. 'All things are possible to him that believeth,' says the Bible (Mark 9:23). We live in a land of make-believe. Your beliefs literally move the world around you. That is why when you rewrite your Success Contract you always get a better deal. Believe it.

Success Intelligence Tip 7 – *Faith*

Everyone is a philosopher. We each have a philosophy about success and about life. What do you believe about success?

Examine:

1. The past: What are the most unhelpful, limiting beliefs you have had to overcome to enjoy your success so far?

2. The present: What limiting beliefs do you now need to let go of for your next level of success?

3. The future: If you could take one positive belief with you – as a centrepiece for your altar of faith – what would it be?

Inner
Dialogue

Who taught you how to think?

How important are your thoughts? What impact, if any, do your thoughts have on your life? Can one new thought make any difference?

James was a junior tennis champion. He was 16 years old and was hoping to enter the professional circuit. He came from a 'tennis family'. He was four years old when he had his first lesson. He won his first competition when he was seven years old. There wasn't enough cabinet space to display all the trophies he had won since then. The media often billed James as a 'future star' of tennis. He was usually seeded number one for the competitions he played in. A lot was expected of James.

James had a perfect mix of natural talent and superb attitude. In tennis you need a great attitude because in every match you play you lose points, commit unforced errors, serve double faults, fail to make returns, and mishit shots, and you still have to remain positive. In fact, in tennis it is possible to lose more points than your opponent and still win the match! In spite of James's great attitude, he had hit what he called a 'mental wall' that he couldn't dismantle. That was when he decided to see me.

James had not won a tournament for six months – his longest dry spell ever. He had reached seven consecutive competition finals, as he was expected to, but each time he had underperformed and lost to opponents he should have beaten.

'It's since gone from bad to worse,' James told me. 'I've now lost in the first round of my last three events.' As I listened more to James's story, I agreed with him that his failure was not a talent gap, but a mental block.

I asked him, 'What do you say to yourself just before you play a match?'

'I just focus.'

'On what?'

'The game.'

James struggled with this line of questioning. He was largely unaware of the inner dialogue of his thoughts. But he eventually identified a single mantra he repeated to himself: 'I must win.'

I asked James, 'Why precisely do you tell yourself, "I must win"?'

He told me, 'It's expected. I'm the favourite. I want to play professional tennis. I must win.'

In our first session, I asked James to say 'I must win' out loud 50 times. Each time James repeated 'I must win, I must win, I must win,' he noticed that this mantra actually increased his physical tension and mental anxiety. He also noticed how saying 'I must win' generated mental pictures of tough points and poor shots.

Next, I got James to repeat 'I can win' 100 times.

'Saying "I can win" feels completely different,' he said. 'I feel no negative pressure, the tension isn't there, and all I feel is positive.' James won his next three tournaments back to back. A different thought, a different result.

Here is the question: 'Can a single thought really make that much difference?' Notice your conversation with yourself as you answer this question. It's important.

Inner Listening

Coaching is about listening. It is about helping people to listen to their inner dialogue – their own personal psychology – so that they can tap into their potential and be more effective. A person's inner dialogue is often the key difference between faith and doubt, courage and fear, success and failure. In essence, the inner dialogue sets the tone for every external dialogue with other people, life events, and creation itself.

People talk to themselves constantly. Psychologists call this behaviour inner dialogue or subvocal speech. They estimate that you speak to yourself at a conservative average of 50 words a minute, 3,000 words an hour. If you listen to your inner dialogue, you will notice an assortment of observations, judgments, commentary, beliefs, doubts, hopes, fears, anxieties, chatter, and general nonsense. Fortunately, it takes only one great thought – one inspired piece of inner dialogue – to create some success.

The most important conversations you
hold in life are the ones you hold with yourself.
Your own inner dialogue is an important key to success.

You think, you live. Your inner dialogue is the key to your perceptions, your decisions, your actions, and how you live your life. A useful metaphor is to think of your mind as being full of fast-moving mental traffic. Each thought is a vehicle that wants to take you somewhere. The thoughts you 'take' to be true and wise are what shape your future experiences. My friend Dr. Chuck Spezzano is a psychologist who has done some excellent pioneering research on inner dialogue. He concludes, 'Your thoughts are the direction you are heading in.'[10]

Notice how often your inner dialogue is a commentary about you. In any moment, you may be praising yourself or putting yourself down; you may be believing in yourself or doubting yourself; you may be encouraging yourself or criticising yourself; you may be acting as your own best coach or your own worst enemy. Inner dialogue is full of 'I am' and 'I am not' statements, 'I can' and 'I can't' statements, and 'I will' and 'I won't' statements. Listening for the wisdom, if any, in each statement is a true test of intelligence.

Inner Choices

The scientist Sir James Jeans wrote: 'The universe looks less and less like a great machine and more and more like a great thought.'[11]

Modern scientists who study the new physics say that the essential 'stuff' of the universe is not atoms, but thoughts. In their explanation of how the universe works they often refer to 'the thoughts of God' and the 'mind of atoms' and the 'dialogue of creation'. They do not relate to the world as a physical place, but as a state of mind. One of the main conclusions from new physics is that life is a state of mind.

The idea that 'success is a state of mind' is very old. 'It is the mind which gives things their quality, their foundation, and their being,' said the Buddha over 2,000 years ago.[12] Thoughts create actions and results. Thoughts make you want to give up; thoughts make you want to keep going. Thoughts make things look hopeless; thoughts make things look better. The lesson here is: *Be careful what you choose to think, because you will not go higher than your thoughts.*

> *The mind is its own place, and in itself*
> *Can make a heaven of hell, a hell of heaven.* [13]
> – **John Milton**

Thought is creative. Hence, if you *know* you never perform well at interviews, you will make yourself very anxious each time you have one. If you keep *believing* you don't deserve a bigger salary, you make it hard for others to think otherwise. If you keep *telling* yourself that 'they don't return my phone calls because they don't like me', you will lose confidence. If you keep *judging* the one mistake you made today as 'unforgivable', you will be more afraid of failure in the future. I think, therefore I am – i.e., I am afraid or I am hopeful or I am nervous or I am confident or I am unable – becomes your mantra. As my friend and mentor Tom Carpenter[14] says, 'Every day you are experiencing the effects of your thoughts.'

There is much talk in psychology about the power of thoughts. I personally believe that thoughts have no power. It is the thinker who has the power. Thoughts only have as much power as a person gives them. All too often we give away our power to our own thoughts. It is a test of true intelligence to know which thoughts to believe in and which thoughts to laugh at and let go. Thoughts are only thoughts. If we took all of our thoughts seriously – as gospel truth – we would all get into a lot more trouble.

Thoughts are choices. The most accomplished people experience doubts every day, but they have learned how to choose a higher thought. Great actors experience huge performance anxiety, but they have learned how to choose a higher thought. Sports champions feel like quitting every day, but they too have learned how not to take these thoughts seriously. The same is true for successful artists, writers, teachers, physicians, and peacemakers. As you choose your thoughts, you choose your experience.

I have coached many very successful people, but I have yet to meet a 100-per cent positive thinker, someone whose inner dialogue is entirely positive. Most people I know experience a spectrum of hopes and fears every day of their lives. The people who experience consistent success have learned how to identify with the thoughts that create the best outcomes. Even these people may still hit rough patches. And when they do, they call someone, they pray, they meditate, they get coached, and they find a way to choose again.

Inner Wisdom

In my Success Intelligence seminars, I often invite people to participate in an experiment called 'Wisdom'. Everyone is asked to stand up one by one, say out loud, 'I am a wise person', and notice their inner dialogue as they do this. They often report that their inner dialogue is cynical and dismissive: 'Not true!' 'Yeah, right!' and 'Who are you kidding!' are not uncommon thoughts. Usually, a few people feel too uncomfortable to participate. The fact is, we do not always take good care of our wisdom.

When I train people to become coaches, I teach them that a coach is not an oracle who dispenses endless wisdom, advice, and teaching. In coaching, the aim is to help the client access his or her own inner wisdom. Graham Alexander, pioneer of the GROW coaching model, with whom I have co-presented many events,[15] says, 'People have the answer already, and all a coach does is help them to hear it.' Graham describes coaching as 'doing nothing, with style'. I like this. A coach holds a space for people to listen to their inner dialogue and their inner wisdom.

I began this chapter on inner dialogue with a big question: *Who taught you how to think?* If you listen to your own inner dialogue you will hear many influences, such as your mother's voice, your father's opinions, your grandfather's humour, a teacher's wisdom, and so on. Alongside all of these 'learned thoughts' there is your innate wisdom, which is like an 'inner coach'. Learning to distinguish between learned thoughts and inner wisdom is an important key to Success Intelligence.

I once coached a man named Michael, an award-winning film director. Michael was a very intellectual man, hugely talented, quick-witted, very erudite, and prone to bouts of depression. He came to see me on the advice of a friend. At our first meeting he told me, 'I am fiercely tempted to give up directing films for good.' He was clearly disenchanted. He was also very ex-hausted.

'Is this your wisdom or your exhaustion telling you to quit?' I asked. Frankly, Michael was too tired to discern the difference. 'As your doctor, I prescribe a heavy dose of holiday,' I said.

When Michael returned from his time off, we had another coaching session. Somewhat refreshed, he described his thoughts of quitting film as 'insane'. Michael had a habit of working himself close to the point of exhaustion. Many people in the Manic Society work like this. They frequently override their wisdom. Exhaustion and thinking do not mix well. It is not wise to think when tired. I explained to Michael that just because he has a thought – like 'I'm going to quit filming' – it doesn't mean he has to take it seriously.

Over the next few sessions, I taught Michael a simple meditation exercise called 'Listening for the Highest Thought.' Michael's instruction was to begin each day by sitting still and listening to his inner dialogue for wisdom and guidance. His goal was to soar high up above the surface ego thoughts of his everyday mind and to visit the heavens where his best thoughts rest. I also asked

Michael to ask himself, 'If God had one thought for me today, what would it be?' I wanted Michael to learn how to listen inwardly for thoughts of God.

Meditation exercises like these are excellent for stopping the manic, busy activity that so often drowns out our inner wisdom. They create the perfect internal environment for distinguishing between an everyday thought and true wisdom. Michael persevered with meditation in spite of some initial awkwardness. He later told me it was the most valuable thing he had ever learned. He found it had a great impact on his life, his work, and his depression.

One day Michael arrived with a gift for me. It was 'The Knight's Prayer', which he had framed especially for me. He told me that this prayer had been his father's favourite prayer, and that he now began his daily meditating by reciting it. Michael's inscription to me read: 'To the Inner Coach in us all.' The prayer reads:

God be in my head,
And in my understanding;
God be in mine eyes,
And in my looking;
God be in my mouth,
And in my speaking;
God be in my heart,
And in my thinking;
God be at my end
And at my departing.

SUCCESS INTELLIGENCE TIP 8 – *DIALOGUE*

Set aside some time to listen to your inner dialogue. Notice how your mind is having a conversation about everything, including success, money, happiness, love, God, sex, health, etc. Focus on your conversation about success.

Listen to your inner dialogue, and see if you can distinguish between 'learned thoughts', 'everyday chatter', and 'inner wisdom'.

What are your wisest thoughts about success? What is your wisdom trying to teach you? And if God had one thought for you today, what would it be?

Let yourself be inspired.

PART III

Wisdom

• • ● • •

Try not to become a man of success,
but rather, a man of value.
– Albert Einstein

Wisdom Is Not an MBA

Success Is Not Always Up

Happiness Is Not an It

Money Is Not Your Purpose

Love Is Not Just an Emotion

I consider myself fortunate to have had a number of great mentors and teachers in my life. In particular I have spent time living and studying with an Indian sage, a Polish scientist, an American mystic, a Hawaiian doctor, and a British business leader. This diverse group of mentors inspired me with their unique shining examples. Also, they each gave me the same priceless gift, which was the confidence to trust in my own wisdom.

I met my first great teacher while studying communications at Birmingham Polytechnic. His name was Avanti Kumar. Ironically, he was a fellow classmate. He was a mature student – at the ripe old age of 24! Avanti was from India. He had studied Indian spiritual texts called Vedas, meaning 'knowledge', since he was 11 years old. He meditated daily, often for up to eight hours. He had a beautiful presence – serene, wise, and happy.

Avanti was the first person to help me think creatively about my life. We frequently engaged in marathon conversations about the nature of self, the psychology of success, the search for happiness, and the truth about life. The first book Avanti gave me was the Hindu text called the Bhagavad Gita, a poem about the human soul's struggle to awaken to true self-knowledge. Under Avanti's expert tutelage, I studied many classic works, such as the Buddhist Dhammapada, the Hindu Upanishads, the Koran of Islam, the Jewish Torah, and the Christian New Testament.

Avanti was also the first person to teach me about innate intelligence and inner wisdom. 'You are born wise,' Avanti once informed me, half smiling. Avanti's style of teaching was always direct and playful. 'You have all the wisdom you need, right now, to be happy and successful,' he said.

'Why is it that I don't feel very wise?' I asked.

'Just because you will not listen to your wisdom does not mean it is not there,' he replied. Avanti, like all great teachers, taught me to listen to myself. Great teachers point not just to the wisdom in themselves, but to the wisdom in us all.

One day I asked Avanti, 'What is wisdom?'

He told me an old Indian story called 'Neti, Neti.' In ancient India, a wise person was known as a *Rishi,* which is a Sanskrit word for 'seer'. A Rishi was someone who could see the difference between truth and illusion. Rishis would often be heard saying, 'Neti, Neti' – meaning 'not this, not that' – because they could distinguish between true happiness and fleeting desires, real success and pointless goals, inner peace and senseless aims.

> *Learn to recognise the counterfeit coins*
> *That may buy you just a moment of pleasure,*
> *But then drag you for days*
> *Like a broken man*
> *Behind a farting camel.*
> **– Hafiz, Sufi poet**[1]

Wisdom is discernment. It is the ability to know what is a true goal or a counterfeit goal. In our Manic Society wisdom is knowing the difference between busyness and success, activity and purpose, shopping and happiness. True wisdom is letting go of what is not valuable – 'not this, not that' – in order to be with what is priceless. This wisdom is the basis of authentic success – it goes much deeper than cultural conditioning, advertising campaigns, social comparisons, media pressure, and social fads.

The 'Neti, Neti' story has another, deeper level. When the Rishis said, 'Neti, Neti', they were teaching that true wisdom – as well as true happiness and success – is not 'out there' in something to pursue or achieve. True wisdom is innate.

'Do not piggyback on my wisdom, Robert,' Avanti would tell me. 'And do not believe what a book tells you just because it has sold a million copies. Test what I say, and test what you read by listening to your wisdom.' Avanti often described this innate wisdom in us all as Universal Intelligence.

Today, much of my work is about helping individuals and teams tap into their innate wisdom so as to live and work more skilfully. Wisdom is a lifesaver in the Manic Society, where so many people complain that they have no time to stop and think. Wisdom is what will save the Busy Generation from a life of meaningless busyness. Wisdom is the key both to authentic success in the Hyperactive Workplace and to genuine happiness in the Joyless Economy. There is never any shortage of wisdom, only of the confidence to use it.

Success Intelligence is about recognising inner wisdom and using it to good effect in your relationships, your work, and everything you give yourself to. In this part of the book, I offer some reflections on five important subjects: goals, purpose, success, happiness, and love. In each chapter I have included something of the spirit of 'Neti, Neti', to encourage discernment and true vision.

All men are born wise, but they do not use this wisdom;
they resemble the blind man who, lamp in hand,
cannot see the road . . .
– A Tibetan monk

Wisdom Is
Not an MBA

First say to yourself what you would be;
and then do what you have to do.
– Epictetus

Jack was a 31-year-old investment banker who had recently been made the youngest vice-president in his company's history. This was Jack's first opportunity to lead a team – in fact, an entire division of 700 people. Jack's success had been in sales, not leadership. So being a leader was new territory. The company believed in Jack's leadership potential and offered him the services of an internal mentor, who was a company board member, plus an external coach, who was me.

At our first meeting, we set some ground rules for our coaching, including confidentiality. I then asked Jack some questions about leadership.

'Are you looking forward to your new leadership role?' I asked.

'Absolutely,' said Jack, who tended to speak in a fast, positive, upbeat way.

'Are you at all nervous about the challenge of leading 700 people?' I asked.

'Not at all,' said Jack.

'Remember, our conversations are confidential,' I smiled.

Jack thought carefully for a moment, and then said, 'Well in that case, I feel completely out of my depth.'

'Why did you take this leadership position?' I asked.

'Well, it was the next thing,' said Jack.

'What sort of leader do you want to be?' I asked.

Jack looked quizzically at me. 'A good one, I guess.' Jack was a first-class salesman who knew his market and how to negotiate a deal. Leadership was new to him, however, and it was clear he had only vague ideas about his vision for leadership and what leadership really means.

I next asked Jack some questions about his life goals.

'My absolute priority is an MBA,' he replied.

'And what are your other goals?' I asked.

'Well, the MBA definitely comes first.'

Jack was clearly very focused on the MBA, so I asked him, 'What topic will you study for your MBA?' Jack didn't know yet. It quickly became apparent that Jack had not done any research into MBAs. It was simply the 'next thing' he felt he had to do.

Jack was a spectacular 'doer' who had achieved a lot in his short career. Most of his goals were what I call 'Achievement Goals'. Give Jack anything to achieve – any sale, any project, any goal, any carrot – and he is your man. Jack was a superior goal-getter who was hugely driven, focused, and resilient; but Jack was an inferior goal-setter in that he had little or no skill in how to choose a goal. Jack's main criterion for goal-setting was simply to go for the 'next thing' in front of him. An MBA was the next thing in front of Jack.

'Has anyone said you must do an MBA?' I asked.

'No,' he replied. He was already working six days a week, doing 14 hours a day, with a wife of two years and a five-month-old daughter, and now he wanted to enter post-haste on a two-year course about which he knew nothing and that would eat up countless evenings and weekends.

'Why do an MBA, and why now?' I asked. Jack's deeper self-enquiry revealed two main reasons. First, MBAs were all the rage where Jack worked. Second, he was the only vice-president without one.

True Goals

I introduced Jack to a programme I created called the 'Intelligent Goals System'. I explained to Jack that Intelligent Goals start with knowing the difference between a true goal and an unnecessary goal. I said to Jack, 'Climbing the Himalayas might be a true goal for someone but is probably an unnecessary goal for you.'

Jack replied, 'Actually, I have always wanted to climb the Himalayas.' This was a perfect answer for a man who focuses mostly on 'Achievement Goals'.

I changed tack and said, 'Intelligent Goals is the difference between trying to achieve every goal and achieving your true goals.'

Whatever you do, do it with intelligence, and keep the end in view.
– Thomas à Kempis

After Jack enquired more deeply about his desire to do an MBA, he realized his true goal was (a) to be a good leader and (b) to be more confident in his new role. I pointed out to Jack that he was now talking about 'Character Goals' (i.e., *being* a good leader and *being* confident) as opposed to 'Achievement Goals' (i.e., *doing* an MBA). Too often, the language of goal-setting is about 'doing', 'having', and 'getting' and not about 'being'. Without some focus on 'being', there is no true way to test if a goal is right for you or not.

Briefly, the Intelligent Goals System identifies various types of goals (see Figure 5), the most essential being 'Spiritual Goals' (What is my vision? What do I value most?) and 'Character Goals' (Who am I? Who do I want to be?). The clearer you are about these goals, the easier it is to set authentic 'Achievement Goals' (What do I want to do?), 'Acquisition Goals' (What do I want to have?), 'Relationship Goals' (How shall I be with others?), 'Destination Goals' (Where do I want to end up?), and 'Present-Time Goals' (What is important today?). See the Appendix for a fuller description.

Jack and I talked at length about his Spiritual Goals and Character Goals. 'These goals can't just be covered with a few sound bites. They take time, but they also save you time,' I said. First, we explored Jack's Spiritual Goals. Jack found this difficult at first because he had never thought about his spiritual values. 'I am not a religious person,' he said. I explained that Spiritual Goals are about vision, values, and what moves a person's heart. Spiritual Goals are what you give your life to. They are as important as life itself. These goals are discovered, not made. Self-enquiry is essential.

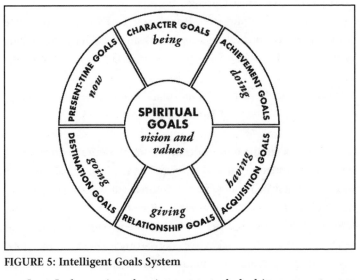

FIGURE 5: Intelligent Goals System

I set Jack a series of assignments to help him connect more consciously to his Spiritual Goals. One assignment was to write an essay entitled 'The Purpose of My Career', in which he had to identify the heart of his work and what truly motivates him. Another assignment was to keep a Leadership Journal in which to record his daily reflections on being a leader. His final assignment was to create 'A Guide to Success' in which he presented his own conclusions about true success. Jack said in one of our sessions, 'These assignments are like doing a spiritual MBA.'

After Spiritual Goals, Jack and I explored his Character Goals, which are about *being*. There are two levels to being. Level One is present-tense and is about being authentic, i.e., *Who am I?* Level Two is future-tense and is about realising potential, i.e., *Who do I want to be?* Your Character Goals are best identified by asking yourself questions like:

- What kind of person do I want to be?
- What kind of son or daughter do I want to be?
- What kind of husband or wife do I want to be?
- What kind of parent do I want to be?
- What kind of colleague do I want to be?
- What kind of leader do I want to be?

Jack learned quickly, as I expected he would. He was particularly motivated to focus on his Character Goals when I explained that the essence of true leadership is all about *being*. I explained that true leadership is not a position, it is an example. Leadership is not about 'do this' and 'do that' sound bites, it is about 'being the goal'. In practical terms, this means that if you want loyalty, you have to *be loyal;* if you want honesty, you have to *be honest;* if you want respect, you have to *be respectful*. Leaders generate possibility through their example. This is the spirit of leadership.

Once Jack was clearer about his Spiritual Goals and his Character Goals, he was in a better position to consider his Achievement Goals. In the time I worked with Jack, he became noticeably less feverish in his activity and more centred in his being. Life was no longer a race to see how much he could get done every day. His pace was more measured, he was more balanced, and he made a positive start in his new leadership role.

I also helped Jack to review his Relationship Goals. Together we identified the most important people to Jack in his work, which included his boss, certain team members, and key customers. In detail, we explored the current status of each relationship, the challenges and lessons of each relationship, and the desired outcomes of each relationship. In addition, we explored Jack's relationships outside of work, particularly with his wife and young daughter. One assignment I gave Jack was to ask his wife about her goals and dreams, and also to explore their goals as a family together.

It took Jack six months to complete the Intelligent Goals System. I wanted him to do it slowly, because I wanted him to do it well. Early on, Jack made a very important decision. He realized that to be the best leader – and the best husband and best father –

now was not the right time to do a two-year MBA. Instead, he drew up a list of support – which included mentoring, coaching, teamwork, and delegation – to help him to be more confident in his new leadership role. In short, Jack was ready to take on the challenge of not just 'doing' leadership, but actually 'being' a leader.

SUCCESS INTELLIGENCE TIP 9 – GOALS

Einstein wrote: 'Perfection of means and confusion of goals seem to characterise our age.' I think his words ring true for our age, also. Set aside time to review your goals. Identify your criteria for setting your goals. How do you decide if a goal is important or not?

Reflect on how you evaluate your success. Use the Intelligent Goals System and review your Spiritual Goals, your Character Goals, your Achievement Goals, etc., as explained in the Appendix. Think wisely about your true goals in work, relationships, and life.

Success Is Not Always Up

The highest reward from your working is not what
you get for it but what you become by it.
– Sydney Harris

I have made a living by asking people a very simple question: 'What is success?' I have asked this question in boardrooms, hospitals, churches, town halls, theatres, health clinics – virtually everywhere. I often find that even the most eloquent, accomplished people can stumble over their answer. Frankly, it is my experience that most people spend less time defining success than, for example, they take to complete a will. This is not much time, really, particularly when you consider that most people don't write a will.

In 1989, at just 24 years old, I founded a government-sponsored health clinic called 'Stress Busters'. For the next five years I offered a free service to people suffering from stress and stress-related illness. I worked with hundreds of people in group settings and one-on-one counselling. It was a massive education for me. One major lesson I learned is that stress is not just a physical ailment, it is also a symptom of deeper issues, such as a lack of self-knowledge, an absence of purpose, and having no clear definition of success.

At my Stress Busters Clinic I once worked with a group of 12 heart-attack survivors on an eight-week recovery programme. They were all men in their early 40s to mid-50s. They had very different backgrounds and were from different cultures, in different professions, and with different incomes. That said, all the men in this group had two major things in common. First, none of them had ever formulated a personal definition of success; second, in the three years prior to his heart attack, each had taken a promotion up the company ladder to do a job he truthfully didn't enjoy.

Graham was one of the group. He was 42 years old, a BBC engineer, recovering from triple-bypass surgery for a massive heart attack that almost killed him.

'I was told that I technically died twice on the operating table,' he told me. Two years earlier Graham had accepted his first management position. 'I hated it,' he told me. 'Something inside me was telling me it wasn't right. My wife told me the same. But I didn't listen.'

Graham was an engineer who worked on live coverage for BBC sports events. He spent much of his time at football fields, athletic stadiums, and horse racing tracks. This was the perfect job for Graham, who was a huge sports fan. After Graham's promotion he spent all of his time in an office pushing paper and making phone calls. He hated his job, his health suffered, and he was difficult to live with. He was eventually prescribed antidepressants for stress.

'Why did you take the promotion?' I asked.

'I felt I couldn't turn down a management position. It was a move up,' he replied.

Graham nearly sold his life away for a goal called 'up'. Like many people, he had been brought up to believe that 'up' is good and that 'up' represents success. He grew up watching his parents keep 'up' with the Joneses. He watched his colleagues, some younger than he, climb 'up' the company ladder. He watched his upwardly mobile friends, who were always shopping for an upmarket lifestyle. Graham decided to give 'up' a go and it led to a serious breakdown. On his way up Graham had lost sight of what he truly valued, and he nearly lost his life as well.

Measuring Success

Graham is an example of someone who had worked hard at success without ever working out what success is. When I asked Graham

'What is success?' he gave me vague answers littered with quantity measurements like 'more,' 'big,' 'bigger,' 'higher,' and 'up'. His thoughts were empty of any value measurements, such as 'happiness', 'love', 'peace of mind', 'service', and 'gratitude'. In short, Graham's definition of success had no heart.

'Up' is not a bad goal. The upside of a goal like 'up' is that it can inspire, stretch, and motivate a person to do great things. Aiming for the 'top', for example, can inspire brilliant performances and accomplishments. Reaching for 'higher ground' can give rise to great creativity and contribution. Up-goals can help a person to evolve and grow in so many ways. I have never told anyone to give up their up-goals, but I have often reminded people that 'up' is just one way – and not the only way – to measure success.

'Up' has its place, but a person must know what that place is. Otherwise, many people who are busy climbing the corporate ladder just keep climbing because they haven't any idea *why* they are climbing. Otherwise, many people who reach the top tax bracket simply continue to earn more money because they don't know what else to do. Many businesses that focus exclusively on increasing company share price *ad infinitum* lose sight of the spirit and purpose of what they do. They focus only on 'up' and so they fall down. 'Up' is not the whole answer to success.

One downside of 'up' is that it is entirely future-focused. People who measure success only in terms of 'up' run the risk of missing out on life along the way. In the chase for success they continue to hurry up, and they keep missing out on important moments, neglecting valuable relationships, forgetting their values, and losing their way. Just as Graham the BBC engineer had done. 'Up' is about a better future, hopefully, but the climb is often at the expense of a better life in the meantime. 'Up' is okay, though, so long as it serves a higher vision.

In the Intelligent Goals System (see the Appendix) there are 'Destination Goals' like 'up', 'next', and 'there'; there are also 'Present-Time Goals', which are about 'here' and 'now'. In my coaching work I like to see my clients strike a healthy balance between Destination Goals and Present-Time Goals. One way to maintain this balance is to ask questions that focus on the present. For example:

- If success is important to me, how can I make a success of today?

- If happiness is important to me, how can I enjoy today?

- If love is important to me, how can I make love count today?

- If relationships are important to me, how can I show that today?

- If health is important to me, how can I be healthy today?

The word *success* is derived from the Latin *succedere*, which means 'to go on well'. This implies that success is a journey and not just a destination. So, if success is a journey, it is important to consider what sort of journey you would like to experience. It is also important to know if you are journeying on a road 'to success' or a road 'of success'. The difference is more than semantic. Graham was traveling 'to success' and his journey was a miserable one. When he began to travel the road 'of success', he had to make sure that his wisdom and his values travelled with him also.

It is my experience that many people relate to success as something to celebrate at the end of their days, when they finally 'get there'. All their energy is invested in a ticket that will get them to a land called 'there'. But life isn't just about 'getting there'; it is also about 'being here' and enjoying your journey. Therefore, when I ask people, 'What is success?' I want to make sure they are using measures for both the journey and the end. Ultimately, the journey *is* the end, anyway.

Questioning Success

In my Success Intelligence seminars, I have a sequence of three questions about success I like to ask. The first question is: 'What is success?' This question is so important. I believe that *how well you answer this question determines how well you will live your life.* Yet many people tell me that they are too busy doing, busy chasing, busy working to have time to formulate clearly their thoughts about success. Only very rarely have I met anyone who has written a personal definition of success. It seems most people prefer to chase something they haven't thought about.

When working in organisations, I often ask teams 'What is success?' This is such a basic question, and yet many teams tell me they have never addressed it. So what have they been doing? It seems that they have been busy achieving goals, executing objectives, and winning deals. But isn't that success? Not necessarily. For example, I once worked for a company whose demise began on the day they won a multimillion-dollar contract that they couldn't deliver. I have also worked for an organisation whose multimillion-dollar turnover could not prevent them from having to lay off another 1,000 people at Christmas.

To answer the question 'What is success?' you have to examine the heart of your enterprise. This question hopefully stimulates some rich conversations about 'Why do we do what we do?' 'What do we enjoy about it?' and 'How could we do even better?' I once coached a CEO who said, 'My company is like every other company: we have a brand, a logo, and products to sell. But what I want to know is why we do it. What really inspires us?' I encouraged him to find out. He immediately set up an off-site meeting with his top team. The agenda had one item on it: *What is success?*

The second question I like to ask is: 'How do you measure success?' This question is designed to help people be clear about the yardstick they are using to measure success. This is important because, if your criteria for success are not clear, you cannot really know if you are successful or not. Most often, people identify quantity measurements, such as 'more', 'bigger', and 'up'. Less often, people mention value measurements, such as 'happiness', 'service', and 'love'. Without a healthy balance between value measurements and quantity measurements, our successes often feel empty and inadequate.

I gave Graham, the BBC engineer, an assignment to write his own obituary. He found this very challenging, especially since he had recently come so close to death. He did a beautiful job. When he read his obituary to the group at the Stress Busters Clinic, several of us were moved to tears by his heartfelt words. Interestingly, obituaries rarely mention the deceased's upmarket properties, their top-of-the-line sports cars, or their expensive china and cutlery. What is mentioned is how well they lived, how loved they were, how much they gave, and the difference they made. Obituaries are full of value measurements.

The greatest irony is that when we chase the up-goals of our lives, we often lose sight of our higher needs. We are so busy upscaling that we forget about higher things, like truth and love. We stop noticing how beautiful our children are; our 'joy of work' gets lost in our in-boxes; we have no time to stop and speak to God; there is no poetry in our lives because it's always one damned thing after another. And there is no love today because we are saving it up for when all of our up-goals are achieved. Graham's obituary began with a quote from the poet Robert Browning: 'Take away love and our earth is a tomb.'

The third question is a little wordy, but valuable nonetheless. It is: 'How do you know at the end of each day if you have been successful or not?' I like this question because it focuses people's attention on each day of their lives. It is about the journey of life and about the journey of success. It also tests the notion that success is in the future and yet to happen. Too often people throw success ahead of them, into the future, and hope to bump into it someday. In the meantime, their lives are full of Destination Goals and no Present-Time Goals.

Success Intelligence is about allowing your inner wisdom to teach you what success is *today*. It is the ability to live life well *now*. There is an old saying: 'The future is made of the same stuff as the present.' Hence, the best way to be successful in the future is to be as successful as possible today. Too often our up-goals are nothing more than a self-serving, desperate cry for significance, attention, and approval. Truly, these up-goals will get us nowhere if we do not learn how to be happy and successful along the way. A successful life can only ever be the one you are living now.

SUCCESS INTELLIGENCE TIP 10 – *SUCCESS*

First, answer this simple question: 'What is success?' Notice the criteria you use to measure success. Make sure that your answer covers these three areas:

1. Success in work
2. Success in relationships
3. Success in life

Second, reflect on the most valuable lessons you have learned about success. Again, make sure your answer addresses:

1. Success in work
2. Success in relationships
3. Success in life

Third, think of a current challenge you are facing and see if you can identify any lesson about success in it.

Happiness Is Not an It

Everyone chases after happiness,
not noticing that happiness is at their heels.
– Bertolt Brecht

Every day in the Manic Society, citizens spur each other on with popular success mantras such as 'Go for it', 'Just do it', 'Make it happen', and 'You can have it all'. What is the 'it' you are chasing? What is the 'it' you must have?

As director of The Happiness Project, I am often asked to participate in national opinion surveys about happiness and wellbeing. These surveys confirm that people value happiness very highly. In fact, most people report that happiness is the most important goal of their lives. Given an option to choose between wealth and happiness, the huge majority of people choose happiness. Similarly, given an option to choose between success and happiness, most people choose happiness.[2]

Most national surveys rely on thousands of self-reports to collect their data. A common question people are asked in these wellbeing surveys is 'What is it that makes you happy?' I have noted that most people's answers are simply a list of 'must haves', such as 'more money', 'ideal home', 'nice car', 'dream holiday', 'more shoes', 'new curtains', 'dark chocolate', etc. Interestingly, many people do not mention relationships, values, faith, or simply being alive.

These public surveys suggest that the public (you and I) believe happiness is something to 'have'. The popular perception is that "I can't just "be" happy; I have to "have" something to make me happy.' The prevailing wisdom is that first you must 'have it' so that you can then 'be it'. Thus, in the Manic Society, we race, compete, and shop for the 'it' that we must 'have' in order to be happy. The media makes a great play on the 'It Girls' and the 'It Boys' who 'have it all' and are apparently happy. The amusing 'It Girl Prayer' reads:

Our Cash
Which art on plastic
Hallowed be thy name
Thy Cartier watch
Thy Prada bag
In Harrods
As it is in Selfridges
Give us each day our Platinum Visa
And forgive us our overdraft
As we forgive those who stop our MasterCard
And lead us not into Next
And deliver us from Benneton
For thine is the Cartier,
The Dior and the Armani
For Chanel No. 5 and Eternity
Amex.[3]

The rise of consumerism has certainly influenced our thinking about happiness and success. The world is a marketplace. We are all God's customers, and we all have purchasing rights. Places of worship are outnumbered by shopping malls. Our number one pastime is shopping. We are making every effort to 'buy, buy, buy!' our way to happiness and success. Erich Fromm was one of the first to comment on the fast-emerging fracture between 'to have' and 'to be'. He writes:

Man is in the process of becoming a homo consumens, a total consumer. [He] has a new religious vision in which heaven is just a big warehouse where everyone can buy something new every day, indeed, where he can buy everything that he wants and even a little more than his neighbour.[4]

The language of happiness is important because how we talk about happiness influences how we encounter happiness. For example, when we talk about happiness as something 'to have', the danger is that we reduce happiness to an 'it' and a possession. Thereby, we externalise happiness, and we end up *pursuing* happiness instead of *being* happy. It is the same with success. In the Manic Society, we are busy trying 'to achieve' success instead of cultivating a deeper sense of inner success.

Consumerism is a theory that promises happiness is an 'it' that can be purchased, i.e., chased and bought. Furthermore, the theory of 'upward comparison' promises that when a person 'ups' his consumption, his happiness is upgraded into some sort of ecstatic bliss. Every day, as you watch TV, listen to the radio, read the papers, look at billboards, or surf the Internet, you are made millions of promises by retailers. Your credit card is the key to the kingdom.

Instant Happiness

At The Happiness Project, we have collected hundreds of happiness and wellbeing surveys that prove that consumerism's guarantee of happiness has bounced. Every day in the Manic Society, we are rapidly increasing our purchasing power, but we are not experiencing any significant increase in happiness. New products are hitting the market faster than ever before, and with overnight delivery they arrive on our doorsteps in record time. Thanks to the 'joy of credit' we don't even have to wait to afford these things. Surely this sounds like instant happiness. But research tells us time and time again that we are not any happier.

Economist Staffan Linder offers a disturbing satirical review of what he calls the 'acceleration of consumption'. He points out that because we consume more things than ever, the consumption time per unit item has been dramatically reduced. We now have less time to enjoy the things we believe we must buy to make us happy. He offers two possible solutions to this problem. One is called 'simultaneous consumption', in which a person tries to enjoy multiple purchases at once. He says this forces a person into 'drinking Brazilian coffee, smoking a Dutch cigar, sipping a French cognac, reading *The New York Times,* listening to a Brandenburg Concerto, and entertaining his Swedish wife – all at the same time, with varying degrees of success.'[5]

The second possible solution is what Linder calls 'successive consumption', in which a person 'enjoys one commodity at a time, but each one for a shorter period.' So instead of playing 18 holes at the exclusive golf club, a person may decide to play only 9 holes so as to make time for a massage at the luxury health club they belong to but never use. Unfortunately, as Linder points out, the challenge for skilled consumers is that they often experience constant time pressure to fit in everything they must have and must do in order to 'have' happiness. Happiness is apparently hard work.

Happiness researchers report that while purchasing can increase short-term pleasure, prior levels of happiness soon return. Like a mild drug, the effects of purchasing soon wear off. One option is further to accelerate one's 'simultaneous consumption' or 'successive consumption'. In other words, we place all our faith in external things to make us happy. The danger here is that we lose sight of inner happiness. We suffer from what Linder calls 'pleasure blindness', which is the ability to generate one's own joy and happiness. We forget how to be happy.

"You're spending the best years of your life doing a job that you hate so you can buy stuff you don't need to support a lifestyle you don't enjoy. Sounds crazy to me!"

Consumerism has many adverse side effects. One is what J. Gordon Lippincott, an industrial designer, described as accelerated 'mass buying-psychosis'. Consumers are spending money constantly in order to feel more satisfied. They are becoming compulsive and addicted to the drug of 'having'. 'Shopaholics' make endless purchases to deaden the pain, the fear, and the depression of 'not having'. The rush of buying is often quickly followed by a crash. Now a new industry has emerged, sometimes government-sponsored, which offers a new kind of therapy called credit counselling.

The insanity of consumerism is that more and more people are spending more and more money they don't have in order to feel more and more temporarily satisfied. The good news, apparently, is that a consumer can now choose from 300 credit-card companies to help consolidate (and increase) his or her debts. The unsustainable pace of consumerism is consuming our finances, trashing our lifestyle, and pillaging our environment. Polly LaBarre, senior editor of *Fast Company* magazine, asks:

> What does all that income and spending add up to? A lot of nothing, it turns out. One of the more shocking measures of our 'prosperity' is the fact that the United States spends more on trash bags than 90 other countries spend on everything. In other words, the receptacles of our waste cost more than all of the goods consumed by nearly half of the world's nations.[6]

Consumerism has so far not produced the goods. It has left us empty, dazed, and confused – and out of pocket. We are left thinking there is so much to want, but what is it I really want? Author Robert Graves wrote, 'When people have lost their authentic personal taste, they lose their personality and become the instruments of other people's wills.' It is imperative that we know what we really value, because as the poet Anne Valley-Fox says:

> *You can never get enough of what*
> *you didn't want in the first place.*

Inner Happiness

I like the story told of Socrates, the Greek philosopher, who was known for his love of marketplaces. He would always visit a market if his schedule permitted. Often, he would alter his schedule to make sure he could. It was noted, however, that Socrates rarely bought anything at the markets. One of Socrates' students once asked him, 'Why do you visit so many markets and make so few purchases?' Socrates smiled and replied, 'I simply delight in looking at all the pretty things I don't need.'

At the heart of Success Intelligence is the wisdom to know what happiness is and is not. The wisdom of happiness must surely be that *happiness is not an it.* Either that or we have all been shopping in the wrong places. How can anyone be truly happy if they believe that happiness is an 'it' that can be bought? We have to think more deeply than this. And how can anyone be truly successful if they do not know what they really value? We have to be wise.

Success Intelligence is about cultivating inner happiness. It is knowing that happiness is not an it; it is a way of being. In interviews about my work with The Happiness Project I am often asked to give a definition of happiness. I have several. One is that *happiness is who you are, minus your neurosis.* In other words, happiness is your original state minus the belief that happiness has to be bought, or minus the fear that happiness is somewhere else. Inner happiness is a release from foolish external conditioning and a return to divine saneness.

The inner happiness I refer to does not have to be manufactured or produced. Nothing needs to happen first in order for this inner happiness to exist. This inner happiness is pre-existent. It is, if you like, pre-packed into a person's being. In fact, this inner happiness *is your being, minus your neurosis.* We are at our most neurotic when engaged in the pursuit of happiness. In truth, you don't go shopping for happiness; you sit and welcome it. Inner happiness – like inner wisdom – is wrapped up inside of you already. The great thing about inner happiness is that there isn't anyone who doesn't already have it.

> *Joy is not in things; joy is in us.*
> **– Benjamin Franklin**

Success Intelligence recognises the value of happiness. It knows happiness is an important goal because happiness is a great teacher. The more you learn about happiness, the better you can distinguish between deep joy and fleeting pleasures. True happiness is an inner guide that teaches a person how to live well. In particular, happiness can teach a person a lot about success. True happiness is valuable because, for example, it is a sign of authenticity, and it is a way of knowing you are on purpose.

Happiness also brings out the best in us. When we are happy we relate better with others. We feel more connected, we are less afraid, and we are more confident. Our inner happiness is attractive, literally, in that it attracts happy relationships. When we are happy we also work better. Occupational psychology research confirms that if you can say 'I am happy in my work', you are likely to be more productive, more creative, and more successful and experience less stress, less depression, and less mental illness.[7] True happiness enables us to be more successful.

My friend and colleague Dr. Chuck Spezzano has written extensively on the wisdom of happiness. In the following passage he sums up the importance of happiness in relation to Success Intelligence. He writes:

> Let us all be students in the school of happiness. As we learn what really makes us happy, we move forward from one step of evolution to the next. Happiness is the only valid measuring stick for our lives. If it is missing, then something is off-centre. We have lost our balance and our perspective. Happiness does not live in the future or the past, but in the here and now. If our lives do not add up to happiness, then we must change if we want to be happy.

Chuck goes on to say:

> As we continuously make the choice for happiness, we learn that we must keep letting go of our past, our attachments, our indulgence, and other counterfeit forms of happiness. With happiness as our goal, we become more educated and wise as we follow its unfolding path. We can have more and more happiness in our lives now, and in all the future nows. As we go, we learn how to bring more happiness into our own lives, and those of other people.[8]

Chuck's thoughts confirm my own view that cultivating inner happiness is an important key to success.

SUCCESS INTELLIGENCE TIP 11 – *HAPPINESS*

Make some time to reflect on happiness. Call to mind the happiest person you know well and ask yourself: 'What has this person taught me about happiness?'

Who else has taught you about happiness, and what did they teach you?

Next, review your own life and identify the major lessons you have learned about happiness. Identify also the main lesson about happiness you currently have to learn.

Finally, if you were asked to give a personal definition for true happiness, what would you say?

Money Is Not Your Purpose

The intelligent man quickly realizes the impotence of gold.
– Hafiz

In my Success Intelligence seminars, I sometimes do an exercise called 'The Money Meditation'. First I ask participants to get out some money. I insist that they use cash, not credit cards. 'I accept every currency,' I tell them. I also ask them to use the most valuable coin or paper bill they have. They reach anxiously for their money, and the room turns quickly into a cauldron of animated side-talk, nervous laughter, and edgy anticipation. Sometimes, if I feel mischievous, I stir the cauldron by saying, 'Now let's explore the joy of giving.'

I begin The Money Meditation by asking people to hold their money in their non-dominant hands. I then invite them to be silent and to focus only on the money. 'Look closely at your money,' I say. 'Notice the design, the detail, the pictures, the people, and the wording.' The room becomes very still, and the participants become very reflective as they continue to focus their attention on money. Money is never far from our mind – some of us are preoccupied with it – yet we rarely stop to think about what money really is and what its true value is.

Next, I ask the participants to explore their relationship with money. I give them some money questions to meditate on. Each question is an invitation to tap into their highest thinking about money. I encourage them explicitly to 'listen to your heart' and to 'use your wisdom'. Below is a sample of the money questions I use. I recommend you not just read these questions, but actually do The Money Meditation. Get out some money. A big bill. Hold it in your non-dominant hand. Focus all of your attention on the money. And then ask yourself these money questions:

- **What is the purpose of money?** Listen carefully. What is the point of money for you?

- **How important is money?** Listen carefully. What influence does money have on your values, your work, your lifestyle, and your decisions?

- **What is more important than money?** Listen carefully. Is money number one in your life?
  Is your work first and foremost about money?

People often report how moved they are by what they experience in The Money Meditation. It usually opens up a deep dialogue and rich interaction. They speak from their hearts, and the conversation about success moves to a whole new level. If you did do The Money Meditation, I recommend that you share your thoughts with someone who is important to you. Better still, it can be very powerful to do The Money Meditation together.

Money Sickness

> *The world is too much with us; late and soon*
> *Getting and spending, we lay waste our powers:*
> *Little we see in Nature that is ours;*
> *We have given our hearts away, a sordid boon!*
> **– William Wordsworth**

I often work for organisations and businesses that suffer from what I call 'money sickness'. Their relationship with money lacks vision, intelligence, and purpose. There is plenty of talk in these places about money. Every day there is a meeting or a report about share prices, quarterly profits, capital investment, projected earnings, price adjustments, etc. In fact, one quickly surmises that all they think about is money. Here is the sickness.

One CEO of a company that suffered from 'money sickness'

actually broke down in tears in one of our coaching sessions. His company had just announced record profits for the ninth straight quarter. He said to me, 'The more money we make, the more money we have to make in order to keep our shareholders happy and the financial press happy. Today that meant I had to make another 400 people redundant.'

'P3' (see Figure 6) is a model I use to talk about three types of activity: profit, positioning, and purpose. Profit is about finance. It is about the intelligent use of money. Money is essential because it is an enabler. No money = no existence. Positioning is about strategy. It is about, for example, building a reputation for talent, giving the best value, offering great service, being the most ethical, providing the fastest delivery, giving more choice, and so on. Purpose is about identity, vision, and a reason for being. It is the soul of the enterprise.

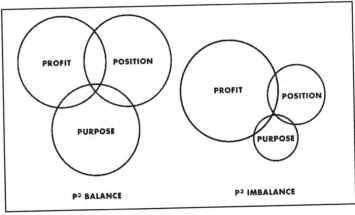

FIGURE 6: P3 Balance

Organisations and businesses that suffer from 'money sickness' tend to have an unhealthy P3 balance. They usually put a lot of creative energy into profit and positioning but give little thought to purpose. They employ brand gurus, logo makers, advertising gods, PR wizards, celebrity icons, and market futurists to push up profits and strengthen positioning. It looks brilliant, but it is often self-serving, manipulative, and meaningless. Also, the success can only be short-lived because, ultimately, it takes a strong sense of purpose to keep growing, to keep prospering, and to keep serving.

Individuals can also suffer from 'money sickness' because their own P3 balance is poor. Once again, profit and positioning compete for pole position, while purpose may do well even to finish the race. Lots of energy and anxiety go into making money, and also into securing the best position in the company (or the best house in town, or the fastest car on the block, for example), but not enough thought is given to what is truly valuable or the end goal. Ultimately, their unhealthy relationship with money will prove to be a major block to success and wellbeing.

'Money sickness' in groups and individuals can lead to all sorts of difficulties and complications, four of which I have outlined briefly below.

1. Impaired Vision

In the Manic Society, people often chase quick success and quick money on the daily money-go-round. Without true vision, this 'chasing all hours' can blur intelligence.

The businessman Henry Ford said, 'Business must be run at a profit, else it will die. But when anyone tries to run a business solely for profit, then also the business must die, for it no longer has a reason for existence.' One of the most important lessons to learn about business is this: *If you always put money first, success rarely lasts.* When people keep putting money first, they usually lose sight of what is truly important.

Any successful CEO will confirm that you can't finance a business just with money; you also have to finance it with a passionate vision, love of purpose, faith in people, a willingness to serve, and a desire to make a difference. Money alone cannot win success. Focusing only on money is like playing tennis while watching the scoreboard and not the ball. Money is a reward for playing the game well; it is not *the game*.

2. Heart Failure

The Busy Generation is full of people who are busy working 'for the money.' They worship the 'Money God'. The Money God comes first because of what they believe the Money God can give them: 'Money is power', 'Money is success', 'Money is freedom'. But money can also be slavery. Leo Tolstoy wrote: 'Money is a new form of slavery, and distinguishable from the old simply by the fact that it is impersonal – that there is no human relation between master and slave.'

The Busy Generation is learning fast that when you work only for money your life does not work for you. The Busy Generation is waking up to the possibility of meaningful work. People no longer want to leave their hearts at home when they go to work. They don't want a job; they want a purpose. They don't just want money; they want to contribute. They don't want just to 'put in the hours'; they want to make a difference.

Love, not money, is the heart of work. Tim Sanders, a Yahoo senior executive, speaks up for the new generation when he says:

> The most powerful force in business isn't greed, fear, or even the raw energy of unbridled competition. The most powerful force in business is love. It's what will help your company grow and become stronger. It's what will propel your career forward. It's what will give you a sense of meaning and satisfaction in your work, which will help you do your best work.[9]

3. High Stress

In the Hyperactive Workplace, if you only do-do-do it for the money, the cost is simply too high.

Working only for money costs too much. When you work only for money, your life becomes all about 'having' and 'getting', not 'being' or 'giving'. And if money is your master, you run the risk of never really taking your place in the world. Money for money's sake distorts vision, blocks inspiration, lacks imagination, feeds fear, and cripples creativity. It also ruins relationships. And how can anyone trust you if your primary motivation is money?

At my Stress Busters Clinic, I saw first-hand the negative cost of working only for money. Stress reports conclude consistently that people who work only for money are very susceptible to stress and stress-related illnesses, such as hypertension, migraines, ulcers, immune deficiency, and insomnia.[10] This is particularly true during challenging times when vision and purpose are what sustain people and inspire eventual success.

4. Joyless Values

In the Joyless Economy, the mistake is to measure success only by money. Think of all the things money can buy. But also think of all the things money *can't* buy. Think what you might miss if you only focused on money.

A 2002 Internet survey entitled 'How Much Is Enough?' tested participants on their goals and values. Participants were asked, 'Would you rather have a $10,000-a-year payrise or an extra hour per day to spend at home with your family?' A staggering 83 per cent opted for the cash, even though 91 per cent had indicated earlier that making their personal lives a higher priority was an important goal to them.[11]

The trouble with 'money sickness' is that it puts your life on hold. Money comes first, and what you really value comes second. Money is now; happiness is soon. Money is now; life is for later. You gamble that once you have made enough money, you will get on with your purpose, your dreams, and your relationships. But how much money is enough? And how long must you wait? Apparently, you really will be the person you want to be once you have enough money – if time doesn't run out first.

The Money Trap

One of my mentors told me, 'Never underestimate the importance of money, and never overestimate it either.' Money is important; let's not pretend otherwise. However, money is not everything. And money is not the answer.

The 'Money Trap' is about waiting to have enough money before you commit to what is true, to what you love, to your real purpose. Many times I have heard people say, 'When I am financially secure, I will do what I really want to do.' But it never happens. Never. Money, by itself, cannot make you secure. Money, by itself, cannot heal fear. Money, by itself, cannot give you faith. And I have never seen money make someone more intelligent. More foolish, yes.

In 1996, I was employed as a consultant for The Body Shop. I enjoyed my time there enormously. Every meeting was a hive of passion, creativity, and contribution. The Body Shop is one of the great business success stories in the modern era. It has an ethical vision, makes quality products, gives excellent service, achieves big profits, and still continues to learn and evolve. And yet The Body Shop would never have happened if its founder, Anita Roddick, had waited to have enough money.

The initial success of The Body Shop was not achieved through big financial backing. On the contrary, there was no money. In her book *Business as Unusual,* Anita Roddick writes:

> The first branch of The Body Shop opened in Brighton in March 1976. Everything was determined by money, or rather lack of it. I hired a designer to come up with the logo for £25 and I got friends to help with filling the bottles and hand-writing all the labels. I painted the whole place dark green, not because I wanted to make an environmental statement – the word 'green' was not a metaphor for the movement then – but because it was the only colour that would cover up all the damp patches on the walls. The cheapest containers I could find were the plastic bottles used by hospitals to collect urine samples, but

I couldn't afford to buy enough so I thought I would get around the problem by offering to refill empty containers or fill customers' own bottles. In this way we started recycling and reusing materials long before it became ecologically fashionable. Every element of our success was really down to the fact that I had no money.[12]

What is money anyway? Money does not define you. Money has no vision. Money does not have your talent. Nor your wisdom. Money cannot guarantee you success. Money cannot buy happiness. Money can't even prevent unhappiness. Have you ever met a millionaire who isn't stressed, under pressure, and experiencing troubles? No. Never put money first. The key to success is to commit first to your purpose, and let the money follow after you. Don't wait. Don't put off your life.

SUCCESS INTELLIGENCE TIP 12 – *MONEY*

Set aside some time to think about money. First, identify five people who have taught you the most about money, both positive and negative. What did they teach you? Explore how their relationship to money has influenced your own.

Second, review your life and name the most valuable lessons about money you have learned personally. How well have you learned these lessons?

Third, consider your current P3 balance. Assess how you could improve your personal balance between purpose, position, and profit. Think how you could be wiser with money.

Love Is Not Just an Emotion

Love broadens vision, love enables creativity,
and love expands intelligence.
– Humberto Maturana[13]

The 11th of September 2001 is a date etched on the heart of modern history. It began as another normal manic Monday. In New York people were already hard at work. In the Twin Towers thousands of people were busy chasing the dollar, doing the deal, making it happen. Until 8:46 A.M. Eastern Standard Time. Then the first plane hit the North Tower. We all remember where we were, what we were doing, and whom we had to speak to first.

My brother David telephoned me immediately. 'Turn on the television,' he said. Over the next few hours my wife and I watched the horror unfold as 2,973 people lost their lives (with 24 still missing). The colossal Twin Towers, the nerve centre of the business world, simply vanished into a pyre of dust and rubble. We made phone calls, too – to America, to Australia, to England, to the people we love.

Personally, the full horror of September 11th did not start to sink in until the day after. It felt unreal at first, like watching an action movie in which New York City goes up in flames again. On September 12th I watched endless replays of the Twin Towers collapsing, and the pain of 'the tragedy', 'the nightmare', and 'the wake-up call' took effect. What I will never forget is listening to the phone calls made by passengers onboard all three aeroplanes. All of the phone calls were to loved ones: 'I love you, I love you forever.'

All of these passengers would be dead in just a few moments. Their last act was to do what is important. They made their phone calls. They declared their love. And millions of television viewers witnessed it. Messages of love. Statements of truth. Famous last words. These were not mere emotional outbursts; they were acts of purpose and courage. These passengers were teaching us all that in the final call, love is the goal, love is the reason, and love is the whole point of everything.

Love Is the Goal

The whole world is a market-place of Love,
For naught that is, from Love remains remote.
The Eternal Wisdom have all things in Love,
On Love they all depend, to Love they all turn.
— **Attar, Persian poet**

The prelude to my Success Intelligence seminars is a slide show featuring inspirational sayings by prominent political figures like Nelson Mandela, business leaders like Anita Roddick, CEOs like Isaac Tigrett, Internet entrepreneurs like Tim Sanders, medical doctors like Deepak Chopra, and spiritual icons like Martin Luther King. These inspirational sayings have one thing in common – they are about love. I use this slide show for seminars to corporate lawyers, cancer patients, technology companies, charity groups, sports associations, drug companies, you name it. Love is always relevant.

Love is central to my work. Every talk I give on success is really a talk about love; every talk on leadership is really a talk about love; every talk on business is a talk about love; every talk on health is a talk about love; and every talk on happiness is a talk on love. For me, love is not just an emotion. Love is an intention. Love is a purpose. Love is our true power. It is what inspires us and what evolves us. 'We are all born for love. It is the principle of existence, and its only end,' said British prime minister Benjamin Disraeli.

Love is the heart of success. I feel strongly about this. Any life goal that is not somehow about love is not really a goal; it is just compensation or a distraction. Love is the ultimate goal and the only real goal. Other goals, lesser goals – such as success, money, happiness, power, and fame – lose all value and meaning without love. What would it profit any man to gain the whole world and lose love? If your success has no place for love, you won't feel successful – no matter what you achieve. This is my standpoint:

*If your definition of success has little or no
measure of love in it, get another definition.*

Success Intelligence is the wisdom to keep putting love first in your life. In the Manic Society, we rarely stop to consider the value of love. The Busy Generation is often too preoccupied to make time for love. The Hyperactive Workplace is full of people working late again tonight. The Joyless Economy cannot manufacture love by itself. With true success, love is not at the finish line of your race; love is the position you start from. Love is the strength you carry with you. Love is your centre.

Love Is Intelligent

*Neither a lofty degree of intelligence nor imagination
Nor both together go to the making of genius.
Love, love, love, that is the soul of genius.*
– Wolfgang Amadeus Mozart

A few years ago a journalist came to my home to interview me for an article on the psychology of success. At the end of a very stimulating interview, the journalist asked if I would e-mail an answer to one final question: 'What is your ultimate secret to success?' I thanked her for asking me such a great question, and I promised her I would compose something within a week.

A few days later, I took the morning off to spend some time with my question. It was a busy week, with several deadlines to meet, but this felt important. I took time to review what my life had taught me about success. I thought about the teachers and mentors who had inspired me so much. I reflected on my meetings with successful people in business, medicine, politics, and sports. I searched for a golden thread. It became clear to me that success is about love and about being deeply inspired by what you aim for.

After meditating for several hours on my 'ultimate secret to success', I wrote something called the 'Love Dedication'. These words have become like a personal mission statement to me. When I e-mailed the 'Love Dedication' to the journalist, I said that I would probably include these words in a book one day. Here is what I wrote:

Before you dedicate your life
to a person, a marriage, a family;
to a corporation, a political party,
a peace campaign;
to a religion, a revolution, a
spiritual path;
make one other dedication first.

First dedicate yourself to LOVE.
Decide to let Love be your
intention, your purpose, and
your point.
And then let Love inspire you,
support you, and guide you
in every other dedication
you make thereafter.

To dedicate your life to love is the ultimate secret to success because love is intelligent. When one studies the effects of love – as opposed to fear, anxiety, or cynicism – it is apparent that every loving thought is a source of strength that helps to create a more beautiful life. Love is intelligent because love inspires vision, love strengthens values, love excites imagination, love expands possibility, and love is creative. The list goes on.

Love is an intelligent archetype. When people call upon love, they are calling upon something higher than their own everyday psychology. No matter how much our cynicism may try to belittle love, the truth is that when you make way for love you tap into something universal and miraculous. The philosopher Emmet Fox famously wrote: 'There is no difficulty that enough love will not conquer; no disease that enough love will not heal; no door that enough love will not open; no gulf that enough love will not bridge; no wall that enough love will not throw down . . .'

> *Love is the ultimate coach.*
> *Do what you love, let love guide you.*
> *Let love inspire you.*

Love Is the Work

> *Love all, serve all.*
> **– Hard Rock Café mission statement**

When I first began to give master classes in corporate-land, I learned that business people classify work skills in two groups: 'hard' and 'soft'. The hard skills are so called because people agree they have a tangible impact on the profits of a business. These hard skills include law, finance, systems, technology, and manufacturing. The so-called soft skills are considered secondary, less essential skills. They are often referred to disparagingly as 'touchy-feely'. They include values, ethics, team spirit, communication, and service. Love is hardly ever mentioned. Love is considered beyond soft – too woolly and too fluffy.

The greatest failure of corporate-land is that work and love appear to have parted company. 'The word love is never mentioned in big business,' wrote Anita Roddick. This is hardly intelligent. We all know, in our heart of hearts, that when love inspires work, it is transformative, creative, and deeply satisfying. We also know from painful experience that work without love is often just busyness, drudgery, and sacrifice. Fortunately, a new generation of business leaders is doing their best to put love back on the agenda in corporate-land. They are working hard, and putting their reputations on the line, to fashion a new language of business that is not afraid to use words like *love, spirit, heart, compassion, story,* and *soul*. This is essential for the future of business and for our own personal futures, too, because, in truth, *love is the work*.

Dr. Humberto Maturana teaches business leaders about the essence of work, which he calls the 'biology of business'. In particular, he teaches that love is essential to business because love expands intelligence. In 1998, he was invited to the Massachusetts Institute of Technology (MIT) to give a paper entitled 'The Biology of Business: Love Expands Intelligence'. In his paper, he wrote:

> If you look at any story of corporate transformation where everything begins to go well, innovations appear, and people are happy to be there, you will see that it is a story of love. Most problems in companies are not solved through competition, not through fighting, not through authority. They are solved through the only emotion that expands creativity, as in this emotion there is freedom for creativity. This emotion is love. Love expands intelligence and enables creativity. Love returns autonomy and, as it returns autonomy, it returns responsibility and the experience of freedom.[14]

In my coaching sessions I often ask clients, 'What do you love about your work?' The immediate response is often a look of surprise followed by quickly spoken words that they hope will pass for an answer. Clearly, many people do not expect love and work to occupy the same space in their lives. They are compartmentalised and reserved for separate occasions. Yet this question I ask has great value because it can help people to explore more deeply what their purpose is, what motivates them, and also what keeps them going in the difficult times.

I think every business card should at the very least carry a watermark of the word *love*. It is possible, of course, to work without love, just as it is possible to have a marriage without love or to have sex without love. However, to join love with work is truly rewarding and represents the major work of our life. Also, love inspires success. Love is what evolves leaders into great men and women. Love is what inspires outstanding service. Love is the secret to marketing. In fact, I firmly believe that an open heart is the greatest form of marketing on the planet. But what use is any of this if we are too frightened even to talk about love at work?

Marianne Williamson, author of the best-selling book *A Return to Love,* writes passionately about love and work. She says:

> You're in business to spread love. Your screenplay should spread love. Your hair salon should spread love. Your agency should spread love. Your life should spread love. The key to a successful career is realising that it's not separate from the rest of your life, but is rather an extension of your most basic self. And your most basic self is love.[15]

Love is an essential soft skill for the work that is not just our jobs but our whole lives. Roger Enrico, a vice-chairman of PepsiCo, said in *Fortune* magazine that 'the soft stuff is always harder than the hard stuff.' That may be so. Nonetheless, Success Intelligence challenges us to love and to be wholehearted in all we do. Ultimately, we have to test the wisdom and power of love by using it. This is necessary for success at work, and also for success in relationships, which I address in the next part of this book.

SUCCESS INTELLIGENCE TIP 13 – *LOVE*

Make some time to reflect on love. Consider how important love is to you and what priority you currently give it. Name the people who have taught you the most about love. What exactly did they teach you?

Review your life and identify the lessons you have personally learned about love. Assess how well you have learned these lessons. What would you teach is the truth about love?

Finally, ask yourself, 'What do I love?' Reflect on the heart of your work, the status of your relationships, and to what you devote your life.

PART IV

Relationships

● ● ● ● ●

How can one individual solve the problems of the world?
Problems can only be solved if one is part of a team.

– Nelson Mandela

The Broken Community

The Independence Myth

The Competition Block

Thin Conversations

A Better Balance

I first met Danah Zohar at a conference hosted by the Leadership Trust Foundation. The conference was entitled 'Leading with Personal Power', and Danah and I were two of the speakers. It was a truly inspiring conference, expertly organised, and it had attracted leaders from government, business, religion, the military, education, and sport. I spoke about Success Intelligence and Danah spoke on spiritual intelligence. It was clear to both of us that we shared a similar vision and had much in common.

Danah Zohar studied physics and philosophy at the Massachusetts Institute of Technology (MIT) and is a pioneer in the field of SQ – spiritual intelligence. Danah and her husband, Dr. Ian Marshall, are co-authors of a book entitled *Spiritual Intelligence,* which explores our relationship with ourselves and with each other. It is a beautiful book to read and reflect upon. They define SQ as 'the intelligence with which we can place our actions and our lives in a wider, richer, meaning-giving context.'[1]

I am fortunate to have Danah and Ian as neighbours in Oxford. We meet up regularly to talk about our work and life in general. Together we marvel at the wonder of creation, despair at how challenging life can be, and also celebrate our hopes and visions for the future. It is a precious friendship. Our conversations are always very stimulating and deeply nourishing. We listen intently to one another and learn so much from each other's experiences and insights.

Danah and Ian are part of a global community of scientists who are challenging humanity to change the way we perceive ourselves and how we relate to each other. They have written several books, including *The Quantum Self* and *The Quantum Society*, that integrate the findings of new physics with perennial philosophy and modern psychology. In all of their writings they encourage a deeper connection with self and society as the key to happiness and success. In one of Danah's works she points out:

> *Logos* has traditionally been translated as word . . . but there is an earlier and more original Greek meaning of *logos*. This is translated as *relationship*. . . . Imagine logos translated in the Bible as *relationship*: 'In the beginning, there was relationship.'[2]

The new physics is urging us to rethink our relationship with self and society. Werner Heisenberg, a German physicist, is a founding father of the quantum physics movement. His famous Uncertainty Principle[3] has enormous implications for how we think about success and how we live our lives. Simply put, Heisenberg took a small subatomic building block of life, called a photon, and showed that it has a dual nature, which is both 'particle' and 'wave'.

To explain further, if a scientist observes a photon with a particle detector, he or she finds that a photon looks like a particle – a small, fixed, singular object that has hard boundaries and is separate from all else. Using this way of seeing, scientists like Sir Isaac Newton and philosophers like René Descartes propounded a theory of atomism in which all living things (that includes you and me) are seen as totally independent of each other. This world view has greatly influenced our thinking and intelligence. As Danah Zohar comments:

> Freud used Newton's atomism as the basis for his tragic view of modern psychology. In his 'Theory of Object Relations', Freud said that each of us is isolated. He

conceived the boundaries of the self as hard and impenetrable. You are an object to me and I just an object to you. We can never really know each other or relate in any fundamental way. I form a picture of you in my mind, a 'projection', and I relate only to that. Love and intimacy are impossible. 'The commandment to *Love thy neighbour as thyself* is the most impossible commandment ever written.'[4]

However, Heisenberg's Uncertainty Principle found that if a scientist observes a photon using another device, called a wave detector, the photon no longer looks like a separate particle floating through space on its own. Now the photon appears as a wave that has momentum and is in connection, flow, and dialogue with everything else. Heisenberg said, 'The world thus appears as a complicated tissue of events, into which connections of different kinds alternate or overlap or combine and thereby determine the texture of the whole.'[5]

Thus the photon may look like a separate, independent entity, but it is never really separate. The Uncertainty Principle is one of many breakthroughs in quantum physics to establish that *relationship* is the basic building block of life – on every level. Nature is really 'a theatre of interrelations'[6]; in truth there is 'separation without separateness'; and, as physicist David Bohm, author of *The Undivided Universe*, explained, we share a 'collective intelligence'[7] and we live in 'a pattern of unbroken wholeness'.[8]

Relationship is at the heart of physics, the heart of life, and the heart of success. Our personal challenge is to be both particle-like and wave-like; in other words, we have to embrace our apparent uniqueness and also realize our deep connection and oneness with all. We have to learn how to live for ourselves *and* for everyone else. Another scientist, Albert Einstein, put it beautifully when he wrote:

A human being is part of the whole called the "universe," a part limited in time and space. He experiences himself, his thoughts and feelings, as something separated from the rest – a kind of optical delusion of his consciousness. This delusion is a kind of prison for us, restricting us to our personal desires and to affection for a few persons nearest us. Our task must be to free ourselves from this prison by widening our circle of compassion to embrace all living creatures and the whole of nature in all its beauty.[9]

The Broken
Community

It takes a village to raise a child.
– African proverb

In the name of success more of us are working harder than ever. In an effort to keep going we routinely sacrifice our relationships, neglect our families, forfeit old friendships, and alienate ourselves from our communities. We promise that in the future it will be different. But the future is a long way off. In the meantime, we struggle on alone. Increasingly we ask ourselves, 'Is this really success?'

I grew up near Winchester in a little village aptly named Littleton. It was a pretty village, quite quiet, with not much traffic. There was a village shop, a village pub, a village church, and a village cricket green. Littleton had a big community spirit, and we were friends with all our neighbours. Children roamed freely with no need for adult protection. I played cricket for the village team from the age of 11. The village policeman was the cricket umpire, and my maths teacher was our opening batsman.

After my father's alcoholism worsened and he left home, my brother, David, and I were the only kids in our village who came from a 'broken home'. I vaguely remember some mention of a woman in the next village who was referred to as 'the divorcée'. The village extended itself to us in a natural and graceful way. I had several father figures on my cricket team. My cricket captain, Jeff Levick, was particularly supportive to me. Our neighbours and our friends' parents all made sure Mum, David, and I were okay.

During the writing of this book, I was invited to give a talk on Success Intelligence to the South East Employers, a government organisation based in Winchester. One of the organisers was Juliet Thomas, whose father used to play on my old cricket team. Juliet kindly offered to organise an informal cricketers' reunion at a local pub. One by one, ten members of the team showed up that night. It had been 20 years since I had last met my old friends. We talked until midnight about the 'good old days', which we enjoyed then but appreciate even more now.

Everything changes, including life in Littleton. I remember two incidents in particular. First, when our closest neighbours had to move away because of work, the local estate agents printed their property details in a colour brochure with the headline '59 minutes by train to Waterloo Station, London.' Second, a brand-new housing development was built in the village on an impossibly small piece of land. The houses were called 'executive homes' and they had no garden, which was considered to be a good selling point. I remember thinking how odd that was.

At 18 years old, I left Littleton for the big wide world. I went to study in Birmingham, just three hours by car, but it seemed much further away. Later I went to live in New York. I then married my first wife, Miranda, who is Australian. And now through work I make regular visits to New York, Hawaii, and India. Every morning in my meditation time I think of friends and family who live all over the world. My village is now a non-local, global village. Creating community is increasingly important to me but also very challenging.

Broken Bonds

Our modern society suffers from what physicist David Bohm called 'the virus of fragmentation'. The increasing breakdown of the traditional family unit, with the resultant broken bonds between children, adults, and the elderly, is well documented and familiar to us all.[10] The new social landscape is complex, full of divided families, high divorce rates, single parents, and more people living alone. We are a society of 'loose connections'.[11]

We live in an increasingly mobile society full of temporary relationships and temporary friendships. In the latter half of the

20th century, as the global economy quickly became a reality, it was considered good corporate policy to encourage managers to move from office to office, town to town, and, eventually, country to country. International mergers made this increasingly possible. With each move, social bonds were broken, best friends lost touch, and good neighbours waved goodbye.

For three years I worked for BAE Systems, the defence and aerospace specialist, which employs one million people worldwide. I contributed to an executive coaching programme for the top tier of senior managers. Many of these managers – 650 in all – have lived and worked in different countries for two or three years at a time. They are also used to living away from home for four nights a week while working in other cities. This is a common practice in the global economy.

The modern workforce also changes jobs and companies more regularly than ever before. The days of a 'job for life' are fast becoming a thing of the past, and yet they were once the norm. At IBM, most people used to describe their work contracts as 'cradle to grave' contracts. At the BBC, they called them 'womb to tomb'. At British Telecom, people described themselves as 'lifers'. Today it seems fashionable to move on every couple of years. Promises to stay in touch with old colleagues are usually broken.

The increase in mobility has certainly challenged the health and status of our relationships. So too has the increase both in the pace of life and the number of hours we work. One recent government survey found that one in eight people now works over 60 hours a week. Also, the number of women working over 60 hours has more than doubled in less than five years.[12] Hence, the busy picture of modern life looks like this:

work, work, work, work, work, work, work, work,
work, work, work, work, work, work, work, work,
work, work, work, work, work, work, family, work,
work, work, work, work, work, work, family, work,
work, work, work, work, work, work, friends, work,
work, work, work, work, work, work, family, work,

work, work, work, work, work, work, family, work,
work, work, work, work, work, work, self, work,
work, work, work, work, work, work, work, work,
work, work, work, work, work, work, work, work.

No space!   We are so busy, so manic, and so saturated that we can barely keep up with ourselves, never mind the rest of the family. We know it is important to make time for family, but we have to soldier on. We may say family comes first, but in practice work comes first, work comes second, and work comes third. The financial welfare of the family is important, but so too are emotional welfare and spiritual welfare. A family needs space together, without which the bonding begins to disintegrate. Space is like a womb that gives birth to new levels of intimacy, togetherness, and connection.

No time!   At work, we hand out business cards that list an office phone number, a cell phone number, a home phone number, a fax number, an e-mail address, and a Website address. There are so many ways to make contact, but do we have the time? Work teams fail to reach standards and achieve goals because they make no time to meet and talk. At home we also appear to be spending less and less time together. Only one out of three families agrees that 'our whole family usually eats dinner together.'[13] Books like *The Sixty-Second Father* and *The Sixty-Second Marriage* are bestsellers.

> *We dream of meeting a soul mate one day,*
> *but doubt we could fit one into our schedule.*

No energy! We are so tired keeping up with the Joneses that we have no energy left to talk to the Joneses, or anyone else, for that matter. We want to connect and socialise, but often the mad dash of modern life leaves us run down, below par, and wiped out. Instead of going out with friends, we stay in and watch *Friends* on television; instead of talking with our neighbours, we watch soap operas; and instead of bonding with people we really know, we settle for another dose of reality TV.

Faith Popcorn, the trend analyst, coined the term 'cocooning' in the 1990s to describe how more and more people are ritually separating out and 'going it alone' in an effort to succeed in our Manic Society. The word 'cocooning' struck a nerve with the public and was soon added to many standard dictionaries. Popcorn described cocooning as:

> The attempt to pull a shell of safety around yourself, so you're not at the mercy of a mean, unpredictable world – those harassments and assaults that run the gamut from rude waiters and noise pollution to crack-crime, recession, and AIDS. Cocooning is about insulation and avoidance, peace and protection, coziness and control – a sort of hyper-nesting.[14]

Cocooning is considered a healthy stress-relief tool if done occasionally. A weekly Sabbath, a personal retreat, or a night in alone can give a person the necessary space for renewal, the time to recharge, and the chance to pause and savour. Occasional cocooning can help to soften the pace of our life. It can help us to punctuate our busyness and connect us again more richly, deeply, and honestly with the people and things that matter most. That at least is the healthy way of cocooning; the unhealthy way is more excessive.

Cocooning is unhealthy when it stops being an occasional retreat and starts being an entrenched, separatist strategy for life. Faith Popcorn identified this danger when she wrote about the 'Armoured Cocoon', who attempts physically to protect and emotionally defend himself wherever he goes; the 'Wandering Cocoon', who wants to control every environment she enters; and the 'Socialised Cocoon,' who connects only very occasionally and very selectively with people.

Broken Hearts

Excessive cocooning has coincided with the sharp rise in individualism and individualistic cultures in the Western world. Most of Faith Popcorn's trends are for one decade at a time, but cocooning is now more prevalent than ever. And so too is individualism. In the Manic Society, people are living an increasingly isolated, particle-like existence, non-local and riddled with the 'virus of fragmentation'. Sociologist Amitai Etzioni, author of *The Spirit of Community*, writes:

> The West is in the cold season of excessive individualism and yearns for the warmth of community to allow human relations to blossom.[15]

The evidence for excessive individualism comes from international surveys conducted at regular intervals since the late 1950s.[16] In fact, individualism has grown so fast in recent decades that it is often referred to as 'hyperindividualism'. Symptoms of excessive individualism include a lot of 'me thinking'. Hence the baby-boomers were described in the 1980s as the 'Me Generation', and every decade since then has been described as the 'Me Decade'. The creed of individualism – look after number one – does not allow for much 'we', 'us', and 'our'.

Excessive individualism is evidenced in social trends, such as more people living alone and people marrying later; more people divorcing and smaller family units; more sole proprietors and people working at home; and people socialising less and reporting a greater sense of isolation and loneliness. Increases in individualism are also well documented in recent sociology tracts like *The Lonely Crowd* and *The Culture of Narcissism*. There is even evidence of excessive individualism now spreading to more Eastern collectivist cultures.

Excessive individualism has risen from the ashes of countless relationships that have crashed and burned. Excessive individualism is so prevalent now because so many relationships have failed. A true diagnosis of excessive individualism – or 'dysfunctional independence', as I call it – reveals that it is often a coping strategy for feelings of grief, a defence mechanism against being hurt again, and a compensation for the lack of intimacy and connection in our lives. The fact is that:

at the heart of excessive individualism is a broken heart.

A closer inspection of excessive individualism reveals a loss of faith in the value and possibility of relationship. Of course we still communicate: we text (it's quicker than phoning), we visit chat rooms (it's safer and we are more in control), and we try speed dating (our schedules are very busy). But we also hold ourselves back more than before, even when trying out new relationships. We are weary and we are frightened; we are lone rangers.

Sociologists like Amitai Etzioni are appealing to our generation to marry the best of individualism (i.e., personal liberty and personal rights) with the best of collectivism (i.e., social connection and spiritual oneness). Etzioni urges us not to give up on relationships, but to find a way to open our hearts and connect more deeply once again. He encourages us to see how our workaholic lifestyles are, at least on one level, a compensation for the lack of social connection and spiritual oneness we feel. He writes:

Nobody likes to admit it, but between 1960 and 1990 American society allowed children to be devalued, while the golden call of 'making it' was put on a high pedestal. Recently, college freshmen listed 'being well off financially' as more important than 'raising a family'. (In 1990 the figures were 74 percent versus 70 per cent respectively, and in 1991, they were 74 per cent versus 68 per cent.)[17]

At my seminars, I often meet men and women who think they have to have career success first before they can consider being in a relationship, getting married, or starting a family. Young executives prefer to go solo so that a relationship does not interfere with work. Big companies make it clear that they want exclusive rights to their young talent. Life must not get in the way of business. Office beds are provided for those who work late. These companies are far from family-friendly. In some ways, they are no better than the Victorian workhouses.

In *The Corporate Eunuch,* authors Battalia and Tarrant document increasing instances of young executives who are pressured into thinking that they have to choose between marriage and career. They quote one report that compares a professional manager to a Janissary, an elite soldier of the Ottoman Empire who was taken from his parents as an infant, raised by the state, and never allowed to marry. The report says: 'A young man considering [a managerial] career might well think of himself as a modern-day Janissary – and consider very, very carefully whether marriage in any way conforms to his chosen life.'[18]

In my coaching sessions, I often listen to 20- and 30-somethings who think they must choose between success and love. In individualistic cultures there is a deep fragmentation between success and love. People do not believe it is possible to have success *and* love.

Lost is the wisdom that an intimate relationship, and a loving family, could actually enhance a career. Loving relationships are seen somehow as a block to success, not a help. Apparently, loving relationships must be sacrificed for success.

Broken Lives

> It's lonely at the top,
> and it's lonely everywhere else, too.

I predict that the fastest-growing disease epidemic of the 21st century will be what I call 'diseases of loneliness'. These diseases are identified as being caused by or producing symptoms of chronic isolation, pained separation, and anxious apartness. These diseases of loneliness include depression, stress, cancer, AIDS, heart disease, narcissism, and suicide – all of which have risen quickly in the 'Golden Era' of spiralling aspirations and excessive individualism.

I recently coached a man called Clive who worked for a global pharmaceutical company. When I asked him what he did, he said, 'I'm in charge of Africa, Europe, and the Middle East.' He had come to see me because he was depressed. 'On my bedside table, I have a copy of *Unlimited Power* by Tony Robbins and a bottle of Prozac,' he said. Clive told me that he wanted to 'stop the craziness', as he put it. He was lonely in his job and lonely in his marriage, and he had thought about leaving them both, but he was afraid of being alone.

Copyright 2001 by Randy Glasbergen.
www.glasbergen.com

**"It's what all the top executives are wearing.
The buttons are available in Valium,
No-Doze, Xanax, or Tagamet."**

Clive is a good example of the people I meet who have taught themselves that in order to be successful they must build tough exteriors and harden their hearts. Clive described himself as being 'between a rock and a hard place'. I told him that I thought he was suffering from a broken heart and that he was hoping more success would somehow mend it.

'The problem is that if your heart is not open you won't feel any success you experience,' I said.

In one session, Clive likened himself to the Tin Man in *The Wizard of Oz*, who had no heart. 'If I don't get my heart back,' he said, 'I may as well die.'

In my Success Intelligence seminars, I present clinical research that proves there is a high correlation between loneliness and diseases such as heart disease. Many doctors identify loneliness as a leading cause of death, describing it as 'a killer'. The loneliness they refer to is: (1) an isolation from other people, (2) an estrangement from our authentic self, and (3) a spiritual emptiness and perceived separation from God. Cardiologist Dean Ornish, author of *Love and Survival,* writes:

> The real epidemic in our culture is not only physical heart disease, but also what I call *emotional and spiritual heart disease* – that is, the profound feelings of loneliness, isolation, alienation, and depression that are so prevalent in our culture with the breakdown of the social structures that used to provide us with a sense of connection and community. It is, to me a root of the illness, cynicism, and violence in our society.[19]

Excessive individualism and the lack of deep intimate attachments is not a formula for success. It breaks up communities and it breaks people's lives. Excessive individualists seek to make an impression, but not to relate. They want admiration, not intimacy. They want to win, not join. They end up lonely at the top (if they ever get there) and suffer from appalling social illiteracy, poor emotional resilience, no spiritual rootedness, and no sense of belonging. They are on their own, and they are afraid.

I believe that it is a spiritual imperative of every human to overcome his or her perceived aloneness. Separation – the optical delusion – is the mental virus that causes so much fear, pain, and disease. My work with Success Intelligence recognises that intimate relationships are the basic building blocks of true success and wellbeing. Several major social research studies conducted across many countries and decades also corroborate that positive relationships promote strength, resilience, and happiness.[20] They conclude, as I do, that the heart of success is about living for ourselves and for others.

Success Intelligence Tip 14 – *Relationships*

Consider this thought: *Relationships are the heart of success.* How true is this for you?

Review your life and name the most important relationship lessons you have learned. Assess honestly how well you have learned these lessons.

Next, name three (or more) of the most important people in (a) your life and (b) your work.

Then review the present status of these relationships. Score the health of each relationship on a scale of 1 (poor) to 10 (perfect). Consider how you could make each relationship even better.

The Independence Myth

No one is big enough to be independent of others.
— **Dr. William Mayo**

Society has always peddled the myth of independent success. In Western cultures, in particular, the highest honour is to describe a person's success as self-made and his or her talent as self-taught. But truthfully, there is no such thing as independent success. No one can create and succeed entirely on his or her own. Every lone genius, original thinker, solo adventurer, and brave entrepreneur has depended on some emotional, financial, or spiritual support for success.

I recently visited Florence, the city where so many Renaissance artists made their names. I spent a day at the Uffizi Gallery, which houses many beautiful works by Michelangelo, including the magnificent *Doni Tondo* painting of the Holy Family with Joseph holding Jesus on Mary's shoulder. Michelangelo's paintings, sculptures, and architecture are everywhere in Florence. He is rightfully called a genius and commended for his unparalleled influence on the development of Western art.

Michelangelo was a prolific, tortured genius who famously claimed that he never had a teacher or mentor. In fact, Michelangelo had an excellent Florentine teacher in Domenico Ghirlandaio, who taught him drawing and painting in both tempera and fresco. William Wallace, author of *Michelangelo,* points out that the *Doni Tondo* offers 'abundant evidence that the young apprentice learned his lessons well.' Wallace comments that many of Michelangelo's biographers 'relate a fictionalised history about a precocious genius who had little or no formal training . . . but who succeeded against all odds to create masterworks without faults or any prior failures.'[21]

Michelangelo was a fiercely independent man. He portrayed himself as a lone artist who was forced to create without any support. And yet he was sponsored by several patrons in the Medici household, the most influential family in Florence. Lorenzo de Medici introduced the young Michelangelo to many great philosophers and thinkers, who clearly inspired him. Also, Michelangelo drew on his religious faith and divine connection, which he shared with us in great works like *The Creation of Adam*.

'By Myself Syndrome'

Children are taught from an early age to take pride in being able to say 'I did it by myself.' Our childhood histories are full of 'firsts', such as the first time we walked by ourselves, got dressed by ourselves, used the toilet by ourselves, rode a bicycle by ourselves, walked to school by ourselves, and so on. Adults applauded our successes on these important occasions. We were growing up, and learning to be self-sufficient gave us the strength and confidence to do so.

Being self-sufficient is often a vital characteristic for success. It teaches us to dig deep for courage and talent; it encourages self-discipline and personal resilience; it also helps us to take responsibility for our lives. And yet too much self-sufficiency can be a block to success. People who suffer from 'By Myself Syndrome' are lousy at asking for help. They are blind to opportunities for support. They are blocked by their inability to get past themselves. Success requires both self-determination *and* letting yourself be aided and inspired by others.

Michelangelo had a fierce rivalry and competition with Leonardo da Vinci, an artist, musician, engineer, and botanist – and the greatest inventor who ever lived. Giorgio Vasari, author of *The Lives of the Artists,* said of Leonardo, 'Heaven sometimes sends us beings who represent not humanity alone but divinity itself, so that taking them as our models and imitating them, our minds and the best of our intelligence may approach the highest celestial spheres.'

Leonardo famously said, 'I wish to work miracles.' He proclaimed that 'The knowledge of all things is possible.' His imagination was awe-inspiring, and his diversity was incomprehensible. Leonardo was one of a kind. Like Michelangelo, he also had a number of great teachers. His role model was Leon Battista Alberti (1406–1472), a painter, musician, architect, mathematician, athlete, and philosopher. Alberti's breadth of vision and talent was clearly an inspiring example to Leonardo.

Leonardo served his apprenticeship with Andrea del Verrocchio, the leading Florentine painter and sculptor of his day. In Verrocchio's workshop, Leonardo collaborated with his master and other artists on many projects. The Renaissance was a time of great rivalry and also great alliance. The *Baptism of Christ,* which hangs in the Uffizi Gallery, is an excellent example of collaboration. The figures of Christ and John the Baptist belong to Verrocchio, the blond angel to the left is the work of Leonardo, and some critics ascribe the second angel to the artist Sandro Botticelli.

Leonardo can rightfully be called a 'pioneer', 'original', 'unique', and 'peerless'. The scope of his inventions is unmatched, and his catalogue of discoveries is without equal. Yet the key to his success was, above all, his boundless appreciation for the connection of all things. I think Leonardo was one of the most connected people who ever lived. His genius came not from being independent of others, but from connecting to them. He learned from everyone he met, he thought of nature as his school, and he related to God as his teacher. He let everything touch him and inspire him.

Michael Gelb, author of *How to Think like Leonardo da Vinci,* pays homage to Leonardo's appreciation for the interconnectedness of all things. He describes Leonardo as the original systems thinker and writes, 'In 1980 Bohm wrote: "Everything is enfolded into everything." Five centuries earlier Leonardo has noted, "Everything comes from everything, and everything is made out of everything, and everything returns into everything . . ."'[22]

'The Original Problem'

To be called 'original' is a true accolade in individualistic societies, where everyone strives for attention and significance. At school, I had a teacher who reprimanded me constantly for not being original. She wrote 'not original' on every piece of homework I handed in. 'Be original, Holden!' she would bark. Unfortunately, none of my classmates was original enough for her either. The trouble was we were only 11 years old, and we didn't know what she meant.

To be original is a healthy goal, if it means to be 'authentic' and to value who you are. However, in individualistic cultures, being original often means setting yourself apart and standing out from the crowd. Thus, originality is confused with superiority. Individualistic cultures also attempt to manufacture and sell originality. Hence, people mistakenly believe that being original is wearing a mass-produced T-shirt with a logo, painting your hair red, or sticking a metal stud through your tongue. Alas, it has already been done.

Success is about being original if it means thinking for yourself and finding your voice. However, if you try to be original for the sake of originality, it often leads to alienation, insecurity, and having no real sense of self. Therefore, success is about being original *and* being collaborative. Success is about connecting with others and finding your team. Even the most original thinkers need to have backing and support for their visions and ideas. Originality without collaboration is mere abstraction and has little value.

Thomas Edison, the American inventor, has been described as one of history's most original thinkers. Edison, dubbed the 'Wizard of Menlo Park', registered more than 300 patents to his name in just six short years, and across his lifetime he registered over 1,000. Edison is rightly acknowledged for his brilliant intelligence and abundant ingenuity. He led the way, but he did not do it all on his own. He was one of a team.

Edison was an excellent recruiter. He assembled a pool of scientific talent at Menlo Park, New Jersey, where he created an 'invention factory' that served the needs of his day. Dozens of expert technicians collaborated side by side on anything and everything to do with radio broadcasting, the phonograph, incandescent lamps, the duplex telegraph, x-rays, long-distance telephony, motion pictures, and more. Edison was the driving force, and he attracted the best minds to work and invent with him.

In 1883, one of Edison's engineers, William J. Hammer, made a discovery that later led to the electron tube. The discovery was patented as the 'Edison effect'. Edison understood the importance of branding long before brand consultants ever existed. Edison was a 'name' that won respect and commercial advantage. Francis Jehl, Edison's longtime assistant, said, 'Edison is in reality a collective noun and means the work of many men.'[23]

Edison's effect on science and society is astronomic. He is truly deserving of the old adage 'We couldn't have done it without you.' Edison achieved his astonishing effect on us through a creative balance of independent farsightedness and creative collaboration.

Your Personal Best

Success is often confused with superiority in individualistic societies. From an early age, children dream of being the best soccer player in the world (just as their fathers still do). The dream of being the best rock star, the best in class, the best at anything, never really dies. Being the best is seen as salvation in individualistic societies because it saves people from the hell of being average and from the fear of being normal. We want to be the best, better than all the rest. We want to have the best, better than the others.

Wanting to achieve your personal best at something is a noble goal. This is how we discover potential and grow talent. However, unhealthy superiority is often a major block to achieving our personal best. A person's superiority drive can only get him so far before extra help is needed. In every hero's story there is a time when he has to set aside his ego for something greater if he is to succeed. To be your best self, you have to be willing to work with other people's strengths and greatness.

Sports halls of fame pay tribute to our sporting heroes, record breakers, world champions, and all-time greats. These people are truly inspirational, and they deserve our respect. But here, also, the storytellers perpetuate the myth of single-handed triumph and independent success as they attempt to deify their heroes. Nowhere is this more obvious than in English football, the game I follow, and in the FA Cup final, which attracts the world's largest television audience for an annual sporting event.

There have been over 120 FA Cup finals in history and many are named after a single player who stood out for one reason or another. The most celebrated final of all took place in 1953. It is known as 'the Matthews final' and is named after Sir Stanley Matthews (often called 'the greatest player ever'), who used his dribbling genius to help his team, Blackpool, come from behind to defeat the Bolton Wanderers 4–3. Geoffrey Green was the *Times* correspondent at the game. He was clearly moved by what he saw:

> Matthews is a superb artist, a football genius beyond compare. He paints, as it were, in watercolours and not oils. His work always has had that beautiful bloom that oils cannot give. He has it within him to turn mice into horses and nothing into everything. Now, in those last 25 minutes, he turned Blackpool into giants at a time when all his inspiration might well have drained away after earlier disappointment.[24]

Fifty years after 'the Matthews final', *The Times* published a report entitled 'Myth of the Matthews Final Revealed'. Reporter Richard Whitehead writes:

> At the age of 38, Matthews finally had won the most coveted honour in the game. Fed by countless reruns of the goals the legend has grown that Matthews defeated Bolton on his own, mesmerising them into submission with that famous body-swerve and providing inch-perfect crosses that forwards could not fail to convert. The facts, however, are quite different. Put simply, the Matthews

Final is a myth.[25]

The Times commissioned a statistical analysis of the match using the modern Opta method of allocating points for every action performed by each individual player. Sir Stanley Matthews clearly had a big impact on the game, scoring a total of 1,295 points for passes, dribbles, tackles, shots, and shooting accuracy. However, the statistics reveal that five other players in the game had a bigger statistical influence. One player, Stan Mortensen, scored 2,601 points, partly because he scored three goals!

Sir Stanley Matthews never once claimed the 1953 FA Cup final as his own. It was not in his nature to do so. Matthews had great individual talent, but was also a magnificent team player. He achieved his personal best through a combination of personal mastery and an excellent team ethic. In the final minute of the match, Matthews provided the cross for the winning goal by Bill Perry. Matthews didn't win the FA Cup final; his team did. And the Opta statistical analysis places Matthews' individual performance in a truer context. The statistics also prove the old adage that 'soccer is a team game'.

Shadow of Independence

Individualistic societies promote independence as strength and as a primary goal to which every individual should aspire. The ethos of individualism dictates that a person should not rely on society or on anyone else to achieve success. The ideal image all individuals are taught to pay homage to is a tall, solitary pose that denotes self-reliance and self-determinism. Of course this image is only an image and does not represent the whole picture.

Positive qualities of so-called independent people include being authentic, original thinking, unique endeavours, pioneering ideas, encouraging diversity, and showing respect for one and all. Independent-minded individuals have inspired the world with their new thoughts and new ways. One such individual, Albert

Einstein, wrote a book called *The World As I See It,* in which he praises the strengths of independence. He writes:

> Only the individual can think, and thereby create new values for society – nay, even set up new moral standards to which the life of the community conforms. Without creative, independently thinking and judging personalities the upward development of society is as unthinkable as the development of the individual personality without the nourishing soil of the community.[26]

Independence, taken out of context, casts a shadow that is full of misunderstanding, insecurity, and fear. A dogged insistence on independence – 'my way or the highway' – is a very common block to success in work, life, and relationships. Total independence makes everything more difficult than need be. Complete self-reliance rules out all offers of help. Excessive individualism cuts us off from our team. Absolute self-sufficiency is unnecessary and egotistical. Going solo alienates us from the collective intelligence and from God.

Einstein extolled the virtues of independence, but he balanced this beautifully with his praise for community and his experience of connectivity and oneness with life. Again, in *The World As I See It,* he writes: 'A hundred times every day I remind myself that my inner and outer life depend on the labours of other men, living and dead, and that I must exert myself in order to give in the same measure as I have received myself and am still receiving.' In truth, independence is part of a greater picture that leads to interdependence and wholeness.

<u>INDEPENDENCE</u>

<u>Strength</u>	<u>Shadow</u>
Free-thinking	Selfish
Pioneering	Egotistical
Liberty	Anarchy
Ambitious	Overcompetitive
Leadership	Superiority
Enterprise	Looting
Assertive	Narcissistic
Diversity	Inflexibility
Autonomy	Hubris
Self-reliant	Isolated

Success Intelligence Tip 15 – *Team*

Stop thinking like a 'particle', and think more like a 'wave'. Make a list of every person who is on your team. These are the people you love and respect, whom you want to support, and who want to support you. Think carefully about this.

Next, explore how you could be more of a team player at work and in life. Whom could you connect more with? Whom could you offer more support to? Whom could you ask for more help from? True success is a collaborative venture that serves the whole.

The Competition Block

Competitive intelligence is about knowing
how to compete and how to cooperate.

In my Success Intelligence one-day workshop, I often run a team challenge called 'Winners'. The workshop participants are divided into four teams of about five people each. The teams spread out to the four corners of the room. Each team is given 50 minutes to start up a business, make a product, and achieve a profit. They receive the same materials, an 8½" x 11" instruction sheet and a short statement of objectives, which reads: 'Use all the resources. Make the highest profit you can. All teams must make a profit.'

I have watched 'Winners' played more than 100 times now, by businesspeople, politicians, teachers, and doctors. Fifty minutes is not a long time, so invariably each team starts at a furious pace. The feeling in the room is manic, busy, hyper – a race against the clock, a competition among each other. There is also much invention and good humour. At the end of the exercise I conduct a review using the S4 Model of Success Intelligence (see Figure 7).

The S4 Model is very useful because it highlights four critical mistakes that most groups make. In fact, only two groups out of 100 have ever won at Winners. Before I point out the common mistakes, I would like to note that the four S's of S4 are covered in the first four parts of this book: the first S is for 'Self', which is in Part II; the second S is for 'Success', which is in Part I; the third S is for 'Strategy', which is in Part III; and the fourth S is for 'Synergy', which is covered here in Part IV.

Mistake 1 – A Poor Sense of Identity: Most teams at my workshops are a newly assembled bunch of strangers who have not met before, yet as soon as the clock starts they jump straight into action. 'How well did you get to know each other?' I ask. The usual reply is, 'There wasn't any time for that.' In other words, there wasn't any time to share relevant skills, identify past learning, and appoint people in appropriate roles. Usually what happens is that an extrovert grabs the instructions and takes charge. Assumptions are made, a culture is formed, and inefficiency commences.

FIGURE 7: S4 Model

Mistake 2 – A Poor Understanding of Success: In the review I ask, 'What was success?' A barrage of answers is given, including 'winning', 'making the highest profit', 'finishing first', and 'having fun'. Usually two or three teams in the room record a profit (the others make a loss), so most teams think wrongly that they have 'won' at Winners. The objectives state very clearly that *all* teams must make a profit. Staggeringly, almost every team misses this important criterion for success, usually because everyone goes straight into competition mode.

Mistake 3 – A Poor Use of Strategy: I usually ask the group questions like 'Other than speed, what was your strategy?' 'Other than effort, what was your strategy?' and 'How did you agree upon the best strategy?' There are many creative and diverse ways to make a big profit in Winners. However, most are missed because strategy is sacrificed for action, wisdom gives way to effort, and intelligence steps aside for the first idea a team comes up with.

Mistake 4 – A Poor Display of Synergy: When I ask the group 'What was the resource?' most delegates point to their own individual teams and not to the entire group, which is unfortunate because every team must make a profit for anyone to win at Winners. None of the teams talk to each other or share ideas, strategy, or success. In fact, most teams automatically go into competition against each other and are very adversarial. Thus, the group fragments early on, separate camps are established, and self-defeating behaviours reign.

The Competition Era

> Winning isn't the most important thing,
> it's the only thing.
> **– George Allen**

One of the biggest obstacles to success is what I call 'the competition block'. A common characteristic of dysfunctionally independent people is that they make everything into a competition. This may be appropriate in some situations, but not all. The independent mind-set, which has a default position set on 'compete', cannot help but translate encounters into 'me against you', turn tasks into a contest, and send relationships (even with team members) into a power struggle.

People who are very independent put up boundaries to protect their position of 'me against the world'. They have a commitment to a one-man army. Inevitably, cooperation, trust, and synergy are difficult to believe in, never mind experience. Competition rules apply in all situations. Success is defined only in terms of winning something such as winning a sale, winning first prize, winning some praise, or winning friends and influencing people.

People who define success only in terms of winning always lose out in relationships. They are deal-makers who do not know how to connect and join genuinely with people. At best, these 'winners' are beneficent in that they will agree to a 'You can win, if I win more' deal. At worst, however, these 'winners' have to have someone else lose if they are to succeed. The writer Gore Vidal famously said, 'It is not enough to succeed. Others must fail.'

The cult of individualism, the golden age of economics, and the rise of global opportunity have all helped to spawn a new era of increased competition. Competition is very much part of everyday life. The upside of this competitive era is that individuals, businesses, governments, and nations have all had to improve their games. Increased competition has been a catalyst for growth and an invaluable spur for betterment. The downside of this competitive era is that when we take competition too far, we end up living and dying in a 'winner-take-all' society.

Increased competition in society: I once coached a man who earned over US$3 million a year and whose chief criterion for success was still to make more money. When I asked him what he was going to do with all his money, he didn't really know. I learned eventually that what really motivated his money-making was a grievance he held about a senior partner in his company who was earning more than he. This man was suffering from what I call 'Social Comparison Sickness'.

I challenged his criterion for success. 'So you want to die with the most money?' I asked.

'Yes,' he said defiantly.

In highly individualistic cultures, the need to win and have more money than others plays tricks with our perceptions. Interestingly, social surveys reveal that most people rate themselves as better than average when it comes to things like 'driving ability', 'job performance', and 'getting along with others'. Very few people say they are average, and hardly anyone admits being below average at some things. This fear of being average causes a self-deception that inhibits learning and blocks growth.[27]

The need to win and have 'more than' others also plays tricks on our values. For example, a person who owns a Mercedes may feel very proud, especially if his or her neighbour commutes to work in an old wreck; but if that neighbour buys a top-of-the-range Ferrari, then a Mercedes is just scrap metal. The danger here, of course, is that excessive competition takes us away from our true values and our real criteria for authentic success. Obsessive social comparison creates a climate in which all of the winners feel like losers.[28]

Increased competition at work: One of the new man-agement tools in business today is what some consultants call 'competitive intelligence'. Competition at its best is an art form. It takes great vision (seeing an opportunity) and intelligence (know-ing the market). It also takes great faith (believing in your cause), strategy (acting on your strengths), and courage (committing yourself wholeheartedly). In this way, competition is noble. It is about being the best that you can be.

Unfortunately, many individualistic cultures have had to put up with an increasing amount of Neanderthal rhetoric from their corporate and political leaders. These people talk of competition as a war and define success as the ability to annihilate the opposi-tion. They want us to believe in their 'dog-eat-dog' world and for us to 'make a killing' at work. But we are not dogs, and we are not killers. Here are some examples:[29]

> *What you do when your competitor's drowning? Get a live hose and stick it in his mouth.*
> – **Ray Kroc**, driving force behind McDonald's, quoted in *The Wall Street Journal*, October 20, 1997

I don't like my competitors. I don't eat with them, don't do anything with them except try to waste them.
– **Hugh L. McColl, Jr.**, CEO of Nations Bank, quoted in *The Wall Street Journal*, July 25, 1996

Competition is warfare. Mostly it is played by prescribed rules – there is sort of a Geneva Convention for competition – but it's thorough and often brutal.
– **Andrew Grove**, CEO of Intel. E-mail exchange quoted in "Only the Fast Survive," *The New Yorker*, October 20 & 27, 1997

If you are a fierce competitor, you want to beat the brains out of the other guy, because that's what you love doing.
– **Al Teller**, president of CBS Records U.S., quoted in *Hit Men*, Fredric Dannen, Times Books (1990)

Increased competition between the sexes: The rise of individualism has also contributed to the rise of feminism. Women are learning how to benefit from their newfound freedom and opportunity – and men are learning how to handle this, also. The true essence of feminism is equality, but some feminists want to prove a point first. Many women want to show men that 'anything you can do, we can do better'. They want to out-earn, outperform, outrank, and outdrink men. Some want to 'out' the need for men altogether – 'we don't need you' – and advances in test-tube science appear to be helping.

With the rise in feminism, men have had to improve their game. Men have had to grow and to learn how to respect women more. Also, women have had to learn how to respect and join with men on a new creative level of equality and possibility. Eileen Gillibrand and Jenny Mosley, authors of *She Who Dares Wins*, offer a positive vision for the future when they write:

In a traditional, competitive, male world the image of 'winning' is often associated with a single person bursting through the ranks and leaving others behind. Let's have a different understanding of the word 'winning'. Winning for women should mean working effectively, confidently, and quickly within a network of supportive people, sharing their aspirations and hopes.[30]

Increased competition in schools: I once coached a woman who told me that she was very worried about her daughter's poor performance at school. As I listened, she told me her daughter had failed three oral examinations and achieved a below-par result in a class test, and was showing early signs of Attention Deficit Disorder (ADD). I assumed my client was talking about a young teenage girl, but in fact her daughter was only five years old.

The competition to get babies smiling, laughing, talking, walking, toilet-trained, and tested for preschool makes it unsafe to be a child these days. Penelope Leach, a child psychologist, reminds us:

> Child development is a process, not a race . . . We behave as if the child who walks earliest will walk fastest, as if exceptionally early single words predict meaningful later sentences, and as if children's prospects as intelligent, independent, and socialised people can be improved by speeding them through the age-appropriate illiteracy, dependence, or incontinence. It is not so and there is abundant evidence to prove it.[31]

School curriculums are packed with an increasing number of entrance exams, midterms, and finals. Who in the final analysis benefits from this intense 'pass or fail' focus – other than the schools that win more funding – is hard to fathom. We are schooling our children to be winners, but winners at what? We are still not sure.

The Tao of Competition

Gil Atkinson, the modern historian, said, 'Thank God for competition. When our competitors upset our plans or outdo our designs they open infinite possibilities of our own work to us.' Competition can inspire new standards, help us lift our sights, and motivate us to improve our game. This happens in sports, business, and politics all the time. For instance, it is often said that a government is only as strong as its opposition. Competition keeps us on our toes.

In the context of Success Intelligence, the issue is not whether competition is good or bad; it is whether competition is appropriate. When a person's only definition of success is 'to win', then that person will over-compete. At best he will practise what David Riesman, author of *The Lonely Crowd*, called 'antagonistic cooperation': 'I'll use you to get what I want.' Or he will do what anthropologist Robert Trivers called 'subtle cheating', in which people appear to reciprocate, but consistently give less than they receive.[32]

When people's only strategy for success is to compete, they often block all sorts of opportunities for mutual support, potential for shared learning, and possibilities for creative collaboration. Those who insist on 'going it alone' miss out on the power of relationships. They are afraid to receive help because it feels like failure. They are reluctant to accept support because it feels like cheating. They don't want to join forces because then it doesn't feel like a victory.

The Tao of competition is about knowing when to compete (which is *yang*) and when to cooperate (which is *yin*). It is also about knowing how to compete. A true champion will work with his or her competitive instinct to achieve a personal best. He will also keep his primary focus on his own personal vision and values so as not to let the competition urge, distract, or derail him. Ice-skating champion Katarina Witt said, 'When I go out on the ice, I just think about my skating. I forget it is a competition.' Herein lies the Tao of success.

The Tao of competition is also about knowing how to 'compete with' as opposed to 'compete against'. The difference between 'against' and 'with' may look small, but it can make every difference to your relationships and your life. To 'compete against' invites many subtle levels of conflict and struggle. But to 'compete with' helps a person to use everything as an aid and valuable spur to greater success. In sport, for example, great champions willingly give credit for their success to the fellow competitors who challenged them the most.

A champion golfer once told me that before every competition, he prays to God that his opponents play their best golf and that he also plays his best golf. He said two things that greatly impressed me. First, he said, 'Winning is not as important to me as playing a beautiful game of golf. I love golf more than winning, and that's probably why I win so much.' Second, he said, 'I cannot play to my best and achieve new personal bests without the help of a strong field and a good contest, and that is why I pray to God we all do well.'

This golf champion's prayer denotes unusual wisdom and courage in our competitive era. It is inspired by an absolute faith in the power of synergy, which states that the whole is greater than the sum of the parts. A very independent competitor believes that 'where two or more are gathered only one of us can do well', whereas an intelligent competitor believes that 'where two or more are gathered we can inspire each other to do our very best.' Synergy sees no lack. On the contrary, the power of synergy sees that success 'for one' inspires success 'for the whole'.

Success Intelligence Tip 16 – *Synergy*

Consider this statement: 'My success depends on the success of others.' Is this nice rhetoric, or is it more powerful than that? Synergy is not just something you do; it is a way of being. It is wisdom that allows the power of the whole to support all the parts.

Over the next few days, aim to be less independent and more interdependent. Identify how you could be less competitive and more effective. Be open to synergy and to opportunities of mutual support. Don't close your mind to greater success.

Thin
Conversations

My life is full of thin conversations.
I am a social anorexic who hungers for deep connection.
I am aching for some real, blissful contact.

– A client

The faster we go, the more we specialise in thin conversations. When we are busy, we communicate mostly on the run, using mobile phones, BlackBerrys, pagers, and e-mail. There is so much to do we barely have time to catch the headlines, digest the sound bites, skim the memos, and read the notes stuck to the fridge door. Everything is abridged, for convenience, so that we can get on with our lives. Occasionally we stop, and we wish our lives could be better than this.

I have been employed as a communications consultant to British Telecom for over ten years. BT is one of the largest communications companies in the world. Like all companies, it succeeds and fails according to how well it communicates. BT works hard at internal communication by achieving a healthy P3 balance between profit, position, and purpose. For external communication, the BT Better World Programme is consistently investing energy and resources in growing the spirit of community.

I have worked with many visionary BT leaders who have been actively involved in community initiatives for the BT Better World Programme, which provides valuable research and support for better communication in the workplace, schools, and family.[33] These leaders appreciate that businesses and communities can enjoy greater success through positive partnership and synergy.

BT has sponsored many national communications surveys that highlight interesting trends and challenges.[34] I am often asked to be a media spokesperson for these surveys, which confirm that the majority of adults and young people think communication is very important. Those interviewed agree unanimously with statements such as:

- Communication is an important skill for success at work.

- Communication skills can be the difference between success and failure.

- Making an effort to communicate is key to happy relationships.

- Talking and listening is the best way to solve an argument.

- Good communication is one of the most desirable qualities for children to have.

It is interesting to note that almost everyone interviewed agrees that communication is important *and* that they could communicate better. People typically report that they would like to 'be a better listener', 'understand people better', 'communicate more clearly', 'speak well in public', and 'spend more time with loved ones'.

In 1997, BT Forum published the results of a communications survey entitled 'Listening to the Nation'. One important finding of this survey revealed that 'although we talk to the people who matter most in our lives, we do not talk about the subjects we feel most strongly about. While nearly everyone (95 per cent) believes that couples need to talk about their deepest feelings and their relationships, the reality does not always live up to the ideal.' For example:

- Approximately twenty per cent of couples rarely talk about their deepest feelings.

- Fifty-three per cent say they are more likely to give up on their relationships than try to communicate.

- Forty per cent say they do not feel comfortable talking about deep feelings or sex with their partners.[35]

Joanna Foster, the director for BT Forum, concluded from these findings: 'We clearly understand that good communication is central to all our relationships, but we don't value it enough to turn our theories into practice.' We say we value communication, but there is little evidence that we try to improve our communication skills. Hence, we talk a good game, but the unhappy outcomes speak for themselves. Reports confirm that more of our relationships suffer from thin conversations, poor understanding, increased conflict, and feelings of apartness.

Thin conversations with the family: Comedian Frank Carson said: 'If you think television has killed conversation, you've never heard people trying to decide which programme to watch.' How true. So many of the TV programmes on offer today are mass media, anti-deep, and designed to appeal to the lowest common denominator of intelligence. We say we don't have the time to talk to each other, but we still manage to watch over 20,000 hours of 'dumbed-down' TV, shallow talk shows, and mind-numbing soaps.[36]

Families may 'small talk' together, but they do not always enjoy open and rich dialogue. At my seminars many people have told me, 'I know my parents want me to be happy, but we have never talked about happiness.' Another common disclosure is: 'I trust that my parents love me, but they have never said so.' Many people report they have never had an in-depth conversation with their parents about faith, spirituality, or God. Many grown-up children say they have never asked what their mother's or father's deepest aspirations are.

Thin conversations at work: A few years ago I had a business card made with the job title 'Conversationalist'. Many companies I consult to suffer from thin conversations about purpose and success. My team coaching events usually begin with a comprehensive Success Intelligence communication survey. Each team member scores – from 0–10 – statements such as 'Success is clearly defined', 'We communicate our successes well', and 'We know each other's strengths'. The scores are usually low.

I once saw a cartoon in a national newspaper that depicted a boss making a hospital visit to a subordinate who was recovering from a heart attack. The boss says, 'Don't worry about your work. We'll organise coverage if you tell us what you do.' I once coached a finance team of a media company, in which all 30 people had business cards that read 'Financial Manager'. They all had different roles and different responsibilities, but they all had the same job title and no idea what each other did.

Thin conversations between couples: Communication is the great enabler in relationships. It is the basis for good things, such as intimacy, trust, love, and sex. Communication breathes new life into relationships. A recent survey interviewed many couples and concluded that 'couples who discuss their relationship regularly discuss their mutual hopes and expectations, and are therefore likely to maintain flexible relationships that adapt and respond to the inevitable life stages they encounter.'[37]

Communication is like oxygen to a relationship; without it something dies. I once counselled a man who was desperate to resurrect his relationship with his wife. He said something I won't forget: 'We lived in the same house for 20 years, but we didn't stay in touch.' Research shows that 95 per cent of people think that many failing marriages could be saved if couples communicated more effectively. In times of trouble, the conversation has to be deeper, more honest, and more naked. This is the key both to healing and happiness.

Thin conversations with children: Research shows that the amount of time mothers and fathers spend each day communicating with their children (while not doing something else at the same time, like cooking, shopping, or watching TV) is as little as eight minutes.[38] The increase in split families, absent fathers, and working mothers has influenced this meagre count. Research also shows that people of all age groups agree that parents could improve their relationships with their children if they took more time to listen to their points of view.

A recent government survey on the communication skills of 'TV children' raised great concern. One newspaper article on this survey reported:

> Youngsters raised on a diet of television and computer games are to be given speaking lessons. Ministers are planning the extra instruction for children who cannot talk properly by the time they start school. Experts blame the decline in language skills on today's 'daily grunt' culture in which parents let their children spend hours in front of the television or computer instead of talking to them.[39]

The survey found that three- and four-year-olds were less capable of speaking clearly, understanding instructions, and reciting rhymes than children of the same age five years ago. Liz Attenborough, coordinator of the 'Talk to Your Baby' campaign run by a national literacy organisation, comments that 'we need a culture shift where parents are not praised for having quiet children but instead for allowing toddlers to speak.'

Social Literacy

In my work I often find that my clients' problems are really communication problems. For example, when a client laments, 'I don't like my job,' what he really doesn't like is that his boss fails to appreciate his good work. Or, when a client complains, 'I have a terrible work/life balance,' the real issue is that she never asks for help. Or, when clients say, 'My marriage isn't working,' what they may really mean is that they need to find a better way to communicate.

A central aim of my work is to help clients achieve success in both the short term and the long term. In coaching, especially, clients are encouraged to understand their situation better and then identify positive actions that can be taken immediately. In my experience, most of these positive actions are important conversations that are overdue with loved ones and work colleagues. When a person is ready to extend his or her social literacy skills, new possibilities emerge. Taking a risk in communication can unblock the blocks to success.

Social literacy is an important key to success in work, happiness in relationships, and wellbeing in life. The positive news is that communications surveys agree no one is too old to learn how to be a better communicator. Also, most of us already know how to communicate well; where we fail is that we don't make time to put our wisdom into practice. And yet many people testify that when they give time to better communication it both saves them time *and* they have a great time doing it.

Joanna Foster, director of BT Forum, has done as much as anyone to campaign for better communication in the community. She encourages us never to stop improving and developing our social literacy skills. She sums up her communication research by saying:

> The message is clear. Our ability to learn and relearn how to be effective communicators makes a crucial difference to our relationships, our employment potential, and to the economic success of our communities and the economy as a whole. Communication is the lifeblood of our existence as healthy, happy, and productive human beings.[40]

Social literacy is a vital component of Success Intelligence. I have coached many talented people whose unskilful communication was their major block to success. This is especially true of people who are constantly too busy to connect properly with others. Their lack of mindfulness has lost them valuable support and/or caused unnecessary conflicts. Each time I coach clients to improve their social literacy, they also improve their chances for success. Relationships are the heart of success, and for that reason better communication always leads to more success in every area of your life.

SUCCESS INTELLIGENCE TIP 17 – *COMMUNICATION*

Make time to reflect on the value of communication in work and life. Ask yourself, 'How good a communicator am I?' Think about what you do well and also what you could improve.

Here are four challenges for the week ahead:

1. Give up your busyness and commit to being more present to one conversation at a time.

2. Speak more honestly with everyone you meet.

3. Think of ways to improve your listening by 10 per cent.

4. Look at a current problem you have and find a communication solution for it.

A Better
Balance

People are longing to rediscover true community.
We have had enough of loneliness, independence,
and competition.
— **Jean Vanier**

My friend Cassius Colman is co-founder of MeWe, a creative production and design agency based in the heart of London. Cassius
heads a diverse team of talented directors, producers, and artists
who help their clients express creative ideas in every medium.
MeWe's clients are equally diverse and include The Happiness
Project, MTV, Sony BMG, the rock star Jamiroquai, and the royal
jewellers Garrard. The key to MeWe's success is their 'me-we' philosophy.

The MeWe Company is named after a poem by world-cham-
pion boxer Muhammad Ali. 'Me We' is the shortest poem in the
English language. The story goes that Ali was invited to give a talk
to the Harvard Business School shortly after his famous victory
over George Foreman in the 'rumble in the jungle' fight in Zaire.
An eager audience member asked Ali to recite a poem. Ali stood
up, pointed to himself, and said, 'Me,' and then he threw his arms
wide open to the audience and said, 'We.' Ali said that 'Me We'
represents his whole philosophy of success.

Cassius and I have spent hours together filming, editing, and
producing DVDs and CDs on Success Intelligence. We have talked
at length about the true meaning of a 'me-we' philosophy and why
a 'me-we' balance is needed in our society. For Cassius, 'me-we' is
like the 'yin' and 'yang' of success, which represents a positive
balance between self and others. On the home page of the MeWe
Website is a vision statement that reads: 'If the *me* is balanced in

mind, body, and spirit, then the *we* will be balanced too.' MeWe is a philosophy of mutual success.

Cassius believes 'me-we' thinking is essential on three counts. First, 'me-we' is about partnership. 'Starting up a creative agency like MeWe is a dream come true for me that I couldn't have done alone,' says Cassius, who pays great tribute to his co-founders. The most important successes of a person's life are rarely birthed alone. Yet many times I have coached talented people whose dysfunctional independence has led to endless sacrifice, caused chronic exhaustion, ruined their relationships, and limited their success.

Second, 'me-we' is about teamwork. Cassius' company specialises in one-of-a-kind projects that involve extraordinary vision and teamwork. Each project requires a new blueprint for success and also a new team. Essential to creating the right team is finding people who believe in the power of teamwork. Talent minus teamwork can cause untold drama and distraction; on the other hand, talent plus teamwork can make success happen faster and easier and also make the whole process more rewarding. Teamwork always outperforms independence in the long run.

Third, 'me-we' is about service. 'MeWe is about the joy of service and seeing our clients do well,' says Cassius. There is much talk about the importance of service in business today. It is still mostly rhetoric, though. Many times I have seen organisations preach the need for better service while they grossly mistreat their own staff. Organisations that are not good at teamwork will not be good at service either. Teamwork and service are mirrors to each other, and they reflect the true value put on relationships.

'Me-we' thinking offers a crucial way forward for the individualistic cultures that fail to teach us that we can access higher levels of success when we live for ourselves *and* each other.

Me-We at Work

At my Success Intelligence seminars, people tell me that they are often too busy working to attend team meetings and they can't find time to visit their customers. I express deep concern at this because I do not know many enterprises that can succeed without teamwork or service. Also, I challenge people to assess the true value of their busy workloads. After all, if the busyness is so damned important, the answer may be to get rid of the colleagues and customers.

We have been working like crazy for too long now. A recent government survey[41] reveals a continuing steep rise in the number of people who work excessive hours. The survey estimates industry loses as much as £370 million a year due to overworking and stress-related sick leave. There are also the emotional and spiritual costs of overworking, which are probably too high to calculate. The findings of the survey reveal that:

- One in six (16 per cent) workers surveyed now works more than 60 hours a week compared to just one in eight (12 per cent) in 2000.

- The number of women working over 60 hours has more than doubled from one in sixteen (6 per cent) in 2000 to approximately one in eight today (13 per cent).

- Three-quarters (75 per cent) of employees currently work overtime, and of these, only a third (36 per cent) are rewarded with extra pay or time off.

- Seven out of ten (72 per cent) highly stressed workers do not have access to any formal flexible working practices.

- One in five (19 per cent) very stressed workers is in their mid- to late 30s; one in five (19 per cent) men has visited the doctor because of stress, rising to one quarter (23 per cent) of men over 40.

- Nearly half of employees (48 per cent) say that their employer will step in to redress a work/life problem only when a crisis looms.

Here is the real issue: many people I coach are forced to over-work because they invest so little in their relationships with col-leagues. It is true that relationships take time, but they can also save time. For example, a good meeting can save people from being unnecessarily busy and dysfunctionally independent. And one honest conversation can avoid wasted effort and/or inspire better cooperation. Thus, the paradox of overwork is that our rela-tionships are not good because we overwork, but we have to over-work because our relationships are not good.

Overworking happens when people make the mistake of tak-ing care of business instead of taking care of relationships. Business is a hoax. It doesn't really exist on its own. Business is all about relationships. There is no business without 'me' and 'we'. Thus, when relationships fail, business fails. This is easy to understand, but a lot of people forget. We increase our chances of success each time we remember to give our relationships more priority. It is the power of relationships that ultimately drives success.

The modern world of work is fast realising that the key to success is relationships. The new economy is described by some commentators as a relationship economy. Why? Because custom-ers don't just want a great price or a fast delivery; they also want a good experience. For example, we love our fast computers, but we hate slow customer-service lines with recordings that drone on: 'Your call is important to us and that is why you must hold for 50 minutes.' Good service is valuable and meaningful to us.

I speak a lot about the relationship economy in my Success Intelligence seminars. In particular, I encourage my audiences to be more relationship-centred in their work. I also challenge them to raise their RQ – relationship intelligence – by giving more of themselves to their relationships with colleagues. This is especially important for the Hyperactive Workplaces where relationships get lost beneath a mountain of daily tasks, to-do lists, and permanent busyness.

In my 'Relationship Intelligence Test', I ask the following questions to help people use their inner wisdom to achieve a bet-ter balance between relationships and busyness at work. Take a few moments to answer these questions for yourself. Extend the questions to include relationships in work and also outside of work. Often, when you invest in your relationships outside of work, it can also increase your success at work. This is because relationships are at the heart of all our successes.

RELATIONSHIP INTELLIGENCE TEST

- Even though I am busy, whom could I be spending more time with?

- Even though I have a lot to do, whom could I be listening more to?

- Even though I don't have much time, whom do I need to communicate better with?

- Even though we communicate okay, whom do I need to be more honest with?

- Even though my schedule is full, whom could I be acknowledging more?

- Even though I can do it myself, whom could I be asking for more help from?

Me-We for Life

People who have poor 'me-we' values invariably suffer from poor work/life quality. They steal time and energy away from their most valuable relationships with family and friends in order to score temporary wins for self and work. They make their loved ones pay for their ambition, greed, and selfishness. Sooner or later, though, they learn that it is not intelligent to trample on relationships to

get to success. Inevitably they run out of relationships and they run out of success.

A healthy 'me-we' balance is essential for sustainable success. A friend of mine, Graham Taylor Chilton, is a role model for me when it comes to being relationship-centred. He likes to say, 'I have friends in high places and low places.' He is the sort of person who aims to make friends with everyone he meets, from the CEO at the top to the receptionist at the front desk. This is not some technique to manipulate performance or outcome. Graham genuinely enjoys putting relationships first, and that is why he will always be successful in life and work.

I have met many people in recent years who have elected to 'cash out' or 'downshift' for a better 'me-we' balance and work/life quality. I have also met many people who felt called to stay where they were and help to rehumanise their workplace. These 'corporate angels' believe in the creative power of relationships; they represent the heart of the organisations they serve, and they contribute greatly to the sustainable success of all concerned. Both of these sets of people agree that our challenge today is to work smarter together.

One recent work/life balance survey reported that 'twice as many employees would rather work shorter hours than win the lottery.'[42] Another Internet poll of over 4,000 job seekers confirms that increasing numbers are voting for more time for relationships. The findings include:

- Almost half of the respondents (46 per cent) chose flexible working as the benefit they would most look for in their next job.

- A third of them would prefer the opportunity to work flexible hours rather than receive £1,000 more pay per year.

- Seven in ten (68 per cent) job seekers would like the chance to work more flexibly when necessary.

- Eight in ten (77 per cent) parents with children under six said that work/life balance is an important factor in deciding whether to apply for a new job.

- Six in ten (60 per cent) workers view work/life balance as an important factor in assessing a potential new job.[43]

Individuals and companies are having to find new ways to help create a 'me-we' balance and work/life quality that supports success all around. More companies are offering flexible working options. BMW, for example, offers more than 300 flexi-contracts. More leaders are also valiantly trying to set an example of true 'me-we' success. Peter A. Smith, a senior partner at Pricewater-houseCoopers, speaks for many companies when he says:

What we are trying to do is develop a culture where people can and will realise both their professional and personal aspirations. A culture which enables a true balance between work and life to be achieved, rather than an 'either/or' culture. And we recognise that, whilst this requires considerable effort to implement complementary policies and procedures, the key input comes from our leaders. It is our leaders who need to 'walk the talk' and live our stated values which embrace work/life quality.[44]

So many of us have grown up with parents who sacrificed their relationships for work. Our challenge is to make sure we do not repeat the same mistake. In my Success Intelligence seminars I give participants a success questionnaire that examines 'me-we' values and work/life quality. Success is not just about self and work; it is about others and life as a whole. I ask people to close their eyes, take a deep breath, and think carefully on the following questions. Don't just read these questions, answer them for yourself, also.

- In the name of success, how many bedtime stories am I prepared to miss?

- In the name of success, how many family dinners am I happy to give up?

- In the name of success, how many dates with my partner can I afford to lose?

- In the name of success, how many friendships am I willing to discard?

- In the name of success, how many weekends have I resigned myself to throwing away?

- In the name of success, how many school plays am I prepared to miss?

- In the name of success, how many kisses good-bye will I not make time for?

- In the name of success, how many beautiful sunsets together will I sacrifice?

SUCCESS INTELLIGENCE TIP 18 – *ME-WE*

Healthy relationships are vital for 'me-we' balance and work/life quality. To enjoy sustainable success you cannot keep putting your relationships on the back burner.

Make a list of everyone you know whose funeral you would attend. Be sure not to leave anyone out. The list of people represents the heart of your life. Therefore, these people should figure in your social calendar every so often.

If you really are going to take time off to attend their funeral, you may as well get to know them first. Relationships are *the work* of your life.

PART V

Courage

● ● ● ● ● ●

The key to success is to go from one failure to the next without any loss of enthusiasm.

– Winston Churchill

Shift Happens

A Failure Policy

Further Education

Higher Learning

Success is letting go of fear.
– **Carl Whittaker**

The word *courage* is derived from a French word meaning 'from the heart'. In my work I meet many men and women of great courage. These people have often experienced the worst of life, such as personal heartbreak, major illness, and financial disaster. They distinguish themselves because they have faced their personal hell, survived their dark nights, and chosen to live. Often these people seem extra alive; they live from their heart and inspire everyone they meet. Carl Whittaker is one such person.

I first met Carl at Zurich airport. We travelled together by train to the picturesque town of Interlaken, which is surrounded by fast rivers, still lakes, and giant mountain peaks like the famous Eiger at the 'Top of Europe'. We were visiting Interlaken to speak at an international conference for Novartis, a world leader in pharmaceuticals and wellbeing. I was speaking on 'New Skills for Success' (Novartis comes from the Latin *novae artes*, meaning 'new skills'). Carl was speaking on 'The Courage to Live'.

Carl began his talk by saying, 'First, I want to say "thank you" to the pharmacologists, the surgeons, the doctors, and everyone else who helped save my life. I would not be here without you.' (Carl had a heart transplant operation in 1984, at age 24.) 'All changed! One minute I was healthy and okay, and then I had a sudden onset of stomach pains and palpitations.' Carl was rushed to the hospital, where he underwent emergency surgery. At the end of the operation his body rejected his new heart. 'I was dead on the operating table,' Carl told us.

Carl captivated the audience with his courageous story of recovery. 'When you are put on the spot like I was, you have to choose whether to live or die. All I can tell you is that I discovered a strength within me, more than I knew I had, that willed me to live.' Three months after surgery, Carl took up running to aid his recovery. Five months later, he entered his first race. He went on to win gold medals at the World Games in Austria, Manchester, Tokyo, and Budapest. At 43 years old, he runs the 100 metres in about 11.8 seconds.

Carl is a champion athlete, a successful businessman, *and* a survivor of heart-transplant surgery. He has travelled the world sharing his courageous story with people who are facing transplant surgery and other critical illness challenges. Carl and I have talked several times about his extraordinary experience. 'In my first life, before heart surgery, I lived a normal life,' he told me. 'But in my second life, after heart surgery, I now live a better life. It is a better life because I am able to serve and help people.'

Put yourself in Carl's shoes for a moment, and imagine what it must be like to live with another person's heart inside you. Carl told me, 'You have to understand that "I" am not a "me". "I" am a "we". As a heart recipient, I carry someone else's heart inside me. It is impossible, therefore, for me to live my life just for me. The way I see it, I live my life for me *and* for my donor, his family, and everyone who gave me a second chance.' For Carl, 'me-we' thinking is not just a philosophy; it is reality.

I once asked Carl, 'After all you have experienced, how would you define success?' Without hesitation he said, 'Success is helping people let go of fear. When we let go of fear, even by only one per cent, so much more is possible. After surgery I was full of fear, but slowly gaps began to appear in my fear, and I found a deeper strength and courage waiting for me. It was there all along, but I had to be open to it. I think everyone has more help at hand than they can see. Success is helping people know this.'

I also asked Carl, 'What is the most important lesson you have learned from your experience?' He replied, 'Life is full of uncertainty, but that is not always bad. When my heart failed I was certain it was the end of my life, but really it was a whole new beginning. My experience has taught me to live in the moment, to appreciate what is here, *now,* and to look beyond fear to the many positive possibilities that always exist. Success is seeing through fear.'

Shift
Happens

It was the best of times, it was the worst of times,
it was the age of wisdom, it was the age of foolishness . . .
– Charles Dickens, *A Tale of Two Cities*

A few years ago I wrote a book called *Shift Happens!* In it I summarised 15 years of working one-on-one with people who faced the challenge *of* change and also the challenge *to* change. I focused mainly on the personal psychology of change and on how to shift inner blocks to change, such as personal fears, self-doubts, old wounds, and dysfunctional independence. Change can often be a deeply unsettling process that tests our faith and our resolve. Yet if we learn to handle change well, we can open ourselves up to new levels of creativity and success.

Shift Happens! struck a chord with many readers who genuinely believe that our modern times are 'the best of times' and 'the worst of times'. Recent decades have certainly witnessed a rapid rise in just about everything, including worldwide democracy and more terrorism, greater personal liberty and more mental illness, increased prosperity levels and escalating crime, higher employment and record layoffs, better health care and more heart disease, more divorces and more out-of-wedlock births, and, of course, more changes and more uncertainty.[1]

Change is all the rage today. Some change is for the better, some change is for the worse, and some change is for change's sake. Shift Happens! is also the title of my most requested seminar, which is about how to be successful and stay sane during times of change. Anyone who wants to be successful in this world must take into account that change is constant. I have presented Shift Happens! to many diverse groups, including some zookeepers who faced a big reorganisation. Change is happening everywhere. As the saying goes, 'It's a jungle out there.'

At my seminars people often tell me that they feel less in control of their lives than ever. The rapid and unrelenting pace of change in our Manic Society makes it difficult to adapt and to live life well. We hope for job security, yet there is no such thing as a job for life any more. We wish to marry for ever, yet many marriages do not last two years. We want economic stability, but there is not enough insurance to cover every eventuality. We want to settle down, but most of us are now moving every five years.

In wellbeing surveys people often report that to be happy it is necessary to 'be in control of life'. This is especially so in Western cultures, which teach that life is about bending the world to your own personal will, as opposed to certain Asian and Oriental cultures that teach a philosophy of flow and flexibility. An important part of Success Intelligence is knowing what we can control and what we cannot. Life is forever evolving on the edge of chaos and yet we do have some say in how to arrange this chaos. In other words, the world is always changing, *and the world changes when we do.*

Some forms of control can be very positive, such as the ability to choose your thoughts, knowing how to handle your emotions, and opening and closing your mouth at the right moments. Success often requires some self-discipline and also the confidence to assert yourself. That said, I have worked with many people who blocked success because they tried too hard to be in control. Too much control can cramp creativity and stifle possibility. Overcontrol can stunt the progress of important projects. It can make you brittle. It can also deaden your relationships. Sometimes the key to success is having the courage to let go of control.

In Hawaii, I once saw a poster in a health shop of a Tibetan monk dressed in maroon and gold robes sitting in meditation on a surfboard that was perched on the edge of a magnificent rolling wave. The caption on the poster read: 'You cannot stop the waves, but you can learn to surf.' The Tibetan monk looked happy. I don't know if he had chosen to ride that particular wave or not. Some waves sneak up on even the best surfer. What was clear, though, was that the monk wasn't fighting the wave. Success isn't always about being in control; it is, however, about being wise.

Constant Change Is Here to Stay

A government agency recently invited me to design a two-year advanced coaching skills course for senior managers in its Department of Strategic Change. At the preliminary meeting, I met with the managing director and his human resources director, who told me of their bold and imaginative plans for the next three years. I gathered all the information I needed and promised to deliver a training proposal within two weeks. All was well, or so I thought.

Ten days later I called the telephone number on the managing director's business card. A woman answered my call.

'Can I speak to Mr. Smith?' I asked.

The woman replied, 'I'm sorry, but that department no longer exists.'

'What has happened to it?' I asked.

'It has been deleted,' she said.

'What does that mean?'

'My computer tells me that that the department has been deleted,' she explained.

'Could your computer be making a mistake?' I asked.

'No,' she replied.

'So how can I get in contact with Mr. Smith?' I asked.

'You can't. He isn't listed here any more.'

Change is constant, change is certain, and change can also be unpredictable. The world is forever rearranging itself around us. In physicality, there is nothing permanent except for change. Today is never completely the same as yesterday. 'You cannot step into the same river twice,' said Heraclitus, the Greek philosopher. Why? Because by the time you take your foot out and put it back in again, it is all new water. Hence, our task is to be both present to what is now and available to what may come.

A deep acceptance of the temporary nature of this world offers a powerful way to live. When we accept the essential truth that nothing physical lasts forever – including jobs, companies, relationships, marriages, good times, and difficult times – we can operate at a higher awareness. When we stop trying to make impermanent things last forever, we can truly appreciate our jobs now, our relationships now, our life *now*. And when we realise that change is only painful because we resist it, we can better cooperate with change. We can succeed better when we accept that the path of our lives is permanently under construction.

Cultivating a deep appreciation for what is timeless is also necessary for success. Here we return to the 'Neti, Neti' principle (see page 87) and the ability to discern between the transitory and the real. Success Intelligence challenges you to dig deep inside yourself and to discover what is changeless about your work and what is eternal in your relationships. 'Go to your bosom: knock there, and ask your heart what it doth know,' wrote Shakespeare in *Measure for Measure* (Act II, Scene ii). The heart knows something about the eternal qualities of life. It is the seat of wisdom, and it can see further than the eye.

When I want my clients to get to the heart of success I ask them, 'If the picture of your life changed completely tomorrow, what would still be the same for you?' A person can only answer this question if he or she speaks from the heart. Inevitably people speak about inner values, about Character Goals, about the spiritual, and about love. Whenever we make space to examine the eternal aspects of life, we bring a touch of heaven to this ever-changing world.

Progress Is Happening Faster Than Before

There is a story that Albert Einstein was holding an exam for his university students when a teaching assistant rushed up to him and said, 'Dr. Einstein, sir, there has been a terrible mistake. This exam is the same as last year's exam. All of the questions are exactly the same!' Albert Einstein smiled. 'Don't worry,' he said, 'this year the correct answers are all different.' A year is a long time in science, a month is a long time in business, and a week is a long time in politics.

The old APR (Annual Performance Review) is fast becoming outdated and obsolete. People working in business, medicine, and education, for example, cannot afford to let an entire year go by before they review their performance. Today most of us need an APR on the last Friday of every month. Many professionals are turning to coaching for support with performance and change because it offers a flexible, ongoing format. One of my clients, the owner of a small business, describes his coaching sessions with me as his monthly AGM (Annual General Meeting).

Medicine is an example of a profession progressing so fast that many of its members can barely keep up. 'Medicine looks likely to change more in the next 20 years than it has in the last 200,' reports the *British Medical Journal*.[2] I work frequently with doctors who are sorely harried by the progress and advances in medicine. 'I do not recognise my own profession now,' one senior surgeon told me. 'At a recent medical conference I attended lectures on breakthroughs in microsurgery, DNA medicine, and a "Virtual Dr. Brown" capable of making home diagnoses online.'

In January 2000, I attended a meeting at a private health-care company. The human resources director told me, 'Our keyword for 2000 is "innovation." Our goal is to be the market leader in innovation.'

I asked him, 'What do you want to be innovative about?'

'Everything,' he said. He also told me that senior managers will be under orders to be more proactive.

'What will they be more proactive about?' I asked.

The director fumbled for an answer. 'Everything,' he said.

I suggested a better keyword for 2000 might be 'vision'.

He said it had to be innovation.

'Why is that?' I asked.

'It's what the boss wants,' he said.

Innovation is not always progress, and change is not always growth. As a client of mine once said, 'Not everything we do in the future will be better, and not everything we do now is wrong.' Success Intelligence is about knowing what progress is and is not. In the name of progress we have made some of our greatest errors. Success Intelligence challenges us to remember what works already and not to lose sight of the truth in our rush for greater success. Otherwise, we may simply use change to create an illusion of progress and nothing more.

The Future Isn't What It Used to Be

We are mourning the death of normal, it is the end of the world as we know it, and our future keeps changing before it even gets here.

In the early 1960s Tom Watson, Jr., CEO of IBM, called a meeting among fellow business leaders to discuss a new intelligence called 'computer literacy'. Most of his peers were excited about the idea but remained unconvinced that this new type of literacy would ever be needed. Last year, in 2002, I attended a government-sponsored conference that identified a new class divide that is emerging in society between those who are 'IT literate' and 'IT illiterate'.

Computers are the new virtual nervous system of modern society. In 1998, fewer than 10 per cent of households had home access to the Internet, compared with 45 per cent of households in 2002.[3] Today, families stay in touch by e-mail, schoolchildren do homework using 'the Web', friends 'surf' to find each other again, the public 'logs on' to read the daily paper, lonely hearts date online, and companies use 'clicks and mortar' multichannel commerce to promote their products. Jobs that require no computer skills are diminishing rapidly.

The corporate landscape is changing beyond recognition. In the past, the longer you worked for a company, the more certain you were of your future. Not so today. Business visionary Peter Drucker sees unparalleled change for the future of business in what he calls the 'next society'. He states: 'The corporation as we know it, which is now 120 years old, is not likely to survive the next 25 years. Legally and financially, yes, but not structurally and economically.'[4] Company restructuring is everyday news; and each time a company restructures, employees and families and communities have to restructure as well.

Peter Drucker also predicts that in the next society (which is really happening now), 'the average knowledge worker will outlive the average employing organisation. This is the first time in history that's happened.'[5] We will outlive the organisations we serve. Thus, we now have to learn how to manage our own careers, update our own skills regularly, and continually reassess our true value to society. Hence, Drucker says, 'The centre of gravity of higher education is shifting from the education of the young to the continuing education of adults.'[6]

With constant change and uncertainty happening at work, it would be helpful if family life were more predictable. It is not, of course. In 2001, a national census recorded the lowest annual number of marriages since 1897.[7] And when we do agree to marry 'till death us do part', many of us part before that contract is up. In a Relate Centre for Family Studies report, P.C. Glick concludes: 'So much is known about recent trends in family life and so little is known with confidence about the future of the family.' The same report comments:

> Although people in all societies continue to place a high value on family life, there appears often to be a tension between familism, in which personal desires may be subordinated to the good of the family as a whole, and individualism, in which personal achievement and fulfillment are paramount: the struggle between 'we' and 'me'. On the one hand, people cherish family living in which marriage demands long-term commitments and fidelity, yet on the other, they subscribe to a culture which emphasises 'getting ahead' and doing what is most satisfying for oneself. People appear to be caught between opposing sets of values . . . [8]

The cumulative effect of so much change can cause what I call 'Change Fatigue'. This term describes the profound tiredness that is brought on by the grief of change, the fear of change, and also the anxiety of change. In my seminars I sometimes recite 'The Anxiety Prayer', which sums up how many people feel about change. It reads:

> *God grant me the strength to be really anxious*
> *about that which I need to change;*
> *The patience to be even more anxious*
> *about that which I cannot change;*
> *And, above all, the wisdom to know*
> *there's no difference.*
> *Amen.*

In truth, anxiety is a call for help. 'Every change is a crisis in confidence,' writes philosopher Eric Hoffer. People often experience some 'inner trembling' during times of uncertainty. However, the key to change is not more anxiety, it is more faith. Change calls us to have more faith in our vision and in ourselves. We have to tap our inner strength to handle change well. Change also calls for more faith in others and in our relationships. Success in times of change is often a team effort. Moreover, change calls for faith in God and in everything else that gives us real strength. What we put our faith in is where we put our power.

We Have to Exult in the Mess

I recently gave an address on Success Intelligence at a conference on 'The Future Society'. The audience of 200 people included senior politicians, city mayors, religious ministers, prize-winning scientists, and business chiefs. The hearts and minds gathered at this conference have enormous influence in society. I began with a question: 'Is anybody here certain what our future society will look like and how soon it will get here?'

No one raised a hand, but one man did shout, 'We are making it up as we go along!' Interestingly, he received a round of applause.

'Thank you for your honesty,' I replied.

Ten years ago a leader would not have admitted so publicly to 'making it up as we go'. The traditional 'command and control' style of leadership was all about 10-year plans and 50-year plans, executed with complete certainty. To alter a plan, to improvise, or even to seek advice was frowned upon as showing weakness. Recently, then-British Prime Minister Tony Blair was harangued by a television journalist for making a U-turn on a policy statement he made over ten years ago. 'Times change, and we must evolve our thinking,' Mr. Blair replied.

Many organisations are now putting a lot of investment into naming and training the new leadership capabilities necessary for managing change well. Emotional intelligence is encouraged for a more creative approach to change that uses both logic and feelings. Emotional resilience is taught for managing adversity, keeping faith, and generating inner renewal. Emotional honesty is also promoted for developing relationships that are truly creative, forgiving, and successful. In work and at home, change often requires us to be wholehearted – and to give more of ourselves, not less.

In my Success Intelligence seminars, I often quote the well-known saying 'The definition of madness is doing the same thing again and again, and hoping for a different result.' Sometimes we have to let go of our old winning formulas to experience new success. For example, we may owe our past successes to being always in control, yet some future successes may require less control and more faith. Or maybe we achieved our past successes by being very independent, yet some future successes may need greater partnership and synergy. Similarly, in the future, we may need to use less effort and more imagination, or we may need to use less logic and more instinct.

David Whyte is the author of *The Heart Aroused*.[9] He is a poet who lectures to leaders all over the world, and he recites from memory a repertoire of classic poetry delivered with great fire and tenderness. Poetry is his device for helping people to connect more consciously to the eternal intelligence of the heart. His poetry and commentary shifts his audiences from their heads to their hearts, beyond logic to wisdom, past perception to vision, above the world to the truth. What David Whyte does is unusual, but these are unusual times, and, as he says, 'the 21st century will be anything but business as usual.'

Shift happens when we are willing to make the inner shifts that create more success. The world does not change because business changes, society changes, or our relationships change; it changes because we do. When we change our thinking, we change our experience of the world. When we show up differently, the world responds differently to us. When we give the world another chance, our chances for success and happiness improve. Furthermore, until we put our whole hearts into our lives we will not know what is truly possible, nor will we reach the hearts of others.

Success Intelligence Tip 19 – *Change*

In every heart there dwells a sage.

– Taoist proverb

Successful people use their emotional intelligence to coach themselves through 'the best of times' and 'the worst of times'.

Name the most valuable changes you have made over the last 12 months in:

1. Your work
2. Your relationships
3. Your life

What inspired these changes, and what helped you make them?

Next, identify the most valuable changes you will make in the next three months in:

1. Your work
2. Your relationships
3. Your life

What/who can help you to make these changes?

A Failure Policy

Failure is only the opportunity to begin again,
more intelligently.
– **Henry Ford**

To be successful, a person must have a 'Failure Policy' that is honest and effective. A Failure Policy is a similar idea to the 'Success Contract' explained in Part II. Both your Success Contract and your Failure Policy sit in the back of your mind beneath a pile of thoughts. Both are metaphors, of course. The Success Contract represents your philosophy and beliefs about success, and your Failure Policy represents your attitude and approach to failure.

Everyone has a Failure Policy. It is 'written' from experience, and it can be 'rewritten' at any time. Most people's Failure Policies begin with a big headline in bold type: 'Try not to fail', 'Don't fail', or even 'Don't ever fail'. This is highly commendable. Unfortunately, most of us do experience failure. What does your Failure Policy recommend now? A less robust policy might advise a defensive 'deny until death' approach, a non-accountable 'run like hell' strategy, a 'blame someone quick' routine, or even a hefty 'be ashamed for ever' penalty.

A Failure Policy that is not wise and intelligent can easily block success and can also invite more failure. People who handle failure badly tend not to succeed well in life. By contrast, people who face failure with courage and openness stand every chance of more success. A good Failure Policy (i.e., a wise mental approach) can deliver the necessary grace to make the best of the worst times. The key message here is: if you work on your Failure Policy your life can work out better for you.

People who want to grow and to live life to the fullest need to have a robust and intelligent Failure Policy. When attempting new things and mastering new skills, a person is a student of a learning curve that includes failures, mistakes, and other lessons along the way. I have helped many people to 'write' and 'rewrite' their Failure Policies in order to experience greater success. A Failure Policy usually has three main parts to it:

Definition of Failure: Often by asking 'What is failure?' a person is better able to answer the question 'What is success?' Thus, when a manager thinks, *What ways could I fail in my job?* it can help her to employ greater vision and strategy in her work. When a person asks, 'How could this relationship fail?' he may gain valuable insights on how to relate more skilfully and how to be more loving. When a parent asks, 'How could I fail as a parent?' he or she can process fears, be alert to possible changes, and even prevent some mistakes from ever happening.

Meaning of Failure: An effective Failure Policy can help a person adopt the best possible attitude to failure. Some people interpret failure to mean 'The End'. Some people judge that failure is proof of 'No Talent'. Some people believe that failure is God's way of saying 'No Hope'. Alternatively, other people can give failure more positive meanings, such as 'I need to commit myself more', 'I need extra support', or 'I need to find a better way'. Attitude creates meaning, and meaning points the way forward.

Uses of Failure: An intelligent Failure Policy can help a person decide how best to use failure. Some people use a failure to write the first line of their resignation letter. And some people use a failure to buy a time-share in their own private wilderness. Alternatively, other people use failure as a chance to learn, adapt, forgive, commit, pray, dig deep, and live more from their hearts. Success Intelligence challenges us to use failure wisely and not to let failure use us up. Failure has its uses.

Talking of Failure

'Failure is not in my vocabulary' is a popular mantra people are taught at big motivation seminars. The high-octane motivational speaker races across the stage, yelling, 'It's negative to talk about failure!' and 'If you focus on failure it will happen!' I have heard this sort of thing many times. The theory is that if you don't talk about failure, it won't happen. The advice, therefore, is to make it a policy never to talk of failure. Such 'power talk' sounds positive, but really it stems from fear. Talking about failure won't make you fail. In fact, a constructive conversation about failure can help you to be more successful.

Your most valuable failure in business: Eight very successful people sat around a large coffee table. We were a diverse ensemble made up of a venture capitalist, a dot-com millionaire, a management guru, a business icon, a Shakespearean actor, a Benedictine monk, a leadership coach, and a best-selling author. It was the first of three meetings arranged by our host, who wanted to share with us his plans for a new organisation to promote spiritual values in the workplace.

After coffee was served, our host talked about the failure of business to engage the hearts and souls of people. He also spoke very personally about his own failure in business. He told us about the burnout he experienced after 15 years of working 'like a machine' in a cold, heartless industry. He said, 'At the height of my success, I was at the lowest point in my life.' He told us how he used his burnout experience as a wake-up call and as a chance to change. After he finished his story, he asked if anyone would like to share their most valuable failure in business. Initially there was silence.

I put up my hand and spoke of a business venture that lost me £50,000 in non-repaid loans. I explained that the failure was twofold. First, I lost money that I did not want to lose. Second, I had made some decisions based on making quick money and not on what my heart was trying to tell me. I used this failure as a lesson to be more heart-centred in all my future money dealings and business decisions. Next, the dot-com millionaire spoke, and then the management guru, and then everyone else. We each shared our most valuable failures and our subsequent learning.

The level of connection between us grew deeper as each person spoke. There was a realness in the room, an uncommon honesty, and a deep respect. There was no posturing and no 'Alpha male' – just eight people being wholly present. We learned so much about each other in such a short time. We had seen inside each other's hearts and learned what we truly value, what pains us, what we believe in, and what we are working for. Since that meeting, I have not been afraid to ask individuals and teams to talk candidly about failure. So much good can come of it.

Your most valuable failure in relationships: At my 'Positive Relationships' workshops, I sometimes ask people to share their most valuable failures in relationships. This doesn't sound very positive, but the resulting conversations often lead to important lessons, insights, and breakthroughs for relationship success.

At one workshop a woman told me, 'The biggest failure in relationships for me was staying in an unhappy marriage.'

'Why did you do that?' I asked.

'Everyone thought our marriage was successful, so I was afraid to leave,' she replied.

'Were you afraid of looking like a failure?' I asked.

'Yes,' said the woman.

Sometimes we fail in relationships because we are afraid to look at failure, and also because we do not want to experience the pain of failure. Unfortunately, this fear only causes more pain.

At another workshop a man told me, 'I came home from work one day to find a note from my wife of eight years that said, "I have finally left you. Good-bye." It was completely unexpected.' He said that, for him, the real failure of the relationship was not that it ended but that he had no idea his wife had been so unhappy for so long. This man told me how he used his relationship heartbreak as a spur to learn more about relationships and how to be a better partner. He finished by saying, 'My second marriage *to my first wife* is so much better because I am better at relationships.'

Owning your part in a relationship conflict is an important first step for future happiness. To be able to admit, for example, 'I am a poor listener', or 'I am too independent', or 'I am afraid of intimacy', or 'I go into sacrifice in relationships' is a good starting point for learning and improvement. The alternative is denial or blame, both of which fail to produce new outcomes. And if couples can find the courage to talk from the heart and listen from the heart, they can join together to experience new levels of intimacy, forgiveness, and success.

Your most valuable failure in life: When I coach clients one-on-one, I sometimes set up what I call 'A Meeting with Failure'. This meeting is usually conducted in three parts. Part I is 'A Meeting with Failures Past'. I ask my client to recall the most significant failures from his or her past, and also the key lesson learned from each failure. I also ask, 'From 0 to 100 per cent, how well have you learned this lesson?' If the lesson is learned well, it does not need to be repeated.

Part II is 'A Meeting with Failures Present'. People's emotional intelligence will tell them if they are currently failing somewhere in their life. Emotions are messages – internal memos – each with wisdom and/or a warning to impart. The better people listen to their emotions, the wiser they will be. Emotions such as sadness, anxiety, and fear all point to making better choices, such as 'I need to rest more', 'I need to communicate better', or 'I need to be more authentic'. When people shut off from their emotions, they may also tune out their wisdom.

Part III is 'A Meeting with Failures Future'. This is an opportunity to visit the future and to anticipate any possible regrets or mistakes. One client I coached was on the verge of taking a new promotion. In her Meeting with Failures Future, she identified a concern that her promotion might conflict with an important new relationship she had begun. We used her concern as an internal prompt to explore how she could create good work/relationship quality. An honest self-confrontation like this can put a person in touch with his or her wisdom.

I once coached a man named Peter, a modern-day Leonardo da Vinci, who was a publisher, designer, architect, photographer, property developer, and, when time permitted, sculptor. Peter was very good at everything he did, *which was his problem*. During his Meeting with Failure, Peter realised that just because he was good at something didn't mean he had to keep doing it.

I asked him, 'If you did what your heart wanted, regardless of being good or bad at it, what would you do?'

Peter listened. Over the next few weeks he kept listening. Today Peter sculpts for a living.

Benefit of Failure

> *Some of your greatest advances you have judged as failures,*
> *and some of your deepest retreats you have evaluated as success.*
> **– A Course in Miracles**

I am considered quite a successful author. I have had ten books published, translated into 14 languages, with gross sales of several million pounds, and I hope that the quality of my writing improves with each new work. I consider myself very fortunate to write for a living, and I never take my success for granted. This is partly because I received 71 rejection slips over a period of five years before I received my first book deal.

For five years the worst sound in the world was the heavy thud of a package landing through my mail slot. I could tell exactly the sound of a returned manuscript (with rejection slip). I quickly developed a policy to have at least three manuscripts out with publishers at any one time. My philosophy was, 'Give someone the chance to say "Yes" to you.' After a couple of years, I stopped talking about my writing to people. My friends felt too embarrassed to ask. It felt like a hopeless mistake.

Anyone will tell you that failure is not as much fun as success, but failure is not as bad as giving up on something you love. Every time I received another rejection slip, I felt the pain of failure and the temptation to give up. The 'gift' of my failures is that they forced me to enquire more deeply about why I wanted to write and about the real benefit of writing. Each failure also led me to ask, 'What is success?' My answer was, 'To keep writing.' If a writer stops writing, he is dead, just as if a person stops loving (or dreaming), he or she is dead.

I now understand that my failures were part of an apprenticeship that taught me to love writing for the sake of writing. Today, my writing is an important ritual for me, as important as my daily meditation and prayers. Writing is an act of listening in which I tune in to my highest thoughts and deepest wisdom. Aspiring authors often write to me for help and advice. I always caution them against writing solely for publication. It isn't worth it. If, however, they learn to love writing, they will always succeed, whether they are published or not.

Whatever people aim to succeed at, it is likely they will experience some failure along the way. An actor does not succeed at every audition he attends. A songwriter never publishes an album of first drafts. An artist usually works and reworks a canvas. No politician wins every election entered. A champion golfer does not win every tournament played. Every public speaker has 'died' at least once. Every true love, sweet as it is, will encounter the test of time.

The term 'successful people' is misleading if one takes it to mean 'people who have not failed at anything'. Successful people are so called not because they have experienced no failure but because they have used their failures well. There are many famous accounts of talented people who experienced failures, rejections, criticisms, and setbacks. They may have been temporarily disheartened, but that was all. Here are a few:

He has no talent at all, that boy. . . Tell him please to give up painting.
  – **Edouard Manet about Claude Monet, 1864**

I'm sorry, Mr. Kipling, but you just don't know how to use the English language.
  – **Editor of *The San Francisco Examiner* to Rudyard Kipling, 1889**

Can't act. Can't sing. Balding. Can dance a little.
  – **MGM executive on a screen test by an aspiring entertainer named Fred Astaire, 1928**

You'd better learn secretarial work or else get married.
  – **Director of Blue Book Modeling Agency to would-be model Marilyn Monroe, 1944**

You ought to go back to drivin' a truck.
  – **Theatre manager who fired a singer named Elvis Presley after one performance, 1954**

We don't think your ideas have any merit here.
  – **IBM executive to a young man named Bill Gates, 1970s**

A good policy for failure is: *You do not have to like failure, but you must learn not to be afraid of it.* Failure happens. Hopefully not too often. When it does, try to benefit from it.

The word *fail* can be an acronym – *f.a.i.l.* – for *first action in learning.* In the spirit of learning, Thomas Watson, the former IBM chief, said, 'The way to succeed is to double your failure rate.' Sometimes we have to risk failure and learn by it in order to achieve success. A reporter once said, 'The real secret of Silicon Valley is that it leads the world in a fast, phenomenal failure rate.' We can all learn from this.

Failure is never fatal; it just feels that way sometimes. Emotional intelligence gives us the inner resilience that is necessary for negotiating our way through feelings of distress, low self-evaluation, internal defeatism, general depression, and even suicidal thoughts. It can be a fine line between giving up and continuing. Each time I received one of my 71 rejection slips I repeated a personal mantra: 'To be continued.' With each new rejection slip I said, 'To be continued' in order to keep my attitude facing the direction I wanted to go. I still use this mantra during difficult times.

Success Intelligence recognises that failure is a teacher if we allow it to be. The real challenge of any failure – be it in work, relationships, or life – is to face up to failure and ask, 'How can I learn from this?' People who are not afraid of failure can go anywhere they want in life. They may experience failure, but they can take instruction and thereby benefit from it. Hence, the key to success is to find an approach to failure that (a) does not kill you and (b) does not kill your chances of success. Failure points to success, if you learn to use it wisely. To sum up, then:

- **Failures are not bad.** As Shakespeare wrote: 'Nothing is either good or bad, but thinking makes it so' (*Hamlet*, Act II, Scene ii). Every person has the divine right to handle a failure wisely or foolishly.

- **Failures can be good.** It takes great learning to realise that every event has some benefit, some wisdom, and some gift. Some of the best gifts may come badly wrapped.

- **Failures are lessons.** Each success and each failure is part of a highly individualised curriculum that teaches you about the true value of all things.

- **Failures teach success.** You can use failure to teach you about success. Failure is not the only way to learn about success, but when it happens, be sure to benefit from it.

- **Failures are not final.** 'Fall down seven times, get up eight,' says the Japanese proverb. A failure is not the end of the story; it can be the start of something new.

SUCCESS INTELLIGENCE TIP 20 – *FAILURE*

An effective Failure Policy recognises that your worst failures can be your best learning opportunities if used wisely.

Recall some past failures in:

1. Your work
2. Your relationships
3. Your life

Identify the lessons of each failure. Assess how well you have learned the lessons, so that they need not be repeated.

Next, think about a current relationship, project, or situation that is not going as well as you would like.

Ask yourself, 'What am I being asked to learn?' Listen and then lead with your best wisdom.

Further
Education

What is a mistake?
Nothing but education,
nothing but the first step to something better.
– Wendell Phillips

A person's curriculum vitae (CV) is an immaculate, well-presented résumé full of successes in work, education, and life. It represents approximately 20 per cent of anyone's personal history. The other 80 per cent is made up of gaffes, blunders, and errors. Normally, people will not mention these mistakes in their CVs, and yet each one of their successes was built in part upon these mistakes.

Success requires an intelligent balance between making the fewest possible mistakes *and* the best possible use of mistakes. A person who is good at relationships is probably very mindful and is also willing 'to go to school' on any mistakes he or she makes. A person who has a great talent for something often has what is commonly called 'a natural ability' (translation: courage) to risk learning by trial and error. A person who is a great leader has often made 'every mistake in the book' *and* has learned how to capitalise on them.

Success Intelligence includes the wisdom to avoid making unnecessary mistakes and also the courage to accept the necessary education when mistakes are made. Mistakes are not 'good' *per se*, but everyone can learn to make good use of them. Hence, a good relationship is one in which both parties are good at honest apologies, genuine forgiveness, and a willingness to learn from mistakes. Also, a good company or organisation is one whose culture supports creative risk, honest accountability, and mutual forwardness.

Even the best people make mistakes. In my Success Intelligence seminars, I show a list of famous mistakes made by very successful people. I do this not to humiliate, but to honour them. How so? I point out that none of these successful people stopped being successful after they made a mistake. Mistakes don't have to mean 'The End'. Mistakes can mean 'Part II' and 'Part III' and so on. Mistakes need not be the final grade in something; they can also be an opportunity for further education.

> *Everything that can be invented has been invented.*
> – **Charles H. Duell**, Commissioner of the
> U.S. Office of Patents, 1899

> *The phonograph . . . is not of any commercial value.*
> – **Thomas Edison**, inventor of the phonograph, 1880

> *I think there is a world market for maybe five computers.*
> – **Bill Gates**, Microsoft founder, 1981

> *My biggest fear is that we will be too successful.*
> – **Robert Fitzpatrick**, Euro Disneyland Chairman, 1992

> *The Internet will collapse within a year.*
> – **Bob Metcalf**, 3Com founder, 1995

A year later, Metcalf took his magazine article, liquidised it in a blender, and ate it with a spoon.

Past Mistakes

Beechy Colclough and I have co-presented together at many corporate seminars and also at a public workshop called 'Positive Change'. Beechy is a 50-something Irishman, a soft-spoken man, brilliant therapist, and inspirational presenter, who speaks with remarkable honesty about his traumatic story of abuse, addiction, and recovery. He touches the hearts of everyone with whom he works, but as he says, 'If you had met me 30 years ago you would not have liked me.'[10]

Beechy grew up in Belfast, Northern Ireland, and he was the youngest of 13 children. From the age of 11, Beechy was addicted to alcohol, then speed, then dope, then prescription drugs, then cocaine, then LSD, and then heroin. He recalls, 'My life was one big mistake after another; and I left behind a dirty trail of carnage, mayhem, lies, and broken promises.' Beechy was a gifted musician who played with Van Morrison and Alexis Corner, but his addictions ruined every good opportunity to grow his talent.

Beechy describes the first 35 years of his life as a 'tortured, isolated existence in which all the low points got lower.' He lived homeless and slept at night in graveyards. He hurt anyone who got close to him. Beechy once fell into a farm trough full of pig's swill after a sudden drink-induced seizure. 'I literally woke up in pig shit. So if you ever think your life stinks, think again,' he says. Beechy used drugs heavily to kill his pain and the shame he felt about his life. He also nearly killed himself. 'I had a priest read me the last rites at least twice,' he recalls.

'Every day I made the mistake of giving up on myself, and so my life got worse and worse,' says Beechy. Fortunately for him, he met people like Josephine, his future wife, who told him it could be different. Josephine encouraged Beechy to attend a local Alcoholics Anonymous (AA) meeting, where he took his first steps to recovery. 'Initially I sabotaged every offer of help, but eventually I got sick and tired of being sick and tired, and I turned a corner,' says Beechy.

In our Positive Change seminars, Beechy and I emphasise the importance of making an honest inventory of past mistakes. The reason most people won't examine their past mistakes is that they are afraid to face their shame. But we explain that the reason to do it is to let go of shame. Unhealed shame causes people to live on the run. When people run away from their mistakes, they generally run into the same mistakes again until the lesson is healed. Paradoxically, running away is a form of holding on. What you run from you run into.

Beechy and I teach that positive change is about 'picking up your own mess'. Our formula for mistakes is:

1. Acknowledge the mistake – look at the mistake to discover the lesson.

2. Learn from the mistake – so as not to repeat the mistake.

3. Account for the mistake – pick up your own mess and clear the way for a better future.

4. Forgive yourself for your mistakes – everyone has to forgive themselves for having a past.

5. Let your mistakes go – shift happens when you let go.

'Let go and let God,' says Beechy. 'No one punished me more for my mistakes than I did, but until I stopped punishing myself I was not able to make amends.' The future cannot be any different from the past if a person will not let the past go. Basically put, shame holds you back and forgiveness takes you forward.

'A person who won't forgive his past is dangerous to be around,' says Beechy. 'Shame can be an addiction, also, and a person who won't forgive his mistakes will keep on making mistakes.' At best, shame can prompt the need for learning, but unless a person can let go of shame he learns nothing of value.

Beechy's story is of a man who made more mistakes than most *and* has learned how to put his mistakes to good use. After being sober for two years, Beechy trained as a chemical-dependency counsellor. He later became treatment director at Promis, a treatment centre for multiple addictions. He holds a Ph.D. in psychology, trains therapists all over the world, and has a thriving practice. He was also awarded the Freedom of the City of Jerusalem for setting up the first treatment centre for multiple addictions there.

Last year, I was present as Beechy, Josephine, and friends celebrated his 20th year of being sober. Beechy's life is an example of how our mistakes need not be the end of our story. His life also teaches us that when we learn from our mistakes it is possible for others to benefit as well. On the other side of a mistake is a chance for growth. Therefore, as Beechy says, the only mistakes to avoid are those that eliminate the chance to try again.

> *Oh God of second chances,*
> *and new beginnings, here I am again!*
> **– Nancy Spielberg**

Present Mistakes

> *A full and candid admission of one's mistakes*
> *should make proof against its repetition.*
> **– Mahatma Gandhi**

Some people have a need to be right about everything and to be right *all of the time.* Wanting to be constantly right is an attempt to be strong and wise but, in truth, it hides insecurity and it blocks success. No one gets everything right always, and anyone who thinks they do is making a mistake. A person who denies he makes mistakes also denies himself the opportunity to learn and grow. What's more, a person can never get past the mistakes he or she won't admit.

People who are always right-right-right fool themselves into thinking they have nothing to learn. In fact, always needing to be right hides a fear of learning. Hence, people who want to be permanently right are often their own worst authority. According to them, there is no curriculum left to learn from; they have learned all there is to learn, and there is no higher authority than their own. However, people who think like this do not feel successful. On the contrary, they usually feel isolated and dead.

Permanently right people are hopeless at communication, feedback, and truth. You cannot tell them anything because either they know it already or you are wrong. Permanently right people wish to win admiration and respect, but they are not good at relationships. Dogmatic 'rightness' blocks success in relationships. It causes power struggles, stand-offs, non-forgiveness, and bitter endings. Hence, permanently right people often complain that 'people are difficult', 'relationships go wrong', and 'it's not my fault'.

People who need to be permanently right invariably sabotage success at work. Any success is usually short-lived and/or a façade. Also, they do not make good leaders. Permanently right people may look strong, but inwardly they feel frail, so they only work or socialise with 'yes men'. Any crony who dares to speak the truth may be fired for insubordination, dismissed from the list of friends, or tortured with thinly cloaked acts of revenge. Dogmatic rightness leaves little opportunity for support, diversity, or inspiration.

'Rightness' is a defence against making mistakes. But, like most defences, it attracts what it aims to repel. Successful people make mistakes, but they also learn how to recover quickly from their mistakes. In sport, for example, champion tennis players will hit an unforced error in every match they play. Immediately, in the space of a few seconds, they have to (1) admit the mistake; (2) process their feelings of disappointment, anger, etc.; (3) identify the learning; and (4) reset for success. Champion sports players are able to process mistakes fast. Honesty is the fastest policy because honesty is the best teacher.

> *Admit your mistakes, and don't let your*
> *mistakes put you off your purpose.*

Permanently right people unwittingly defend themselves against success by not admitting their mistakes. They try to 'save face', but at the expense of the truth. They allow themselves to be put off by mistakes and by their fear of making mistakes. They end up risking nothing, and therefore they stop learning and growing. Permanently right people have to be willing to drop their personal arsenal in order to move forward. In particular, they have to learn to let go of three defences: excuses, blame, and complaining.

If you have an excuse, don't use it: A common reason why people fail – in relationships, work, and life – is that they have a good excuse. In my work I help people to discover the 'hidden excuse' they are using not to live more, risk more, and love more. Often they identify an old mistake, heartbreak, or wound that they are still holding on to and that keeps them afraid.

Making excuses has an effect similar to taking drugs like cocaine: the more a person uses excuses, the stronger the habit becomes, and the weaker the person becomes. 'I never knew a man who was good at making excuses who was good at anything else,' wrote Benjamin Franklin. Excuses are a way out, but not a way forward.

If a person who makes a mistake can tell the truth, instead of making an excuse, he will grow stronger. He may also discover the extraordinary power of making a sincere apology. Refusing to use excuses commits a person to being more mindful and to giving the best always. I also believe that if you don't make excuses, you don't need them.

When you blame others, you suffer: If you are running late for a meeting, do you blame traffic or do you confess you started out ten minutes late? If your spouse is unhappy with you, do you first explain what he or she is doing wrong? If you make an error, are you a 'victim of circumstance' or can you apologise? If you fail at something, do you intellectualise that 'it wasn't meant to be,' or do you examine your part and draw some learning?

Life is full of 'traffic gridlock', 'market forces', 'computer crashes', 'parental mistakes', and 'my DNA', which can make life challenging. From an early age, we learn how to play the 'blame game', pointing the finger away from ourselves and never holding up our hands. Blame, however justified, wins a person nothing of value. It is a consolation prize. Ultimately, blame makes you a victim of your own consciousness.

When people blame others or something else, they forfeit an opportunity to learn and grow. Each time we use blame, we

"Congratulations, Bob...you've won a Pulitzer Prize for excuses."

also give up the opportunity to respond creatively. Blame never fixes anything, no solution is found, and nothing is ever learned. Blaming is like casting a personal vote to have everything stay the same. Nothing improves.

Complaining is a form of projection: People who believe they are permanently right complain frequently about how 'wrong' everyone else is. It is wise to check from time to time that you are not spending too much time in the 'Complaints Department'. It is okay to go for an occasional visit, but a person should not spend most of his or her life there.

Complaining can be a projection in that the mistake you see someone else making might also be the mistake you are making. A client once said to me, 'My boss has not once acknowledged my good work.'

I asked him, 'How often do you acknowledge your boss for her good work?'

The client was shocked. 'I have never thought to acknowledge any boss I have worked for,' he said. Sometimes other people's mistakes mirror our own.

Complaining can also be a call to leadership. In other words, it is a signal to give what is missing, to do what is not being done, and to create something new by your example. People who are chronic complainers are afraid that they cannot make a difference. Their complaining highlights the problem but offers nothing better. The challenge is to stop complaining and take the lead by being giving and saying and doing something better.

Aiming to be permanently right is a small-minded goal that can block bigger successes. Success Intelligence gives the wisdom and humility to know the difference between 'being right' and 'being successful'. Sometimes a person has to give up needing to be right in order to experience greater success. In other words, to be successful you have to be willing to give up your pride. And if you can admit your mistakes you can literally gain admission to new levels of learning and possibility.

Future Mistakes

I am always doing that which I cannot do,
in order that I may learn how to do it.
– Pablo Picasso

A major goal in life for many people is to 'look good'. To live in a well-appointed home looks good. To work in a high-profile job gives you a certain image. To drive a classic Mercedes looks elegant. To wear Armani makes a strong impression. To own 'successories' like a Mont Blanc pen or a Cartier watch makes a statement. Wanting to look good and needing to look good are two different things, though. In fact, needing to look good can be a major block to success.

A person who needs to look good at all times usually has a low frustration tolerance for setbacks and challenges. He or she does not have the heart to be vulnerable, to sweat for success, to risk a failure, or to speak the truth. These people are rarely found at the scene of an accident. The need to look good translates as 'if at first you don't succeed, destroy the evidence'; 'if at first you don't succeed, exit quickly'; 'if at first you don't succeed, blame someone';

or 'if at first you don't succeed, pretend you didn't care anyway.'

People who need to look good are afraid of making mistakes. They play it safe because they don't want to risk their prime directive. They take no risks because to look bad is the ultimate failure. They are at a serious disadvantage, though, because creative risk-taking is an essential key to growth and success. Taking risks is in vogue in the modern workplace. *Forbes* recently announced: 'If you are not bloodying your nose in today's warp speed economy, we have a name for you. Dead.' A calculated risk, personal accountability, and intelligent review make for success.

The need to look good is a defence against getting hurt. Anyone who has a heartbeat knows how bad it can feel to experience failure and heartbreak. If our feelings of disappointment are not processed well, we may be tempted never to risk ourselves again for anything. Hence, we do not give ourselves fully to any situation, which eventually causes our demise. In relationships, we edit ourselves. In work, we edit ourselves. In life, we edit ourselves. To be authentic and wholehearted is perceived as being too risky, so we settle instead for looking good.

True success is about finding something you believe in so much that you will risk giving your heart for it. True wisdom is knowing you have to put your whole heart into any situation, any failure, and any conflict in order to find a way through to success. You have to open your heart to give your relationships their best chance; you have to work from your heart to achieve your personal best; and you have to follow your heart in order to live your best life. In essence, then, the biggest risk a person can take is not to live from the heart.

In my Success Intelligence seminars, I show a slide of a tombstone that has written on it: 'Died at 30; buried at 60.' This is the risk we take when we stop taking risks. Every person's Failure Policy includes a section on risk assessment. There are two types of risk: (1) the risk you can afford not to take and (2) the risk you cannot afford not to take. Wisdom is knowing the difference. 'Then the time came when the risk it took to remain tight in a bud was more painful than the risk it took to blossom,' wrote the philosopher Anaïs Nin.

As a person stands on the threshold of a risk, he or she may well ask, 'What if I risk my heart and it all goes wrong?' Another good question would be, 'What if I risk my heart and it all goes well?' To risk is an act of faith. A person who puts his faith in looking good will be less courageous than a person who puts his faith in something he values and believes in. Looking good is all about faith in 'me'; it is an independent form of thinking; it does not allow for synergy, partnership, or miracles. Looking good has no room for 'me-we'.

A hundred times a year I stand up on a stage to give a talk. As I am about to speak, I am aware of a desire to look good and to gain acceptance from my audience. Occasionally, I also notice the temptation to edit myself for fear of disapproval. In these moments, I remind myself how safe it really is to speak from my heart and how unsafe it would be not to. I pray for the courage to speak my unedited truth because I believe that otherwise I cannot be of true value to anyone else. Onstage and offstage, the same truth applies.

The best things in life are worth giving your heart to *and* worth looking bad for. Giving yourself wholeheartedly is a risk, but as the poem called 'Risk' suggests, it is a risk that a person cannot afford not to take.

To laugh is to risk appearing the fool.
To weep is to risk appearing sentimental.
To reach out for another is to risk involvement.
To expose feelings is to risk exposing your true self.
To place your ideas, your dreams before the crowd
is to risk their loss.
To love is to risk not being loved in return.
To live is to risk dying.
To hope is to risk despair.
To try is to risk failure.
But risk must be taken, because the greatest hazard
in life is to risk nothing.

The person who risks nothing does nothing, has
nothing, and is nothing.
He may avoid suffering and sorrow, but he simply
cannot learn, feel, change, grow, love . . . live.
Chained by his certitude, he is a slave, he has forfeited
freedom.
Only a person who risks . . . is free.

– **Unknown**

Success Intelligence Tip 21 – *Forgiveness*

Forgiveness is the great masterstroke that helps a person release past mistakes and reset for success. First, we have to forgive ourselves for the mistakes we have made; otherwise the shame and denial is too heavy to carry. Second, we have to forgive others for their part in our heartbreaks, betrayals, and disappointments. Why do this? Because our purpose is not to carry grievances; it is to grow and live. A person cannot think of him- or herself as a victim and be successful. Forgiveness releases us from the past and makes us strong again.

Higher
Learning

There is guidance for each of us,
and by lowly listening we shall hear the right words.
– **Ralph Waldo Emerson**

When I finally met Peter, I had already heard a lot about him. He was a vice-president of BAE Systems. He had a 'Deep Gold' performance rating, which put him in the top 3 per cent of 100,000 employees. His track record in transforming ailing parts of the business into successful new brands had earned him the nickname 'Mr. Alchemy'. Peter's colleagues described him in glowing terms like 'a business genius', 'an inspirational leader', and even 'the best man I know'.

Peter attended a three-day leadership programme in Washington, D.C., run by a team of presenters that included Beechy Colclough and me. At the close of day two, Peter stayed behind to thank Beechy and me for our contributions, which he said resonated deeply with his own values and beliefs.

'I would like to show you something,' Peter said. He then took out a picture from his wallet. 'This is my beautiful daughter, Angela.' He paused for a moment. 'Angela was born with a hole in her heart.'

Angela lived to the age of five before she passed away. Peter talked intimately with us about the best and worst times of those five years. 'Angela is my greatest teacher,' he said. Angela's pain, his wife's pain, and his own forced Peter to examine his life more deeply than before. 'I had to rethink success, rethink my purpose, and rethink my spirituality.'

Peter told us he owes all of his success to the lessons he learned from Angela's life. 'Angela is a gift from heaven,' he said. 'She lives in my heart every day.'

A true definition of success must embrace a profound truth about life: *there is suffering*. Literally every moment of the day, somebody somewhere is coming to terms with pain and loss. Right now, as you read this book, people all over the world are being told they are HIV positive, are receiving chemotherapy treatment, are being downsized, are attending funerals of loved ones, are filing for bankruptcy, are ending marriages, are facing career-threatening injuries, and are learning that their child has a drug problem. Suffering happens.

'All the world is full of suffering, it is also full of overcoming it,' wrote Helen Keller. When suffering happens it brings all of our fears and doubts to the surface; it also necessitates that we go deeper, wider, and higher than ever before. The emotional anatomy of pain has two distinct parts: one part includes the temptation to give up and die; the other part includes the call to wake up and live. Beyond every pain, a higher school of learning awaits. Every adversity can teach us something valuable if we will let it. This is the test of true courage. This is how shift happens.

The Stoics of ancient Greece referred often to the 'intelligence principle that pervades the Cosmos'. The 'intelligence principle' states that every individual has access to the collective wisdom of creation. In practical terms this means that every person has the answer to every challenge he or she faces. Many schools of philosophy and psychology acknowledge the existence of 'inner wisdom' and an 'inner teacher'. The true work of a psychologist and a coach is to teach people the art of 'inner listening' so that they can be receptive to the best guidance available.

In my book *Shift Happens!*, I explored the power of inner alchemy, which describes a person's innate ability to transform setbacks into lessons, problems into opportunities, and pain into wisdom. We are all alchemists. We can 'turn straw into gold' if we are willing to listen deeply and follow our wisdom. Alchemy happens when we are prepared to look with new eyes, think new thoughts, make better choices, and act differently than before. Every problem has a message for us. Every adversity hides some gift. Every conflict points to a better way. Fortunes change, as we do.

To find the answer to a challenge or problem, a person has to first find the right question. The following 'Straw into Gold' questionnaire is a useful tool I use with individuals and teams. Each question is an invitation to think deeper, wider, and higher than before. Each question is also a challenge to reach past your own familiar psychology and allow for higher guidance and grace.

'Straw into Gold' Questionnaire

The 'Straw into Gold' questionnaire is designed to help people use the 'intelligence principle', which states that everyone has the answer to every challenge they meet. I often use this questionnaire in my Success Intelligence seminars. Each question is based on a principle of inner alchemy, such as the 'vision principle', the 'wisdom principle', and so on. I recommend that you not just read this questionnaire, but actually use it. Begin by calling to mind a challenge, then ask yourself each question, and listen inwardly for guidance.

1. Vision Principle: What Is the Fear?

Dr. Karl Menninger said that the real challenge of adversity and suffering is that 'the voice of intelligence is drowned out by the roar of fear.' On one level, every problem is an encounter with fear. Hence, some *fear management* is essential if you are to make way for vision, wisdom, and inspiration. The better you manage fear, the better you will manage the situation. Remember also that fear is a call for extra help.

Complete the following sentence: 'If I was to know what fear is at the heart of this problem, it is . . .'

Define the fear, and you will learn what the real challenge is. A good question to ask is: 'What fear prevents me moving forward with this challenge?' Is it the fear of rejection, the fear of speaking out, the fear of failure? It is important to listen carefully to your fears because some fears carry wisdom, and other fears are just fear.

2. Wisdom Principle: What Is the Truth?
Any problem calls for you to remember your true purpose and to be more honest. There are three levels to the wisdom principle:

1. Be honest about the real issue. We are never upset for the reason we think. For example, stress is not the problem, it is a symptom; relationship conflict is not the problem, it is a symptom; and poor work/life balance is not the problem, it is a symptom. What is the hidden agenda? A problem well defined is half solved.

2. Be honest about your part in any problem. Be willing to give up your excuses, complaints, and blame for greater accountability and responsibility. There is no progress otherwise.

3. Use any pain as a challenge to be more honest with yourself and everyone else. Avoiding the truth only delays an outcome; it does not solve anything. In ancient Greek, the word for *truth* is *aletheia,* which means 'not forgetting'. Any problem or difficulty challenges us to remember our real intentions and values.

3. Intelligence Principle: What Is the Highest Thought?
Perhaps the greatest block to success and happiness is a person's own familiar psychology. A person cannot go further than the thoughts onto which he holds. But if we change our thoughts, we can change our life. Thus, our problems are really an invitation to think at a higher altitude. 'The significant problems we face cannot be solved at the same level of thinking we were at when we created them,' wrote Albert Einstein.

In any situation in which you find yourself, pleasant or otherwise, it is a good discipline to ask, 'What is the highest thought here?' This question invites wisdom, insight, and appreciation. A client of mine who had been through terrible adversity told me, 'I used to think and then pray; but now I pray and then think.' Allow the highest thoughts to drop into your mind and heart. Let wisdom lead the way.

4. Choice Principle: What Choice Do I Have?

It can be very easy to lose sight of our choices in the middle of pain and adversity. In truth, there are always choices, but they can be difficult to see. Psychiatrist Viktor Frankl wrote: 'Everything can be taken away from a man but one thing; the last of human freedoms – to choose one's attitude in any given set of circumstances, to choose one's own way.'[11] Choosing a new thought, a new belief, and a new perception can create new possibilities.

I once coached an actor who had failed 50 consecutive auditions. All of his fears and doubts came to the surface. I told him he had ultimately one choice, which was to handle the situation either badly or well. First we explored some ways to handle the situation badly. His options included giving up acting, becomingmore cynical, and murdering all the casting directors. He successfully vented his grief and frustration. Next we explored how to handle the situation well. One option he had was: 'Maybe I should only take auditions for parts I am really interested in.' Now he was listening to his wisdom.

5. Learning Principle: What Is My Lesson Here?

'There cannot be a crisis next week. My schedule is already full,' said Henry Kissinger. No adversity ever feels convenient. At first we may interpret a new problem as an interference with our schedule, but later we learn it is our schedule. Every problem has a lesson for us. It is part of our curriculum, our life education. Everything can help us to advance if we use it wisely.

My friend Susan Jeffers, the author of *Feel the Fear and Do It Anyway*,[12] has taught herself to live by the mantra 'I can learn from this.' She finds that this mantra inspires an attitude of courage and victory that has helped her to cope with divorce, survive breast cancer, and overcome many other challenges. By reframing every trial as a learning opportunity we stop being victims and we become students.

6. Alchemy Principle: What Is the Gift Here?

I once gave a lecture at an international cancer conference entitled 'The Gift of Illness'. Before my talk, I asked every cancer patient in the audience to complete a short questionnaire. The first question was 'Is cancer a gift – yes or no?' Out of 325 answers, 303 people checked 'yes'. What a testimony this is to the human spirit and to human courage. In truth, I do not believe any illness is a gift, but I do believe we have the intelligence and courage to turn illness into a gift.

Almost everybody agrees with the following two statements: (1) life is full of gifts, and (2) I often forget that life is full of gifts. It is especially easy to forget about gifts when facing adversity. Asking the question 'What is the gift here?' during difficult times may initially draw a blank. But continuing to ask the question can help a person to work with the adversity rather than against it. Alchemists look for the advantage in every adversity.

7. Reciprocity Principle: What Do I Commit To?

During difficult times, we often focus on everything we are not getting – such as enough support, understanding, lucky breaks, etc. However, it is also important to focus on what we are not giving. Conflicts and problems are often caused by a subtle lack of commitment on our part. They are a sign we need to give more – more energy, more attention, more honesty, more trust. Giving your whole self to a situation usually inspires greater creativity and success.

It is tempting to withdraw and resign when faced with problems and setbacks. It is also tempting to go on the attack, to find blame, and to issue more complaints. The courageous thing to do is:

1. Commit to *being* ("What can I be more of in this situation?' such as more patient, more honest, more receptive, etc.).

2. Commit to *doing* ('What can I do more?' and 'What can I do less?' such as more listening, less talking, more rest, less busyness, etc.).

3. Commit to *giving* (giving more appreciation, giving more time, and giving more of yourself).

8. Synergy Principle: Who Can Help Me?

One of my own favorite mantras is: 'If you are alive, you need help.' Some people would rather die than ask for help. People who suffer from dysfunctional independence are often held back by the failure to ask for help. Dysfunctionally independent people believe that needing help is a failure. They rely solely on their own familiar psychology for new answers. This is a bit like reading only one book in the library for the answer to everything.

Any problem or conflict is a signal to try something new. There is an old saying, 'Keep doing what you are doing, and you will keep getting what you have got.' You don't need a high IQ to know how to ask for help, but it may test your pride and your courage. A common fear of asking for help is that we may not receive any; yet, by not asking, the outcome is certain. Each time we ask for help we set new possibilities in motion.

9. Trust Principle: What Shall I Trust?

Trust is what creates success or failure in any situation. In a nutshell, what you place your trust in is where you put your strength. In difficult times it is imperative to ask yourself, 'What shall I place my trust in?' People fail because they put all their trust in their fear and not in their wisdom. They do not trust themselves to succeed. Also, people fail because they will not place their trust in other people, their team, and in God to help them out.

Trust can transform any situation. Trust can turn a failure into an opportunity if you trust that there is a lesson in all things for you. Trust can turn every ending into a new beginning if you can trust in your wisdom to see you through. Trust can turn every enemy into a friend if you will place your trust in the highest wisdom in both of you. Trust can transform tired minds and broken hearts when you place your trust in heaven's help and God's grace.

10. Purpose Principle: What Is My Real Goal?

In the middle of a fight or disagreement, it can be difficult to remember the real goal of the relationship. In difficult times at work, we can spend so much time fighting fires that we forget our real purpose. In the midst of any setback or difficulty, we can be so distracted that it distorts vision, fragments purpose, and weakens intention. In any difficult situation it is wise to keep asking, 'What is my real goal here?'

Success Intelligence is the ability to process pain and choose success, feel fear and choose wisdom, be sad and choose hope, acknowledge anger and choose creativity. It is important not to let life's setbacks sidetrack you or derail you from your true purpose. And a wholehearted commitment to your real goals is a powerful immunity against unnecessary distractions arising in the first place.

SUCCESS INTELLIGENCE TIP 22 – *ALCHEMY*

As the saying goes, 'Some people *go* through life; other people *grow* through life.' True success is about growing your awareness of who *you* are and what your *strengths* are. It is also about placing your faith and your power in what will help you to grow beyond the mistakes, failures, and setbacks you encounter by seeing them as opportunities, not blocks. It fashions everything into a gift. A simple alchemy practice is to ask yourself in every situation, good or bad, 'What is the gift here?'

PART VI

Grace

• • ● • •

The soul should always stand ajar,
ready to welcome the ecstatic experience.

– Emily Dickinson

Destination Addiction

Insane Busyness

The Failure of More

The Energy Crisis

Three weeks before I was due to deliver my final manuscript for *Stress Busters,* the hard drive on my computer seized up. I spent four frantic hours on the phone to a technical-support operator who tried everything to revive it, before he finally pronounced last rites. My book had died and gone to cyber-heaven. My heart was on the floor. My despair was extreme because I had not made a backup. I prayed to God – the ultimate backup – for help. 'Dear God, guess what just happened!' The word 'RELAX' echoed through my mind, followed by a great wave of peace. I honestly wondered if God had grasped the enormity of my situation.

I had only 20 days left to write my book, 8 of which were booked with conferences. So really I had less than two weeks to write 50,000 words. I prayed, 'Dear God, if my purpose is to write this book, please help.' Ten minutes later, the human resources director for BT phoned to tell me that our three-day conference for the following week had been cancelled. She was very apologetic. 'Of course we will pay you in full,' she said. Later that day, two more cancellations came in. This was a record. Then a colleague at my Stress Busters Clinic generously agreed to take a large workload off my hands. A space had appeared.

The key to writing is to begin, and to keep beginning again until you are finished. A writer is never totally ready to begin because no map of the full territory ahead exists. The supreme joy of writing is that once you begin, a path unfolds one step at a time and signposts appear along the way. When a writer is completely absorbed it is as if the whole world sponsors his or her efforts. Into the writer's space appears all manner of help, including timely conversations, chance meetings, a relevant newspaper article, and even some lyrics in a song. Everything speaks to you. It is one big dialogue. For 20 days the whole world helped me to write my book.

At 11:30 A.M. on day 20, I finished *Stress Busters*. It had been an amazing flow experience. Each day at some unpredictable hour the flow would take me to meet new ideas I had not considered before. Insights, epiphanies, and answers fell like cherry blossom petals into my garden. Sentences would spring forward, and whole paragraphs would write themselves. Often it was effortless; occasionally I had a crisis of faith, but the flow kept finding me, especially when I would relax. *Stress Busters* was co-authored with everything around me. This beautiful sense of flow is what moves a writer, an artist, and a visionary to participate.

After I clicked 'save' for the final time, I did something I wouldn't normally share, but for the purpose of this story I must. This is eccentric, but in my mind I imagined a thousand angels, like in a Gustave Doré painting, circling above me and applauding wildly. I soaked up the applause from my heavenly crowd, as if I had scored a last-minute goal in a soccer match. My next thought was *I need chocolate*. As I got up from my desk I heard a package drop through my mail slot. The postman had already visited that day. I went downstairs. On my doorstep was a free trial sample for a chocolate bar called 'Applause'. God's honest truth.

Broadly speaking, there are two schools of thought about my experiences with *Stress Busters*. The first school, called 'Chance', would explain that I merely witnessed an unusually high cluster of random experiences called 'coincidences'. This 'luck theory' is favoured by Cartesians, Newtonians, and other individualists who subscribe to non-unity and to the separateness of all things. Their self-sightedness arranges the world in a way that leaves no possibility for a universal dance or an infinite intelligence. Apparently, every man is an island, the world is a lonely place, and life is not interested in you or me.

The second school, called 'Grace', would explain my flow experiences as moments of connectivity that prove that life is a theatre of interrelations. Grace cannot be fully grasped by the ego. 'What is grace?' wondered St. Augustine. 'I know until you ask me; when you ask me, I do not know.' Grace has something to do with the universal dialogue between all things. People who believe in grace believe that life is a collaborative adventure and a joint effort. Grace is the meeting point between an open-minded individual and the whole of Creation. It is the experience of being moved or inspired by something bigger than your ego.

Ben Renshaw, my co-director at The Happiness Project, writes eloquently about the relationship between success and grace in his book *Successful but Something Missing.* He explains that if we subscribe only to 'chance', our standpoint must be 'me against the world' and we have to rely only on our independence to navigate us through space; whereas if we subscribe to 'grace', we also make ourselves available to collective assistance and infinite possibility. Grace is a realisation that you live in a friendly universe and that life wants to work with you. Ben Renshaw writes:

> The truth is the world wants you to succeed and to be happy. The responsibility lies with you to open yourself to the possibility. The Greek philosopher Heraclitus wrote: 'There is only one wisdom: to recognise the intelligence that steers all things.' It is this intelligence that causes our bodies to function, birds to fly, and flowers to grow, and which brings dreams and desires to fruition. It has infinite organisation power, so the more tuned into it you are, the more access you have to unlimited creativity. By consciously connecting with this intelligence your relationships, work, and life will be transformed.[1]

Like many people, I have had countless experiences of grace. Each time I commit to a new book, a new project, or a new way forward I feel 'something bigger than me' lending a hand. Sole credit for any of my successes is out of the question. It has been a central feature of my life that I am continually inspired to be 'in the right place at the right time'. Psychologist Carl Jung defines these fateful experiences as 'synchronicity', which he describes as 'meaningful arrangements and coincidence which somehow go beyond the calculations of probability.'[2]

I teach a model of human potential that focuses on the interplay of personal psychology and universal grace. It is a psychospiritual model that teaches that success is easier when we trust in our inner wisdom and accept God's helping hand. Indeed, a chief goal of psychology is to make way for grace and God's help in every situation. I teach this synthesis of psychology and grace at The Interfaith Seminary, which runs a two-year training programme for ministers and spiritual counsellors.[3] I also teach it at The Happiness Project and in all my corporate and public programmes.

SUCCESS

Psychology	Grace
Thought	Inspiration
Perception	Vision
Intellect	Intuition
Logic	Eureka
Inner dialogue	Guidance
Readiness	Connection
Understanding	Trust
Concentration	Flow

School of Grace

If the school of grace had its own motto, it would surely be: 'When the student is ready, the teacher appears.' This ancient proverb appears in many spiritual texts written by Buddhists, Hindus, Taoists, Christians, and Theosophists, each of whom claim it as their own. It is a spiritual truth, a success mantra, that is practical and relevant to modern life, work, and relationships. It conveys great wisdom in a few words, and the closer you inspect the words the more wisdom you find. This proverb can teach us a lot about success.

'When the *student* is ready, the teacher appears' begins by affirming that everyone is a student. Albert Einstein called himself a pupil who wanted to know the thoughts of God. Leonardo da Vinci said he learned everything from the school of nature. Thomas Edison said he studied the laws of life. He said, 'I know this world is ruled by Infinite Intelligence. It required Infinite Intelligence to create it, and it requires Infinite Intelligence to keep it on its course. Everything that surrounds us – everything that exists – proves that there are Infinite Laws behind it. There can be no denying this fact. It is mathematical in its precision.'[4]

Success requires each of us to be a student *of* life and a student *for* life. Learning is living; there is no difference. We are all students of life, students of happiness, students of love, and students of success. When we learn well, we live better. Success is continuous learning. This applies to the modern world of work as well. Arie de Geus, the author of *The Living Company,* has pioneered the model of 'the learning organisation'. He teaches that success is a result of learning. He also states: 'The ability to learn faster than your competitors may be the only sustainable competitive advantage.'[5]

'When the student is *ready,* the teacher appears' affirms that 'readiness' is the key. Note that it does not say, 'When the student is *lucky,* the teacher appears.' Readiness is the ability to be present in the moment called 'now' and to receive every precious gift that is here. Readiness is the willingness to engage fully with what is happening and let every small detail speak to you, teach you, and lead you. Readiness is the ability to be spontaneously available for unplanned opportunities – not to be too busy, on autopilot, or preoccupied. Readiness is the willingness to drop your old learning and let grace inspire you with better ideas.

In business today the conversation is about diversity and inspiration. Tom Peters, in *The Circle of Innovation,* says that 'we

are all Michelangelos' and that our daily task is to keep opening to new levels of success. Peters is a student of possibility. He
reveres the art of the possible. He quotes another student of possibility, Benjamin Zander, conductor of the Boston Philharmonic,
who says, 'I make myself a relentless architect of the possibilities
of human beings.'[6] Readiness creates possibilities.

'When the student is ready, the *teacher* appears' affirms that
there is a teacher for all of us. If you accept that everyone is your
teacher, then everyone can teach you something. A student of success might reflect deeply on what his parents have taught him
about success, both positive and negative. He might even initi-
ate a conversation with them about success. A student of success
might ask his partner and friends, 'What is success?' He may also
examine carefully what his children are teaching him about success. Every relationship is a curriculum, and the lessons we learn
in relationships can create more happiness and success.

The 'teacher' can appear in many different forms. One of my
greatest teachers is a book called *A Course in Miracles*.[7] I study this
book every day, and it inspires my work and life. *A Course in Miracles* encourages its students to cultivate appreciation for every
person, every moment, and every thing. A central lesson is, 'All
things are lessons God would have me learn.' Your teacher may
appear as a book, a film, or a beautiful piece of music. Patience is
also a teacher, just as stress is a teacher, failure is a teacher, your cat
is a teacher, illness is a teacher, and so on. Grace moves in mysterious ways.

'When the student is ready, the teacher *appears*' is a categorical
statement. It does not say 'sometimes appears'. Also, the word is
appears, not *arrives*. This is an important distinction because *arrives*
suggests that the teacher is currently somewhere else, but *appears*
implies that the teacher is already here waiting to be noticed. Carl
Jung had a Latin saying inscribed over the front door of his house:
Vocatus Atque non Vocatus Deus Aderit. It translates as 'Bidden or
not bidden, God is present.' Grace is present wherever it is made
welcome. Therefore:

When the student is ready, the teacher appears.
When the thinker is ready, the idea appears.
When the artist is ready, the inspiration appears.
When the servant is ready, the purpose appears.
When the athlete is ready, the performance appears.
When the leader is ready, the vision appears.
When the lover is ready, the partner appears.
When the disciple is ready, God appears.
When the teacher is ready, the student appears.

In the four chapters that make up Part VI of this book, I will examine some of the blocks to grace with which I am most familiar. I will focus on the Destination Addiction of the Manic Society and how we can make way for more grace and inspiration in our everyday life. I will explore the Insane Busyness of the Busy Generation and look at how we can supplement our efforts with more imagination. I will look at the Failure of More in both the Hyperactive Workplace and the Joyless Economy and what alternatives we might consider. I will also reflect on the Energy Crisis that is both personal and global, and how to choose between burnout and wisdom.

Destination Addiction

'Do you eat a banana only to get to the end of it?' I was once asked this question by my friend and teacher Tom Carpenter. We had just finished picking tropical bananas from his garden, and we were sitting out on the deck watching the sunset over Hanalei Bay in Kauai, Hawaii. I laughed the question off initially, thinking it didn't merit any deep enquiry. However, Tom was serious. He wanted an answer. 'How a person eats a banana can teach you a lot about how they live their life,' he said. Most of my teachers have had an eccentric sense of humour.

Two weeks later I was in Ireland presenting a workshop called 'The Way Ahead' to business leaders. I took a box of bananas with me. After introductions, I handed a banana to each participant and explained that the first exercise was to eat a banana. This they all did. I then asked, 'Do you eat a banana only to get to the end of it?' My research found:

1. 16 per cent (four subjects) reported the best part is unpeeling the banana.

2. 24 per cent (six subjects) rated the first bite as the best moment.

3. 48 per cent (twelve subjects) enjoyed every bite.

4. 12 per cent (three subjects) preferred the last bite.*

'What does this have to do with "The Way Ahead"?' one participant asked.

Do you live your life only to get to the end of it? Most people answer this question with a 'no', but not everyone lives like they mean it. In the Manic Society, people exhibit a frantic, neurotic behaviour I call 'Destination Addiction'. This addiction is a major

---

*These subjects confessed they did not like bananas.

block to success. People who suffer from Destination Addiction believe that success is a destination. They are addicted to the idea that the future is where success is, happiness is, and heaven is. Each passing moment is merely a ticket to get to the future. They live in the 'not now', they are psychologically absent, and they disregard everything they have.

Destination Addiction is a preoccupation with the idea that happiness is somewhere else. We suffer, literally, from the pursuit of happiness. We are always on the run, on the move, and on the go. Our goal is not to enjoy the day, it is to get through the day. We have always to get to somewhere else first before we can relax and before we can savour the moment. But we never get there. There is no point of arrival. We are permanently dissatisfied. The feeling of success is continually deferred. We live in hot pursuit of some extraordinary bliss we have no idea how to find.

Destination Addiction is a nonstop approach to inner peace. We are like runaway trains bound for a station called NEXT. We embark on fast-track careers that are all about the next position, the next payrise, and the next stop. Our current work is just a stepping stone or a parking lot, where we hang out waiting for the next good opportunity. In the meantime we celebrate the end of the day, we say 'Thank God it's Friday', and we recover on the weekends. Everything will be better soon. The life we dream of is in the future somewhere, and we hope to catch up with it any day now.

Destination Addiction causes us to rush through as many experiences as quickly as possible. We like to be able to say 'Been there, done that!' A typical example is the popular package tours that visit eight European capital cities in a week. Surely, though, life isn't just about getting things done. Surely, life is not all about endings. If it were, we would read only abridged novels; we would attend only the final act of a play at the theatre; the last note of a symphony would be best of all; the best restaurants would serve only petits fours; and sex would have no foreplay.

Destination Addiction is an attempt to get on with life faster in the hope that we will enjoy our lives better. And yet our constant speeding means we frequently run past golden opportunities for grace and betterment. We are so harassed by the insecurity of our forward-seeking ego that we have no idea what it means to live by the grace of God. We seek, but we do not find. If only we could stop a while and let wisdom and grace show us a better way. 'One's destination is never a place but rather a new way of looking at things,' wrote novelist Henry Miller.

I think of grace as being *the potential for a better way that is present in every situation*. Grace is the ability to let yourself be inspired. It is letting yourself be touched by the highest intelligence and wisdom available. Our job is not to acquire grace, it is to accept it. We simply have to make it welcome. In other words, we have to be receptive. Our Destination Addiction often works against us, however, because we are too busy running to be receptive. Hence, we always feel empty. Here are some more symptoms of Destination Addiction:

- Whatever you are doing, you are always thinking about what comes next.

- You cannot afford to stop because you always have to be somewhere else.

- You are always in a hurry even when you don't need to be.

- You always promise that next year you will be less busy.

- Your dream home is always the next home you plan to buy.

- You don't like your job but it has good prospects for the future.

- You never commit fully to anything in case something better comes along.

- You hope the next big success will finally make you happy.

- You always think you should be further ahead of where you are now.

- You have so many forecasts, projections, and targets that you never enjoy your life.

The German mystic Thomas à Kempis observed, 'Whatever you do, do it with intelligence, and keep the end in view.' This is a great truth. It is similar to the popular aphorism 'Begin with the end in mind.' The words 'the end' have two different meanings. One meaning is 'the finish', i.e., the end of a project, or the end of your career. The other meaning is 'the purpose', i.e., your vision, your values, etc. The trouble with Destination Addiction is that it focuses purely on finishes and not on purpose. To live intelligently is to live with purpose, to make the means the end, and also the end the means. The end is in every moment.

Living in the Not-Now

> Like the Prodigal Son, we all eventually return to
> 'NOW' to find our spiritual home.
> – *Shift Happens!*

'How are you, Bob?' asks Bob's neighbour.
   'Oh, getting there,' says Bob.
   'Got to go,' says his neighbour.
   Destination Addiction is all about 'getting there'. As soon as we 'get there', everything will be all right. Hence, we intend to enjoy our successes, but not now; we will enjoy our life, but not now; we mean to be a better partner, but not now; we want to spend more time with the kids, but not now; we like the idea of stopping to smell the flowers, but not now.

The problem with Destination Addiction is that we are not fully present in our own lives. We suffer from psychological absenteeism. We are 'not here'; we are missing in action. We exist somewhere between the 'there' and 'now', in a netherworld devoid of any real inspiration and grace. We are but a shadow of our true selves. No now, no life. No now, no connection. Grace knocks on the door, but we are not here; opportunity knocks, but we are out; success knocks, but we do not answer.

'Getting there' is a dream of success that runs ahead of you, always in your future. Thus, you continually try to close the gap between there and now. 'Getting there' propels you forward towards a destination, but it does not teach you how to stop and enjoy the destination when you arrive. As the artist Gertrude Stein remarked, 'Whenever you get there, there's no there there.' Or, just when you get to 'there', another 'there' appears for you to chase. Almost there, but not yet. Almost successful, but not yet. Almost satisfied, but not yet.

Part of the Latin root for the word *grace* is *gratus,* which means 'welcome'*. Classical literature is full of great thinkers who taught that the key to a rich life is to welcome the 'here and now'. enjoy the 'precious present', remember the 'holy instant', and meditate on the 'eternal now'. Mystics, philosophers, and quantum physicists agree that the stuff of now is the stuff of the future. 'Nature is a living unity of living units in each of which the power of the whole is present,' wrote Bruno, the Italian philosopher. This is why grace is possible in every moment.

If love is the heart of Success Intelligence, then grace is the spirit of Success Intelligence. Grace is the awareness that life is always lived in the present and that 'getting there' really means being here. At a recent meeting with my bank manager, Kevin, I noticed his coffee mug had the words 'Be here NOW' printed on it.

'I bought this mug after reading your book *Happiness NOW!*' he said. 'It appeared, of all places, on a shelf at my local post office.'

Kevin uses his 'Be here NOW' mug to remember to be present.

---

*The Sanskrit word *gurtá-s* also means 'welcome'.

He told me, 'When I remember to "Be here NOW" I am more effective in meetings, I have more energy, I am better with customers, and I enjoy my day more.'

NOW is your goal: To be successful you have to find your NOW. Your NOW is the timeless values you carry with you. Your NOW is the constant principles that inspire your actions. Your NOW is the inner wisdom that coaches you in every moment. Your NOW is also your portal to grace and inspiration. 'The little word *grace* is like a small window that opens out on to a great landscape,' wrote Reverend Alexander Maclaren. Your NOW is your Unconditioned Self. It is your truth, and it is what you love with your whole heart. Success is being with your NOW wherever you go.

NOW is your teacher: It is true we can learn a lot from our past; it is also true that the present moment has much to teach us. Indeed, the 'Class of NOW' has every lesson a person needs in order to move ahead in life. A commitment to continuous learning can be as simple as stopping on occasion to inquire 'Am I living well NOW?' 'What is life teaching me NOW?' and 'What do I need to learn NOW?' My own day planner has a prayer printed on the top of each page that reads: 'Dear God, what is the best use of my time today?'

NOW is your gift: In the English language, the word *present* also means 'now', 'here', and 'gift'. Is this merely chance, or is this grace speaking? Dr. Chuck Spezzano says, 'When the receiver is ready, the giver appears.' Wisdom is knowing how to maximise the enjoyment of each moment. Being fully present enables people to give their best and also to receive the best on offer. I know people who consciously live as though each day is full of gifts to enjoy, and they are not disappointed. Every day is a gift for those who really believe that every day is a gift.

The Cost of Impatience

Do you have the patience to wait till your mud
settles and the water is clear? Can you remain unmoving
till the right action arises by itself?
– Lao Tzu

The 'honkosecond'[8] is, according to one UCLA professor, the smallest unit of time – it measures the time between when a traffic light changes from red to green and when a driver behind you 'honks' his horn. In our Manic Society everyone has to hurry up. We all need to get somewhere fast, but we are constantly thwarted by slow drivers, slow lifts, slow computers, slow coffeemakers, and a slow world.

Destination Addiction makes people feel as though they should always be further ahead of where they are now. They constantly fear they are not progressing fast enough with their lives. They believe they are 'running behind' with their careers, their commutes, and their schedules. They are always chasing the next goal, by the next birthday, by the next whatever. They are hypercritical and are forever 'should-ing' on themselves – 'I should be further in my career by now', 'I should be married by now', or 'I should have achieved more by now'.

Destination Addiction causes us to be permanently impatient with ourselves. The schedule we set for ourselves is so demanding that we end up driving ourselves harder and faster. We refuse to forgive ourselves if we cannot keep up. Our diaries are so full we will not give ourselves ten minutes in the day. 'In your patience possess ye your souls,' reads the Gospel of Luke (21:19). But we are too impatient for success, so we promise to catch up with ourselves somewhere up ahead. We press on, and we lose touch with ourselves. We keep going, and we leave ourselves behind.

We have no time for ourselves, and we are permanently impatient with everyone else. We are a society of fast impressions. If a relationship does not develop fast enough, we drop it. If a person cannot speak in sound bites, we 'tune out'. If people do not get to the point quickly, we make their point for them. If a relationship hits trouble, it is difficult to trust it has any further value. We are uncomfortable with pauses in conversations. We often interrupt conversations to get to the end faster. We need to move on.

We are permanently impatient because we are addicted to the pursuit of progress. Success Intelligence would have us examine, 'What is progress?' According to Destination Addiction, to progress is to move along a timeline from 'here' to 'there' as quickly as possible. But to what end? Impatience impedes real progress if the focus is only on getting to the future faster. Real progress is a real-time goal that is about the here and now – living well today, being more present, caretaking this moment, and enjoying the time of your life.

Real progress is not living life faster; it is about living life better. We are often impatient because we do not know the value of patience. In fact, we may be afraid of patience, for we fear that patience means deferment, forfeit, or loss. Sometimes, however, *patience is opportunity*. Patience helps us to be more receptive and more deeply engaged and to find the treasure at the spot on the map marked 'here'. Patience keeps us in the moment longer, and we are thereby better able to welcome grace and good fortune on our journey.

Progress is the intelligent use of experience. Impatience means you often only touch the surface of any experience and exit none the wiser. Patience brings you more immediate results because you commit more fully to where you are and you give your best to each moment. You are 'instant minded', not 'distant minded'. Patience teaches you how to welcome and to receive each instant. Ironically, you make faster progress because you stay around longer.

Theologian Henri J.M. Nouwen describes well the value of patience. He writes:

The word *patience* means the willingness to stay where we are and live the situation out to the fullest in the belief that something hidden there will manifest itself to us. Impatient people are always expecting the real thing to happen somewhere else and therefore want to go elsewhere. The moment is empty. But patient people dare to stay where they are. Patient living means to live actively in the present and wait there. Waiting, then, is not passive. It involves nurturing the moment, as a mother nurtures the child that is growing in her.[9]

The Joy of Slow

'God Spede' was once a common Old English blessing used by friends and travellers. It is out of fashion now, heard only in classic black-and-white films featuring swashbuckling musketeers, heroes of war, and kings and queens. If 'God Spede' were still used today, it would mean 'live as fast as you can', 'work as quickly as possible', and 'don't stop till you get there'. But in Old English, 'God Spede' did not mean 'fast'; it meant to 'prosper', 'be wise', and enjoy 'the highest success'. The word *spede* is from the Old English *spedan,* which means 'success'.

The day before I began writing this chapter, I was in London giving a talk on Success Intelligence to Accenture, a global consulting firm. Upon departing, I hailed a taxi to take me from Trafalgar Square to Paddington Station. The interior of the taxi was decorated with inspirational sayings like 'You must be the change you want to see in the world' (Gandhi), 'Each day provides its own gifts' (Martial), and 'Be still and know that I am God' (Psalm 46:10). There was also a 'God Spede' sticker with a picture of an angel sitting in repose.

I told the taxi driver how much I appreciated the words of wisdom in his taxi. 'Thank you for noticing,' he said. We talked about the Manic Society and the need to slow down from time to time. He said, 'Most people think this taxi is an ambulance. They act like everything is a life-or-death emergency. I should fix a siren on my roof.' My taxi driver told me he drives for 10 hours a day in London and never logs more than 80 miles. 'Everyone is in a hurry and the fastest we go is eight miles an hour. It's bloody madness,' he said. As we said farewell, we wished each other 'God Spede'.

The 'paradox of fast' is that *doing things fast isn't always the quickest way to success.* 'Fast' has its advantages when used appropriately, but it is not the only strategy for success. Success Intelligence appreciates the importance of fast *and* slow, movement *and* stillness, pursuit *and* pause, action *and* rest. The wisdom of fast is knowing when and how to change gears, because living fast does not guarantee quicker happiness and working fast does not guarantee more quality. Success requires a strategic balance between fast and slow. Think about it:

- Are the best musicians those who can play their instruments fastest?

- Are the best actors the ones who can say their lines the quickest?

- Are the wisest people you know the fastest thinkers?

- Do the best golfers swing their clubs faster than the rest?

- Do the best athletes force the pace from the front for the entire race?

- Are the best leaders the ones who have had overnight success?

- Are the best companies the ones that grow the quickest?

- Do the best friendships develop fastest?

- Are the most successful people on the planet always in a hurry?

Success Intelligence is knowing when to go fast and when to take things slowly. The ability to go fast becomes counterproductive when you try to do *everything* fast. The joy of slow teaches you to discern between busyness and wisdom, effort and grace, progress and truth. Slowing down can help you to stay true to your vision during the fast times. Slowing down can help you to sharpen your focus, adjust any blurring, and be more perceptive. In fact, going slow can help you to go fast better.

The hurry and the busyness are not our real lives; they are just what we do with our time. Our real lives take place in the spaces between hurry and busyness; it is here that we connect to what inspires us and moves us. It is here that grace exists. The joy of slow is that it helps us to remember our true goals, and to know what we really want to be busy about. The joy of slow is that it creates space for clearer guidance and new possibilities. In the slow moments we are often more receptive, more economical, more astute, more strategic, and wiser.

"I'm learning how to relax, doctor— but I want to relax *better* and *faster!* *I want to be on the cutting edge of relaxation!*"

The joy of slow is that it helps you to fully inhabit where you are now and to savor each moment. The ability to slow down brings more flavor and richness to your life. It helps you to be grateful and to enjoy what you have already. The words *grace* and *gratitude* share the same Latin root, *gratia*. Ultimately, slowing down can help to connect you more immediately with what you truly value. The Philosophy of Slow states that *if something is worth doing it is worth doing slowly.* If you cannot afford the time to do something slowly, it may be a sign that there is no value in it, even if you were to do it quickly.

Be Still and Know

> *Be still and know that I am God.*
> **– Psalm 46:10**

I once spoke at a conference on 'The Spirit of Business' held at the majestic Stock Exchange buildings in Vienna. Following my talk, Professor Singh, a business analyst and a scholar of Eastern spirituality, gave an inspiring talk on 'The Wisdom of Success', for which he received a standing ovation. In his question-and-answer period, Professor Singh was asked, 'What does the Western business world most need to learn?'

I remember his answer for its brevity and its power. 'Stillness,' he said. Instantly, a great stillness descended on the room – as if an invisible angel had arrived – and grace filled the air.

The most successful people I know have learned how to cultivate a quality of inner stillness. They use stillness to quiet the mind, to punctuate the busyness, to manage the pace of the day, and to listen to their best wisdom. They are like the 'eye of the storm' inside a twister or hurricane, perfectly still and immune from the chaos around them. These people are busy and relaxed, active and unhurried, passionate and calm. They have a natural grace about them that allows them to participate in the world and keep sane.

D.H. Lawrence wrote: 'One's action ought to come out of an achieved stillness, not to be a mere rushing on.' I begin each day with an hour of meditation. This is my time for stillness. In meditation I surrender any agitation or disquiet, and I allow my mind to become still. The stillness is like a lift that takes me to my highest thoughts, my deepest values, and my innermost sanctuary. In the stillness, I set my intention for the day, listen for inspiration, and make way for grace.

Stillness is a way to log on to the universal intelligence. It helps you to transcend the horizontal thinking of the everyday mind. It leaves behind the usual thoughts, the daily news, the normal ideas, and the business data. In the stillness, we turn off the ego, and we listen for news from the silence. Beyond the ego, we listen for God. As the poet Henry Wadsworth Longfellow wrote:

Let us labor for an Inward Stillness.
An inward stillness and an Inward Healing;
That perfect Silence, where the lips and heart
Are still, and we no longer entertain
Our own imperfect thoughts and vain opinions;
But God alone speaks in us and we wait
In singleness of heart, that we may know
His will, and in the silence of our Spirits,
That we may do That alone.[10]

Sam, a graphic designer, uses the word *stillness* as her password when she logs on to her computer. She first heard me speak about the power of everyday stillness at a 'Coaching Success' seminar I gave in London. She told me that since my seminar she had made a personal collection of pictures, sculptures, art, poems, and wise sayings that remind her of the power of stillness. 'Stillness' is literally the password to her creativity and her imagination. This is how Sam accesses grace.

The best coaching sessions help people to 'stop the world' and know themselves better. People who meditate regularly find the everyday stillness they need to live more effectively. Churches, mosques, and temples also offer sanctuaries of stillness and healing. The best museums, theatres, and symphony halls are like temples of grace and inspiration. And the lakes, rivers, woods, fields, and gardens of Mother Nature also encourage us to be still and know.

Be still and know God.
Be still and know who you are.
Be still and know what is true.
Be still and know what is success.
Be still and know what is joy.

Be still and know how to listen.
Be still and know how to receive.
Be still and know how to love.
Be still and know.

Success Intelligence Tip 23 – *Gratitude*

Count your blessings. First, make a list of everything you most appreciate about your life. Gratitude is a training in vision. Before gratitude we are in the dark and there is little to appreciate; after gratitude a greater awareness dawns.

Second, list all the people to whom you are grateful. Do these people know the full extent of your gratitude? Do you realise how grateful they will be when you tell them? Gratitude invites more grace and success into your life. It restores a feeling of abundance, and it attracts what you most value.

Insane Busyness

If you want to make God laugh, tell Her your plans.
– Anonymous

The first New Year's Eve that my first wife, Miranda, and I spent together did not go according to plan. We had started dating in October, and by our third date we both knew for certain that we would be married. Miranda moved in a week later. The week after that she met my mother and brother for the first time. The next day I asked Miranda if she would spend Christmas with me and my family. 'Your mother and brother have already invited me,' she said. Things were moving fast.

Miranda and I had received several invitations to some great New Year's parties. Hesitantly I told Miranda I preferred to spend New Year's Eve quietly, taking time to recall gratitude for the old year and planning ahead for the next.

'I'm happy with that,' said Miranda. We discovered we both enjoyed the stillness of New Year's Eve, and we wanted to be sober, quiet, and alone together. I suggested that in the lead-up to New Year's Eve we both compile a list of gratitude and future plans to share. We appeared to be on the same page.

On New Year's Eve, Miranda and I shared our gratitude for all the gifts of the past year, including gratitude for meeting each other. Next we shared our future plans. I was so excited because I had not shared my planning system with anyone before. First, I showed Miranda my five-year plan, with categories for 'work', 'family', 'health', 'money', 'spirituality', 'travel', and so on. Next I shared my three-year plan, my one-year plan, my quarterly plan, my monthly plan, and my weekly plan. Miranda appeared to be as fascinated as I was until she suddenly blurted, 'You are freaking me out!'

Miranda's style was different from mine.

'No plans!' I said, in disbelief. 'How do you know what to do?'

'Well,' said Miranda, nervously, 'I pray every day.'

'And?' I asked.

'I believe in grace,' she said.

Miranda had left Australia on a one-way ticket to England because she 'knew' she had to. She had only £400 to her name, but she 'knew' she would be looked after. She had given up a prestigious job as a television newscaster because she believed that life had another plan for her. Miranda is a talented, successful woman whose wisdom and grace inspires everyone she meets.

Planning had always played a major part in my game plan for success. The upside of my planning was that I was exceptionally focused, well organised, and very efficient. The disciplined execution of my plans had kept me very busy. By the age of 27, I had founded two health clinics; authored three books; lectured internationally; run a private practice; and given over 1,000 television, radio, and press interviews. I believed in the power of planning.

'Every day of your next five years is booked,' said Miranda. 'How can God do anything with your schedule?'

The downside of too many plans is that there is no room for anything else. There is no 'room at the inn' to welcome new birth and new ideas. There is no space to accommodate new gifts and better plans. Ironically, too many good plans can block higher inspiration and greater success. Overplanning can exert too much control and not enough openness. The calendar is full already. The mind is closed. The heart has a sign over it that reads 'Do Not Disturb.' There is no improvisation. Grace waits on our welcome, but we have too much to do.

Sometimes a plan is good.   I have since thought a lot about the psychology of planning and the wisdom of plans. Clearly there can be many benefits to having a good plan. For instance, a good plan can support vision, unify intentions, and also provide necessary direction for the journey. A good plan can also sustain a person's faith and enthuse a weary heart in difficult times. However, every good plan must be a servant, not a master. It must yield to a greater teacher, to new inspiration, and to a better way when necessary. In business today, the old three-year plan is called a 1+1+1 plan, which means that it is constantly up for review.

Sometimes no plan is good.   A vice-president of the World Bank once told me he owed his success to having never had a career plan. He said, 'My mother taught me to trust that God has much better plans for me than I do. The first thing she taught me to read was the words on a dollar bill, "In God we trust."' He also told me, 'I wake up every day knowing today will be wonderful.' He has absolute faith that each day will provide gifts for him and also opportunities to serve. 'God is my CEO,' he says. This uncommon thinking may sound odd to some, and yet he maintains it is the key to his success in leading a global enterprise.

Sometimes a new plan is good.   Sometimes you have to be willing to let go of your old plans in order to allow something better to happen. This is especially important today in a world that moves so fast and changes so frequently. Sometimes our old winning formulas and our old plans simply stop working for us. What made you a success in the past – your independence, your busyness, your work ethic, your always being in control, for example – may in fact cause you to fail in the future. Sometimes you have to be willing to ditch the old trip planner and travel the open road.

> *Whatever made you successful in the past won't in the future.*
> – **Lew Platt**, former CEO of Hewlett-Packard

The Space Programme

> *God is in the interruptions.*
> *I plan my day but He has the power of veto.*
> **– Joe Mills**

In May 2003, the designs for a new Microsoft 'iLoo' were leaked to the media. The iLoo is a portable toilet equipped with a wireless keyboard, plasma screen, and high-speed Internet access. Every article I read was in favor of this 'www.c.' After all, it is common now to hear people making mobile phone calls from inside toilet stalls. Multitaskers think nothing of sitting on the toilet and making a phone call, sending a text message, and updating a Palm Pilot. The iLoo is a truly modern convenience.

I think the iLoo is the ultimate space invader. I fear it may signal the death of private space. We will be online and available for meetings everywhere. The toilet is our last sanctuary in the new impersonal open-plan workspaces with 'hot desks' that workers share in shifts. The restroom is where we take a breather and let go, so to speak. One chief executive told me he gets his best inspiration when he sits on 'the wisdom seat'. He said, 'I get more good ideas on my wisdom seat than at any board meeting.' Microsoft's original plans to showcase the iLoo are currently on hold. Our private space is safe – but for how long?

Many people suffer from personal space deprivation in the Manic Society and the Hyperactive Workplace. Michael, a New York lawyer, came for coaching after he had suffered a nervous breakdown. He had been a highly successful attorney for ten years, and then he snapped. He told me, 'This might sound nuts, but I curse the day I installed my car phone. My car was my thinking space. I got all my best ideas driving to work. It was also my space to unwind. I used to listen to Vivaldi on the freeway home. But my car phone made my car into another office, and I became insanely busy, and I lost my space.'

Most of us are either very busy or insanely busy. Our busyness eats up our space. There is no space in our schedule. Our schedule is a never-ending to-do list. In my Success Intelligence seminars, I ask participants to read 'Today's Schedule' (see box below) and then invite comments. The usual comments include 'Who gave you my diary?' 'That's my schedule', and 'Just a normal day'. People also observe 'There are no full stops', 'There is no space', and 'There is no content'. It is just busyness as usual.

TODAY'S SCHEDULE

Most of the time I am very busy and the rest of the time I am insanely busy – every day I wake up and shower and make coffee and get the kids to school and commute to work where I look at my calendar and listen to my voicemail and check my in-box and read my e-mails and then I create a to-do list and prioritise my actions before going to my first meeting after which I make appointments and send e-mails and midmorning I have a cup of coffee and then I listen to my voicemail check my in-box read my e-mails and review my to-do list before lunch after which I listen to my voicemail check my in-box read my e-mails update my to-do list and then I go to meetings make appointments send e-mails drink more coffee and have a heart attack and self-medicate and fill out a time sheet and do what needs to be done before going home to get dinner ready for the kids and catch up on outstanding stuff before either passing out or falling asleep.

In my coaching work I help my clients create their own space programme. I find that most of my clients' problems are caused or exacerbated by space deprivation. I make sure their schedule is emptied of unnecessary busyness and filled with space for vision, strategy, and grace. I also encourage them to book space for themselves, with their families, and with God and whatever else inspires them. When I coach teams, I often facilitate team meetings with no agenda, just open space. Too often an agenda makes a meeting busy but not effective. A good coach helps a client find space where there was no space before. A coach is a space worker.

Psychologists have not found any positive correlation between permanent busyness and peak performance. Nor is there any evidence that permanent busyness supports inspired work or contributes to sustained success. On the contrary, permanent busyness often causes diminishing returns, but unfortunately we are usually too busy to notice. Space helps to undo permanent busyness. Space clears away the old plans and invites new possibilities. Emily Dickinson once wrote in a poem: 'I dwell in possibility.' I love the sound those words make. 'I dwell in possibility.'

Space is oxygen for the soul. It invites grace, it welcomes inspiration, and it births possibility. Successful people make wise use of space in their lives. They are like artists who paint with the space on the canvas, or like musicians who work with the space between the notes. They are like architects who incorporate sacred space into every design, or like sports champions who always find extra space on the field of play. The best leaders, the best parents, and the best lovers always make space for what is most sacred.

I once knew a young man who was the Clark Kent of the New York Stock Exchange. On one day he floated seven new companies on the stock market, and he still kept his appointment for a game of squash at lunchtime. Another day he had breakfast in Paris, lunch in London, and dinner in New York, and he still made a visit to his health club. He always made space for himself. 'Every day I make space so as to find the best in me and give my best to others,' he told me.

Many people complain to me about the lack of space in their lives, yet when space appears they are terrified of it. Nothing frightens us more than a night in alone, a free weekend, no work in the calendar for the next month, or no one to go on vacation with. Once a space appears we panic and fill it with more busyness. We must learn to befriend space, to greet space as a gift. Space empties out the old, but it does not leave us empty. Space helps us to die to the old, and it is also pregnant with new possibility.

Too often our daily busyness hides a fear of what might happen if we were to stop. It is a block against inspiration and a compensation for a lack of grace. If you ever come to a Success Intelligence seminar you will hear me talk about the need for a personal space programme. I will talk about the importance of a Sabbath, meditation, prayer, quiet time, and other natural space workers. I will also urge you the next time you are insanely busy to remember the wisdom of St. Francis de Sales, who said:

> *Half an hour's meditation each day is essential –*
> *except when you are very busy.*
> *Then a full hour is needed.*

The Effort Trap

'Success is one per cent inspiration and 99 per cent perspiration.' A majority of us have been raised to believe in this old Work Ethic mantra. We live as if it is the whole truth about success, and we never question it. Maybe, though, the reason that your success takes 99 per cent perspiration is that we only allow for one percent inspiration. I believe that if people are courageous enough to go for 2 per cent inspiration and 98 per cent perspiration, their lives will be blessed with at least double the grace and success. A one-per cent increase in inspiration can make a world of difference.

The Work Ethic deals in one currency, which is *effort*. It teaches that we have to spend effort to buy success and anything else we value. If you ever experience a setback or a failure, it is a sign that you are not spending enough effort. Effort plus more effort, plus more effort, is the key to success. If that does not work, invest a bit more effort. Effort is the 'real money', for 'in Effort we trust.' Effort is what makes things work.

The Work Ethic, at its most extreme, is about struggle, not grace, and about sweat, not success. We must work harder and harder and conclude we need to work harder still. There is not a minute to lose, but there are no free minutes available. The Work Ethic advocates a full-time effort that consumes our lives and spares no time for inspiration or recovery. Everything we have, including our time, is taken up with effort.

People who believe only in the Work Ethic are uneasy with grace. If success is easy, it feels unnatural. We believe in 'easy come, easy go.' If success is easy, we feel guilty. We believe in 'no pain, no gain.' If success is easy, we do not value it. We believe "there is no such thing as a free lunch.' If success is easy, we find a way to make it more difficult. We have been educated at the 'school of hard knocks'. We believe that struggle is the only learning curve. The bottom line is that we never let anything be easy.

Many of the people with whom I work are held back by the effort trap. Simply stated, they 'over-effort' and thus perform below par. The average executive habitually overworks; the successful executive doesn't. The average athlete overtrains; the great athlete doesn't. The average artist forces his talent; the inspired artist doesn't. The average chef overcooks her food; the genius chef doesn't. The average performer tries too hard; the best talent doesn't. Whereas intelligent effort attracts success, excessive effort blocks it.

The Work Ethic fails to teach that too much effort can actually block success. When you stop trying so hard, you are often easier to live with, you are more attractive, and your relationships blossom. Similarly, your work flows, you perform better, and you catch yourself enjoying your life. Have you ever heard about people who found their soulmate only after they stopped trying to get a partner? Have you ever heard about couples who finally got pregnant once they stopped trying so hard to conceive? When the student is relaxed, the breakthrough appears.

Excessive efforting hides compensations that block success. For example, maybe people over-effort because they are dysfunctionally independent and never ask for extra help. Or maybe they over-effort because they are trying too hard to control a situation. Or maybe they are afraid of what might happen if they surrender to their creativity. Alternatively, they may not believe that they are worthy of effortless success and abundance. Or they may simply be afraid to stop efforting and try something new. Sometimes effort is just fear.

Success requires commitment, particularly the commitment to balance effort with grace. I love to watch world-class sprinters in action. True champions like Linford Christie or Michael Johnson (dubbed 'the fastest man alive') look so relaxed as they glide across the track. They are fully committed and perfectly poised. They are in the zone, which is the meeting point between effort and grace. In the post-race interviews, the winners always comment on how relaxed they felt. Clearly, the relaxation they speak of is not idleness or apathy.

Great dancers like Rudolph Nureyev and great singers like Maria Callas found a way to balance effort with grace. So too did great artists like Leonardo da Vinci, who believed in the need for work and rest. Great orators like Martin Luther King, great politicians like Mikhail Gorbachev, and great servants like Mother Teresa also demonstrated grit and grace in their own way. They know how to give their best and also make space for grace and inspiration.

> *Every now and then go away,*
> *have a little relaxation,*
> *for when you come back to your work*
> *your judgment will be surer;*
> *since to remain constantly at work*
> *will cause you to lose power of judgment . . .*
> *Go some distance away*
> *because the work appears smaller,*
> *and more of it*
> *can be taken in at a glance,*
> *and a lack of harmony*
> *or proportion is more readily seen.*
> **– Leonardo da Vinci**[11]

Less Is More

Business leaders are trying to expand and downsize in an era of global competition; teachers are struggling to educate children in bigger classes with fewer full-time staff; doctors are trying to speed up patient waiting times and also reduce hospital budgets; charity organisations battle with epidemic increases in famine and woefully little political support; and ecologists are pioneering better essential services that require less energy and destruction of the planet.

The key to success has traditionally been 'more' – more funding, more resources, more people, and more effort. However, today there appears to be a worldwide 'shortage of more'. Companies say they cannot afford to employ more people; governments claim they have no more funding to give; environmentalists tell us the earth's resources are running out; and most people are already working 'all the hours God gave' and have no more energy to give.

How can we achieve more with less? This is a difficult question, especially if you have always thought that the answer to success is 'more'. Success Intelligence challenges us sometimes to adopt a 180-degree shift in our thinking. The answer to success may still be 'more' (more vision, more wisdom, more inspiration, etc.), but the answer to success may also be 'less' (less busyness, less waste, less greed, etc.). Success Intelligence encourages a flexible balance between the 'wisdom of more' and the 'beauty of less'.

The Lord's Prayer	=	56 words
The Ten Commandments	=	297 words
The Declaration of Independence	=	300 words
Directive of European Economic Community import of caramel and caramel products	=	26,911 words

Jon Davis, a senior manager at BT, was given a goal to reduce his new team from 90 to 50 people and also maintain customer service levels and annual profits. Jon and I drew up a plan to maximise his team's performance. Jon soon learned he had inherited a team that had been rewarded for effort, not effectiveness. 'For example, my six senior managers each produce a big monthly report that takes at least a day to read,' he told me. Jon's plan – his own idea, I hasten to add – was to buy a set of weighing scales for his office desk. He wanted thinner reports.

Jon weighed the first monthly report that arrived on his desk. He informed his colleague that the report was 'too heavy'.

'I told him I wanted a thinner report so as to save time and effort,' said Jon.

'It sounds a bit eccentric,' I said.

'Yes, and it didn't work either,' said Jon.

'Why not?' I asked.

'Well, he came back with a report that weighed less, but only because he had reprinted it in a smaller font size.' Clearly, the challenge of 'less is more' takes some practice. Jon was undeterred and continued to implement new ways to cut out the bureaucracy and improve effectiveness.

To be successful, it is important to keep asking questions like 'What more can I do?' and 'What more can I give?' It is also important to shift your thinking 180 degrees and to ask questions like 'What could I do less?' and 'What could I do differently?' To help my clients make this shift in Success Intelligence, I devised a '180-degree "Less Is More' Test", which is printed below. Once again, I recommend that you not just read this test but apply it.

180-Degree 'Less Is More' Test

Less busy; more effective: *How can I be less busy and more effective?* Make a regular appointment with yourself to conduct a Busyness Audit. The ego is a random busyness generator that creates unnecessary busyness if unchecked. Keep asking yourself 'When is less more?' in order to exercise mental fitness and to cut out the fat in your day. Investigate if your busyness is a compensation and/or a block to more grace and inspiration.

Fewer tasks; more value: *How can I do less and be more valuable?* As the saying goes, 'Even on your deathbed the tray will still be full.' Cultivate better in-box wisdom. Clearing the in-box is not success if it is full of tasks that are not valuable. The purpose of life is not to get *everything* done. To have time for what is valuable, you have to stop giving time to what isn't. Keep thinking, *What do I value?* and *Am I adding value?*

Less urgent; more wise: *How can I be less hurried and more wise?* In the fast lane there are plenty of speed traps, such as confusing adrenaline with purpose, urgency with importance, and speed with progress. Remember to take a pit stop every so often. Manage the pace of your day better by including time to rest and review. Check if your constant speeding is fuelled by wisdom or anxiety. Ask yourself, 'How can I live even more wisely?'

Less activity; more vision: *How can I be less adrenal and more economical?* Everything is dressed up as a priority these days. Take time today for some priority management. Identify your most important priorities in life and work. Ask yourself, 'What comes first?' and 'Who comes first?' Don't make the mistake of losing your priorities in your 'pending file'. Commit to your priorities now.

Fewer hours; more success: *How can I work fewer hours and be more successful?* Success is not working late again, being last to leave the office, or having another breakfast meeting with your boss. Recent research shows that 51 per cent of people are working longer hours than five years ago; and yet 75 per cent of peo-

© 1999 Randy Glasbergen.   www.glasbergen.com

GLASBERGEN

**"I'm sending you to a seminar to help you
work harder and be more productive."**

ple would choose a four-day work week over a 20 per cent pay increase.[12] What would you have to do more of and less of to work only a four-day week?

Less effort; more imagination: *How can I be less laboured and more creative?* Create time in your schedule for thinking outside the box. Set meetings to have more 'What if?' conversations. Make space for less doing and more possibility thinking. Keep asking yourself, 'How could I be working smarter, not harder?' Consider your options, book a coaching session, do something different, and take a leap.

Less struggle; more ease: *How can I experience less struggle and more ease?* Make a list of all the ways you could make your life and work even easier. For example, take a regular sabbatical, stop working weekends, delegate more often, ask for help, become more organized, tell the truth, have some 'me time', eliminate your commute, don't attempt to answer all your e-mails, and trade perfectionism for wisdom.

Less waste; more efficiency: *How can I be less wasteful and more efficient?* Once a month put a date in your calendar for waste management. Identify any time-wasters that are drawing attention away from your purpose and priorities. Look for any energy vampires that are eating up your energy. Identify any financial waste and how to use your money more intelligently. Look for any personal strengths you are wasting by not using them.

Less stress; more peace: *How can I be less stressed and more peaceful?* Identify three effective stress-busters that you can incorporate regularly into your schedule. For example, yoga classes, daily meditation, lunch breaks, white space, health clubs, golf courses, body massage, herbal tea, inspirational reading. Discipline yourself to 'switch off' mobile phones, BlackBerrys, laptops, and any other 24-hour technology.

Less ego; more God: *How can I be less independent and more inspired?* Add up all the benefits of being less self-centred, less proud, less controlling, less defensive, less competitive, and less egotistical. Be willing to let in more grace and inspiration. Be open to letting God work through you more, even if you don't know what that means. Ask God for help, and be willing to receive.

SUCCESS INTELLIGENCE TIP 24 – *SIMPLICITY*

In our Manic Society we constantly cram and multitask in order to manage the pace. And yet we are often slowed down by the complexity of our lives. The decision to simplify things is a gift because it returns you to your essence and to what you most value. Greater simplicity helps to avoid excess busyness and unnecessary effort. It increases effectiveness, and it welcomes grace and inspiration. It also preserves your sanity. Take time to reflect on how you could simplify your life and work to enjoy greater success.

The Failure
of More

We enjoy a thousand material advantages over any
generation, and yet we suffer a depth of insecurity
and spiritual doubt they never knew.
– Tony Blair

I was writing notes for a public seminar called Everyday Abundance when the phone rang. I didn't want the interruption and
was tempted not to answer. Somewhat reluctantly, I answered the
phone and spoke to a man who sounded 'old school' – like a but-
ler, very formal.

'My name is Morton,' he said. 'You are cordially invited to
give a speech next Thursday in Scotland.'

I thanked Morton but said it was very short notice. 'Who is
my speech for?' I asked.

'I am not at liberty to say,' replied Morton.

'Well, I need more information than that,' I said.

'I have been authorised to pay you a £10,000 fee.'

I liked Morton and he now had my full attention.

The following Thursday a chauffeur-driven car took me to a
local airport where a private jet was waiting for me. Two hours
later I was in Ayrshire at the Turnberry Hotel, home of the famous
Turnberry golf course. I met my host, who told me about the club
he had formed, which he described as 'an informal learning circle
for very successful business leaders.' Every member of this club was
a millionaire several times over. They met once a month to listen
to talks on subjects that interested them. Recent topics included
the global economy, Greek philosophy, business ethics, and the
Kabbalah.

My host had read an interview with me in the *Financial Times*, in which I talked about the difference between 'achieving success' and 'feeling successful'.

'This is what I want you to speak about,' he said.

After lunch I was introduced to my learning circle of million-aires, which comprised ten men and six spouses. My host then invited me to, in his words, 'say some words about success.' As always, I said an inner prayer for guidance, and then I began to speak about Success Intelligence. Mostly I talked about the need for meaningful success. I also defined success as 'something we feel when we allow the grace of God to inspire our endeavours.'

A lively discussion followed, in which the group shared their intimate thoughts about success. One man bared his soul about his lack of fulfilment and inner peace.

'I have never felt successful,' he confessed. Others nodded in agreement. We did not talk much about business that afternoon; instead we talked about meaning, enlightenment, and God.

'What do you think is God's definition of success?' I was asked.

'Love,' I said. I noticed a beautiful stillness in the room as we continued to talk.

That evening there was a formal black-tie dinner at which the deep conversation continued. One man asked me what I thought was the cause of his depression. 'I have been on antidepressants for ten years and they don't work,' he said. He had hoped that making enough money would silence his persistent anxiety. 'Yet the more money I have, the more I worry about it,' he said. He had been successful at making money, but he felt valueless inside.

'What if money isn't your purpose?' I asked.

'Then what is?'

I suggested that the answer to this question might help him with his depression.

In another conversation a wife begged her husband to have some private coaching with me.

'Chris never stops working and his family never sees him,' she said. She also told me that her husband had recently spent two weeks in hospital recovering from a stomach ulcer.

I asked Chris, 'What drives you so hard?'

He told me, 'No matter how much more I have, it never feels enough'.

I listened further, and then I asked him to give me a definition of 'enough.'

'I don't know,' he said. 'I'll have to think about it.'

The deep and meaningful conversations I had with the millionaire learning circle are a common experience for me. In fact, I am so used to having conversations like these that my brother David and I named our company 'The Deep & Meaningful Training Company'. We traded in 'D&Ms', as we called them, in which we coached individuals and teams to explore more honestly their vision of success and also any blocks or issues they faced. These conversations are not like the normal thin conversations we experience every day. They are more truthful and raise our life to a new level.

How Much More?

The accumulation of material goods is at an all-time high, but so is the number of people who feel an emptiness in their lives.

– Al Gore

We live in a 'Culture of More'. We clamour every day for more of everything. We have faith that 'more' is the answer to success and happiness. Our God is 'more'. Modern hymns like 'More', sung by Madonna, the material girl, tell us:

Each possession you possess helps your spirits to soar.
That's what's soothing about excess
Never settle for something less
Something's better than nothing, yes!
But nothing's better than more, more, more.

We have all prayed that one day we would have more, and actually we do. More than ever, we have more wealth, there are more jobs, we have more cars, there are more TV channels, we are more educated, there is more equal opportunity, we consume more, there are more Starbucks, we have more plastic surgery, we are 'more' healthy, and more men and women are living longer. There really is so much more. Strangely, the only thing there isn't more of is happiness. This is especially true for those who have more than others.

Social psychologists have amassed a large body of research on the 'failure of more' to make us happy and fulfilled. One study, 'Happiness of the Very Wealthy',[13] found that millionaires in the *Forbes* 100 (with a net worth of $125 million plus) reported only a slightly higher average of happiness than people on average incomes. In fact, 37 per cent of the millionaires were *less happy* than the national average. One very wealthy millionaire reported that he could never remember being happy. It seems that even the 'winners' feel like 'losers' in the culture of more.

A famous study of lottery winners found that after an initial short-term rise in reported happiness, their happiness levelled off and was no higher than that of people who live with disability, blindness, and other serious illnesses.[14] Some lottery winners have also reported that having so much money ruined their lives. I once appeared on a TV show about lottery winners in which one winner said, 'Money corrupted my relationships and caused me to question everything I value.' She also said, 'I thought it was money I wanted, but now I just want some peace.'

The question 'How much is enough?' is on everyone's mind today. I put this question to Chris, the millionaire, again when we next met.

'What is the point of this question?' he asked.

'Well, it looks like you are not going to relax and enjoy your life until you have enough, so I want you to quantify it,' I said. I meet many people who put their lives 'on hold' until they get enough done at work or until they make enough money, for example. The trap is that there is always more to do, more to earn, and more to purchase. Without Success Intelligence, our never-ending clamour for more can distract us from what is truly valuable.

Every now and then someone is able to sum up the thoughts of an entire generation. This is true of Lee Atwater, the campaign manager for former President George Bush, who was interviewed for *Life* magazine shortly after a diagnosis of terminal brain cancer. His reflections are about the 1980s and 1990s but are still relevant today. He said:

I acquired more wealth, power, and prestige than most. But you can acquire all you want and still feel empty. What power wouldn't I trade for a little more time with my family? What price wouldn't I pay for an evening with friends? It took a deadly illness to put me eye to eye with that truth, but it is a truth that the country, caught up in its ruthless ambitions and moral decay, can learn on my dime. I don't know who will lead us through the 90s, but they must be made to speak to this spiritual vacuum at the heart of American society, this tumour of the soul.[15]

The Real More

Today, we have more economic growth than ever before, but we still do not feel rich enough. Economists estimate that a year's worth of economic growth in 1830 now takes place in a single day. Today, we get more done than ever before but still don't have enough time for family and friends. Statistics tell us the number of business transactions made in all of 1949 now happen in a single day. Today, we communicate more than ever before, but we also report we feel more lonely. The equivalent of all the telephone calls made worldwide in 1984 now take place in just one day.[16]

Today, we consume more than ever before. People across the world have consumed as many goods and services since 1950 as all previous generations put together.[17] Today, more of us own more than our parents ever had, and yet more of us are more in debt than at any time in history.[18] Today, we continue to manufacture and purchase while turning a blind eye to the daily news that present levels of consumption are not sustainable on a personal or global level. We still want more. And yet, it appears that enough is never enough.

What am I really trying to buy? This intelligent question can lead to a greater insight into true success and happiness. When you identify your true motivation for wanting something, you can make more intelligent choices. For instance, do you want a Mont Blanc pen because it writes well, or because you want to feel successful? Or, do you wear Manolo Blahnik shoes because they are so comfortable, or because you want to feel good about yourself? The musician Ry Cooder said, 'All the money in the world is spent on feeling good.'

What is the 'real more' I want? There are so many types of 'more' to pursue in our Manic Society, such as more money and wealth, more status and attention, more education and wisdom, more credit and shoes, more meaning and happiness, more spirituality and a deeper connection to God. Success Intelligence encourages you to think wisely about what it is you really want. It teaches you to distinguish between an 'illusory more' that has no permanent value and a 'real more' that is in alignment with your values and success.

When I asked Chris, the millionaire, to identify his 'real more' it prompted a deep personal enquiry. In particular, he had to distinguish between wisdom and desire. I introduced him to the Intelligent Goals System (see page 345) and coached him on his Spiritual Goals and Character Goals in order to clarify his true purpose and values. Chris recognised that he could go on doing more and earning more *ad infinitum,* but that on some level this would be a compensation for a lack of inner peace and grace in his life.

There are many schools of thought about what the 'real more' is that most people want. I have summarised six philosophies of the 'real more' below. I share the views expressed by these thinkers and recommend their work wholeheartedly.

More vision: Ben Renshaw, co-director of The Happiness Project, writes in *Successful but Something Missing,* 'We often spend our lives in the fast lane, yet we still don't seem to be going fast enough. One of the greatest lessons for experiencing true success is to know when enough is enough.'[19] Ben and I co-present seminars at The Happiness Project, such as Success Intelligence, which teaches that 'enough' is an attitude, not a destination. When you lose sight of who you are and what you most value, you end up chasing more of everything else.

More wholeness: Tom Carpenter, the author of *Dialogue on Awakening,* says, 'Our ego thinks something is missing in us, and that we are not enough. We hope if we acquire more things we will feel more whole. However, feeling whole and being at peace with yourself is not something you can buy. The key to success is to know that *you are what you seek*. You have to remember you are whole already.'[20] Tom teaches that unless you let go of the thought 'I am not enough', you will never experience enough success or happiness in the world.

More authenticity: Sarah Ban Breathnach, the author of *Something More,* writes: 'Something More is not about money or fame, a home featured in *Architectural Digest,* or a love affair with a movie star. Something More is repose of the soul. Something More is self-worth. Something More is self-knowledge. The knowledge that your passion is holy and that the only way you'll be able to live authentically is to be true to your passions.'[21] The 'real more' Sarah writes about is being more authentic, knowing yourself better, excavating your wisdom more, and accepting yourself more.

More meaning: Danah Zohar, the co-author of *Spiritual Intelligence,* believes people do not really want 'more things', they really want 'more meaning'. She writes: 'The major issue on people's minds today is meaning. Many writers say the need for greater meaning is the central crisis of our times. I sense this when I travel abroad each month, addressing audiences from countries and cultures all over the world. Wherever I go, when people get together over a drink or a meal, the subject turns to God, meaning, vision, values, spiritual longing. Many people today have achieved an unprecedented level of material well-being, yet they feel they want more.'[2]

More connection: Nick Williams, the author of *Unconditional Success,* states that our primary goal is not 'more wealth' but 'more connection'. He writes: 'Most of our problems in life come down to one basic issue – a sense of separation and lack of connection. Perhaps loneliness and isolation are the biggest diseases on the planet. The universe is one song, one creation in which everything is connected and part of the whole, yet in the rush and chaos of everyday life it is easy to forget this basic principle.'[23] Nick Williams encourages us to 'become more universal and less individual.' He teaches that 'our purpose is connection' both to our true selves and to each other.

More spirituality: Miranda MacPherson (nee Holden), the author of *Boundless Love,* says that at the heart of 'wanting more' is the 'holy longing' for more soul and more of the divine. She writes: 'It is easy to make obtaining a bigger house, a swankier car, a more prestigious job, and more money your god. Your god is that which you make most important, your homing beacon. What's yours? Although material goals and possessions are not inherently bad, they become traps when you make them more important than the inner gold.'[24] Miranda encourages us to think deeply about what our soul truly longs for.

I would like to finish this section with a passage from *A Course in Miracles,* which my wife and I study every day. This passage suggests that the 'real more' we long for is a direct experience of God. It reads:

THE FAILURE OF MORE

In this world, you believe you are sustained by everything but God. Your faith is placed in the most trivial
and insane symbols, pills, money, 'protective' clothing,
influence, prestige, being liked, knowing the 'right' people, and an endless list of forms of nothingness that you
endow with magical powers. All these things are your
replacements for the Love of God. Put all your faith in
the Love of God within you; eternal, changeless, and forever unfailing. This is the answer to whatever confronts
you today. Through the Love of God within you, you can
resolve all seeming difficulties without effort and in sure
confidence. Tell yourself this often today. It is a declaration of release from the belief in idols. It is your acknowl-
edgement of the truth about yourself.

– A Course in Miracles[25]

SUCCESS INTELLIGENCE TIP 25 – *GOD*

A person's thoughts about God will significantly influence his or her capacity for success. Some people say they
owe all their success to God; others say their success has
nothing to do with God. What do you say? Here are three
questions to reflect on:

1. What do you think is God's definition of success?

2. How successful do you believe God wants you to
   be?

3. What else can you do to enjoy a more direct
   and meaningful experience of God?

Success requires a creative mix of psychology and grace.

The Energy Crisis

Modern man is a knackered ape.
– **Patrick Holford**

I arrived at the Old Parsonage Hotel in Oxford for a 4 P.M. meeting with my client Joe, who was travelling up from London. At 4:15 P.M. Joe phoned to say he was running 30 minutes late. At 5 P.M. he phoned again to say his car had broken down on the motorway. Joe told me he had left London late and on less than a quarter of a tank of petrol. He said, 'I kept thinking I'll stop at the next petrol station I see, but I didn't want to arrive even later for our meeting. So I kept going and soon I was running on empty.' Joe's story is a perfect mirror for the energy crisis in the world today.

On a global level, ecologists warn us the world is 'running on empty'. Our old fossil fuels – oil, coal, and natural gas – are fast being depleted. These non-renewable forms of fuel are not economical and also cause much toxic waste. Many ecologists estimate that at current consumption levels the world will run out of fossil fuels by the end of this century. The war to acquire the last barrels of oil is taking place now in the Middle East and elsewhere. The world's Earth energies are close to empty.

Scientists who study eco-literacy are pioneering the use of cleaner, abundant energies like solar energy and wind power. Eco-designers are also testing more efficient ways to use fuel. The car is often targeted as a major fuel waster. Fritjof Capra, director of the Center for Ecoliteracy, writes:

> Like many other products of industrial design, the contemporary automobile is stunningly inefficient. Only 20 per cent of the energy in the fuel is used to turn the wheels, while 80 per cent is lost in the engine's heat and

exhaust. Moreover, a full 95 per cent of the energy that is used moves the car, and only 5 per cent moves the driver. The overall efficiency in terms of the proportion of fuel energy used to move the driver is 5 per cent of 20 per cent – a mere one per cent.[26]

On a personal level, physicians report that more of us are 'running on empty'. Feeling 'tired all the time' is such a common complaint now it has its own medical acronym: TATT. As well as TATT, there are the medical conditions known as Chronic Fatigue Syndrome (CFS) and Myalgic Encephalomyelitis (ME). Symptoms of these conditions include constant lethargy, poor concentration, muscular weakness, sleep deprivation, and feeling depressed. The word *burnout* has recently been added to several English dictionaries. Our adrenaline – the fossil fuel of the body – cannot cope with our manic, busy lifestyles.

Exhaustion is endemic. We live our lives in the fast lane, and every day we search for extra energy to stop us from falling asleep at the wheel. Supplements like 'Busy B vitamins', special protein powders, and miracle Amazon herbs are popular with fast-laners. Other stimulants like nicotine and alcohol – which cause more toxic waste in the body – are also fuel for the road. An increasing number of people now use illegal 'uppers' like speed to help manage the pace.[27]

Many of the people I work with suffer from a personal energy crisis. They are either exhausted or at the edge of exhaustion. Their permanent tiredness inhibits success and intelligence. A client of mine who was recovering from burnout once told me, 'My problem is that when I have energy I get busy, and when I am tired I make decisions.' Chronic exhaustion often traps us in an ineffective 'effort economy' in which we keep on trying harder and doing worse.

Success Intelligence encourages a wise balance between adrenaline and grace. I often ask my clients, 'How do you manage your energy?' I want to know about their physical diet, as well as their mental diet and spiritual diet. I also want them to acknowledge what truly nourishes and inspires them. When I coach leaders I

Copyright 2002 by Randy Glasbergen.
www.glasbergen.com

"Don't be alarmed. After 4 cups, I switch to decaf."

ask, 'How do you manage the energy of your team?' This question is vital because if there is no energy, there is never enough time, and performance slows, morale suffers, and inspiration disappears. Chronic exhaustion and sustainable success do not compute.

Sustainable Success

> *Many of the best people are worn out by lunchtime.*
> – Dr. Peter Nixon

I first met Dr. Peter Nixon, a cardiologist at Charing Cross Hospital, London, in the spring of 1988. Dr. Nixon was pioneering a holistic model of health care – called The Biopsychosocial Solution – to help treat coronary heart disease. His work was based on a central thesis that *exhaustion is the most prevalent health epidemic in modern times.* I was greatly impressed by Dr. Nixon's insights on exhaustion, performance, and success. With his permission, I often relate his theories in my clinics and seminars.

Dr. Nixon originated the 'Human Function Curve' (see Figure 8) to illustrate the stations of health that go from healthy tension to fatigue to exhaustion to becoming ill and, finally, to breakdown. Dr. Nixon taught his patients how to read the Human Function

Curve in order to help them manage their personal energy better. He believed that sustainable success is possible only if a person learns how to use his or her physical, mental, and spiritual energy more wisely. If a person uses these energies poorly, without intelligence, it will cause dis-harmony and dis-eases like heart attacks.

In my Success Intelligence seminars, I encourage participants to assess their current position on the Human Function Curve. I recommend that you do the same. Register your current energy levels. Notice if your tank is full or close to running on empty. Reading your energy levels is the first step in positive energy management. Notice also what sort of energy you are running on. Is it primarily adrenaline or are you also open to grace, inspiration, and flow?

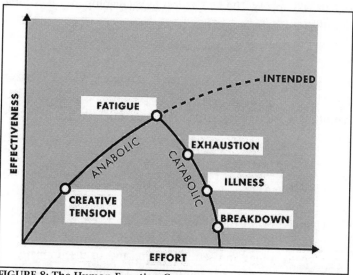

FIGURE 8: The Human Function Curve

Healthy tension: This is the ideal state for best performance, sustainable success, and personal wellbeing. Physically, your body is in an anabolic state, which means that your endocrine, immune, and nervous systems are working at an optimum level. Mentally, you are balanced in the left and right hemispheres, which means you can be logical and intuitive, rational and imaginative. Spiritually, you are receptive to grace and open to inspiration. Essentially put, you are relaxed and energised. You have a good balance between work, rest, and play. You attend to self and others well. Your life flows.

Fatigue: The function of fatigue is similar to red lights on a car dashboard that indicate your fuel tank is low or your brake lights are not working. If you do not pay attention to these red lights, more red lights will appear, and then more, and eventually your car engine will stop. The key to sustainable success is early awareness of personal fatigue signals such as headaches, irritability, palpitations, and poor concentration. You can override these signals for a while, but you will progress more slowly and more signals will appear. The temptation to keep going may be strong, but there is no wisdom in it.

Exhaustion: In an interview I conducted with Dr. Nixon for the health journal *Caduceus*,[28] he gave the most accurate and haunting account of the effects of exhaustion I have come across. He said:

> To be exhausted is to court danger from every point of view. There are no reserves of energy for coping with the unexpected and unfamiliar, and it is difficult to adapt to change. We lose the ability to habituate, to enjoy the benefits of the decreasing tension which is part of getting used to things and settling down, and to discriminate between the essential and inessential demands upon our energy.
>
> Self-esteem fails, and the consequent rise of unpleasant tension generates more arousal. Aggression flares up, often inappropriately, and destroys the good will of potential allies. Ill-advised coping tactics flourish. Particularly serious is the acceptance of long-term sleep deprivation as normal.
>
> Leadership comes to depend more upon age and seniority than ability, and defences are erected against

any change of routine which might call for initiative and energy. It becomes impossible to live and work with the chronically exhausted individual and social cohesion is disrupted. In the severest forms of exhaustion the individual bogs himself down in rage and despair: he cannot go on, he cannot opt out, everlasting discussions never produce an acceptable compromise, and hyperventilation increasingly threatens the order and stability of homeostatic control.

People who are exhausted are often disoriented because when they step on the accelerator it activates the brakes. In other words, more effort equals less energy in the exhausted state. Over-effort only carries a person downhill more quickly, towards illness and breakdown. More effort also blocks grace and inspiration. In my experience, people who rely solely on effort to get past exhaustion end up digging a deeper hole for themselves. Exhaustion is not smart, and we are not very smart when we are exhausted.

Ill health: Dr. Nixon explains that people who suffer chronic exhaustion 'tend to lose all sense of proportion – committed to finishing the job, to carrying on, to doing, no matter the cost. They exhibit irrational, self-defeating behaviours which are without intelligence. They are deemed alexithymic because they have no proper awareness of their position, their deterioration, or their thinking.' The body is in a catabolic state in which the immune system degenerates. The mind is off-centre and there is little Success Intelligence. The person is unable to access any grace or flow. A breakdown is imminent.

Spiritual Fitness

I count Diane Berke and her husband, Tony Zito, among my dearest friends. I stay with them whenever I visit New York. One Christmas, Diane gave me an article she had written, entitled 'A

Simple Programme of Spiritual Fitness.'[29] It was the first time I had heard of the idea of 'spiritual fitness', and I have since incorporated the concept into a vitality programme I teach, which is based on physical health, mental balance, and spiritual fitness.

What is spiritual fitness? For me, it begins with knowing your Spiritual Goals. To stay spiritually fit a person needs to make regular appointments in order to work out his or her vision and strengthen his or her values. Spiritual fitness is about staying on track with your purpose and also exercising your wisdom. Making time for meditation and reflection, prayer and inspirational reading, is vital in this regard. Spiritual fitness is also about staying agile and open-minded in order to accommodate grace and inspiration. It is about dropping your ego and letting God in.

The need for spiritual fitness is greater than ever. George Gallup, Jr., of the Gallup Poll, has tracked the public's renewed interest in spiritual matters in recent times. In his book *The People's Religion,* published in 1990, he wrote:

The new frontier of social research is, I believe, the inner life. The last half of the current century has been dedicated to the exploration of outer space. The next century, I think we may assume, will be dedicated to exploring inner space. There are undoubtedly many exciting discoveries ahead as we seek to probe beneath the surface of lives.[30]

Success Intelligence interprets exhaustion as a vital lesson in how to care for ourselves better. Taking another vitamin B tablet is convenient – it certainly means we don't have to stop – but it is usually not that effective. Exhaustion is a call to be wiser. We are being called to balance effort with wisdom, adrenaline with grace. Exhaustion is also a sign there is a better way. It is a chance to take a higher path and to be more inspired. Exhaustion is about new beginnings.

Spiritual Intelligence sees exhaustion as a symptom of a deeper underlying cause. Therefore, when you are exhausted, a good question to ask is 'What is my exhaustion trying to teach me?' Exhaustion is rarely just physical; it is mostly mental and spiritual. Your task is to let wisdom and inspiration restore your balance for you. Exhaustion is an education, and the more you learn from it the better you will live. Below is an audit called 'Success Intelligence on Burnout' that I use with clients who suffer from chronic exhaustion.

Success Intelligence on Burnout

Vision: Exhaustion is sometimes a sign you have lost sight of what you truly enjoy about your work and life. Joy is a state of pure energy. Without it you will feel like you are 'running on empty' no matter how many energy bars you eat each day. Make time to review your vision and your values.

Hurry: Do you experience a seemingly endless and continual state of time pressure? Exhaustion is often a sign you are relying solely on adrenaline to run your life. Remind yourself that life is not an emergency. Remember also that 'God Spede' doesn't mean to live as fast as possible. It means to live wisely.

Busyness: Exhaustion is an opportunity to be less busy and more effective. It is a sign to reconnect to your heart and to listen to your wisdom more. If you are too busy to relax, you are too busy. If you are too busy to pray, you are too busy. If you are too busy to be happy, you have definitely lost it.

Authenticity: Exhaustion is often a sign you need to be more true to yourself. For instance, if your heart is not in your job it will not inspire you; and if you are not honest in a relationship it will feel as if something is missing. Also, when you do not listen to your inner guidance, you will experience a loss of energy and power. Integrity is energy.

Absenteeism: It can be exhausting trying to live in the past and the future as well as in the present. Too much living in the 'not-now' will scatter your energy. Now is your point of power. It is the only time in your life that you can always influence. The more attention you give to each present moment, the more energised you will feel.

Grievances: Holding on to old wounds and disappointments uses up a lot of personal energy. It is important to be honest about how you feel *and* also to let go of any pain or anger as soon as possible. Forgiveness is a great energiser because it helps you to release the past and focus on the present again.

Sacrifice: Exhaustion is a sure sign that you are sacrificing somewhere in your life. Look for ways to experience less sacrifice and more effectiveness at work. Who could help you with this? Resolve to be a better friend and partner by giving up unhealthy sacrifice in your relationships. Notice also if you deprive yourself of time for self and for spiritual renewal.

Independence: Exhaustion is a sign you are suffering from dysfunctional independence. Identify where you are currently experiencing any struggle or pain and be open to the possibility of greater help. Remember that whenever you feel you cannot do something on your own, it is a sign you are not meant to.

Defences: Dysfunctional independence can be a defence against letting God in. The ego always overspends on its defence budget. It invests all its energy in fear, cynicism, busyness, and other armour. We are literally weighed down by our defences. When we relax and align ourselves with God's energy we feel strong again.

Oneness: Do you always juggle two, three, or four things at once? Too much multitasking creates the illusion of productivity and also impairs vitality. Meditate on the idea that the best things in life are worth doing one at a time. Also, be open to letting universal intelligence and God's grace help you with your efforts.

SUCCESS INTELLIGENCE TIP 26 – *INSPIRATION*

Make an inventory of everything that inspires you. List all of the people in whose company you delight. Reflect on why they inspire you and what they have taught you.

Make space in your calendar for lunch dates with weird and wonderful people. Spend more time with the people you love.

List also all the writers, artists, and great thinkers who have inspired you. Again, make space in your calendar for inspirational reading and learning seminars.

List everything else that inspires you. Do not deprive yourself of the inspiration you need to succeed.

PART VII

Renaissance

• • ● • •

Man's main task is to give birth to himself,
to become what he potentially is.

– **Erich Fromm**

Be the Goal

The Big Fear

A Ph.D. in Happiness

Saying Yes

When I was last in India I stayed in the small town of Bodhgaya, which is where the Buddha realised his enlightenment. During my stay I made several visits to the Mahabodhi Temple, which marks the site of the original Bodhi tree the Buddha sat under when he received his vision. I engaged in many rich dialogues with the learned monks and professors at the Temple. I also sat for many hours beneath the Bodhi tree, where I reflected on the relevance and importance of the Buddha's story for our modern times.

Buddha, which means 'Awakened One', was the name given to Siddhartha, who was born into a royal family in India in 563 B.C. Soon after Siddhartha's birth, the king summoned fortune-tellers to the palace to read the young prince's future. The fortune-tellers agreed that Siddhartha was a man with two potential destinies. One destiny was to acquire the earthly trappings of wealth and success; the other destiny was to realise inner wisdom and eternal joy. The king wanted Siddhartha to succeed him on the throne, and so he lavished his son with every earthly pleasure in the hope that this would be enough for him.

Legend has it that Siddhartha grew up in the confines of his father's palace. The king organised it so Siddhartha never witnessed disease, aging, death, or poverty. He also arranged endless entertainment for Siddhartha and bestowed upon him silk and gold and palaces and dancing girls. In short, Siddhartha was the man who had everything. But he soon learned of the transient nature of life and became dissatisfied. His life was full of passing pleasures, but empty of any lasting peace; he knew only fleeting desires, but never deep joy.

At 29 years old, Siddhartha embarked on his 'Great Going Forth' into the world in search of true wisdom. He journeyed to many destinations, sat with many teachers, endured many trials and sacrifices, but all for no real success. Tired and disillusioned, Siddhartha arrived at Bodhgaya. He sat beneath a Bodhi tree where he resolved to give up his search. Siddhartha had surrendered, and in a holy instant he discovered that the wisdom he longed for existed in him already. Siddhartha had awoke to the truth that life's answers exist not in the world, but in the self.

The Buddha's story exemplifies the primary goal of Success Intelligence, which is to be enlightened and wise. Siddhartha was the original yuppie, the man with the most toys, who had a yearning for something more. Like Siddhartha, we all have to learn that true success is not just about acquiring more stuff. Siddhartha went in pursuit of true happiness, but only once he searched inside himself did he find the truth he sought. Success Intelligence teaches us, ultimately, that we carry with us the answers we seek, and that our innate wisdom can discern what is valuable or not.

Across the river from Bodhgaya, there is a small temple called the Suraya Temple. To get there you have to walk across rice fields and through a small village with homes made of wooden poles and corrugated iron roofs. Next to the Suraya Temple is a lake where the water buffalo graze and also a new school – a small white hut, with a brown door and a single window. The name of the school is The Siddhartha Free Children Educational Center. Here I met Pramod, the head teacher, who has since become a good friend of mine.

Pramod saw me sitting at the Suraya Temple and invited me into his school. Inside the hut I met 40 angelic Indian children, all young Buddhas dressed with big smiles and in blue uniforms.

The children stood up as I entered, and we all bowed to each other as we recited the Indian greeting *Namaste,* which means 'The Light within me recognises the Light within you, and together we are One with this Light.' Pramod then asked the children to sing a song in English, which began, 'Thank you, God, for my life / Thank you, God, for this day / Thank you, God, for all I have . . .'

Pramod is in his mid-30s. In his childhood there were no schools in Bodhgaya. He told me, 'The Buddha's message is that right education is the way to end suffering and to know happiness, but we had no schools and no teachers.' Pramod hoped things would change and that one day a school would be built, but nothing happened. Eventually Pramod decided, 'If there are no teachers here, I shall become a teacher.' Pramod taught himself to read and write, and then he left Bodhgaya to study and become a teacher.

Pramod's dream was to set up a school in Bodhgaya that would educate, feed, and clothe all the village children for free. 'To begin with my classes were small, with only one or two children,' said Pramod. 'There was no school, so I held my classes under a tree. Also, there was no money, but I did it anyway.' Pramod stayed committed to his dream, and in time the villagers began to support his vision. 'Today, the whole world helps me to run my school,' says Pramod, who told me many stories of unsolicited help that has arrived from all over the world.

Pramod showed me the curriculum he created for his children. The academic part covers the basics of reading, writing, arithmetic, and English. The rest of the curriculum covers spiritual ethics and the essential teachings of the Buddha. Pramod teaches, like the Buddha, that true wisdom is within 'like a splendid jewel in the heart'. Pramod is an inspiration to the people of Bodhgaya. 'My aim is to represent hope,' he says. Pramod encourages his children to become teachers one day, too. He tells his children, 'If I can be a teacher, we can all be teachers.'

I include Pramod's story here because it is an example of a new renaissance that is emerging in the world now. The new renaissance is not about canvases and sculptures, but about hearts and minds. It is not about a time in history; it is a movement in consciousness and the birth of 'a better way'. Everywhere in the world today more people like Pramod are inspired to be leaders and to serve in some way. They teach us by their example that everyone has it within themselves to make the world a better place.

The new renaissance is an invitation to be a social artist, to be as fully human as possible, and to be a friend to the world. Who will inspire us, if not us? In the new renaissance the world will be different because we will be the difference.

> *If mankind is not to perish after all the dreadful things*
> *it has done and gone through, then a new spirit must emerge.*
> *And this new spirit is coming not with a roar but with a*
> *quiet birth, not with grand measure and words but*
> *with an imperceptible change in the atmosphere – a change*
> *in which each one of us is participating . . .*
> **– Albert Schweitzer**

Being the Difference

I have met many people like Pramod who want to contribute in a better way. They are participating in a renaissance that is building a compassionate future and an enlightened world. They are interested not only in their own success, but in the success of their communities and the world. They contribute to projects that are literally evolving the consciousness of humanity, such as fair trade and world health, ethical politics and respectful ecology, and interfaith dialogue and servant leadership.

Success Intelligence is a journey that can be mapped over three distinct stages of consciousness. The first stage is called 'Determinism', the second is 'Adaptation', and the third is 'Renaissance'. Pramod's story, and maybe all of our stories, can also be mapped across these three worldviews. As we journey from Determinism through Adaptation to Renaissance, we change the way we see ourselves and how we see success. We learn more about the innate potential of our

Unconditioned Self. And we realise that success is less about gain and more about contribution.

The Determinism Stage: Determinism is the Dark Ages of the human consciousness. A formula for this stage is: the world = my life = me. Here, the external world completely determines how good your life can be, and it also determines what sort of person you will be. Apparently, you are just a conditioned reflex with no will or imagination of your own. Determinism is a bleak 'I can't make a difference' mentality. If Pramod had stayed here, he would have waited for ever for someone to build a school in Bodhgaya.

Determinism is hell because we believe we have no choice in our life. Apparently, it is the economy that determines if we can create a profit or not. Apparently, the company culture has to change before we can make a difference. Apparently, it is our bosses who will decide whether or not we can have an original thought. Apparently, a relationship can only improve once someone else changes first. Apparently, it is our childhoods and our pasts that decide our fate. We believe that the world must change before we can.

Determinism is a lie. In Paulo Coelho's story *The Alchemist,* the young shepherd boy, Santiago, meets a mysterious old man who tells him, 'Everyone believes the world's greatest lie.'

Santiago asks, 'What is the world's greatest lie?'

The old man replies, 'It's this: that at a certain point in our lives, we lose control of what's happening to us, and our lives become controlled by fate. That's the world's greatest lie.'[1]

Determinism is the avoidance of choice. It is a failure to be accountable for the life you experience. Success Intelligence grows once we are willing to see through this lie.

The Adaptation Stage: Adaptation is the New Dawn of the human consciousness. It opens us up to a world of choice. A formula for this stage is: the world + me = my life. External circumstances and other people's actions can strongly influence how you think and how you live. However, it is your internal response to your circumstances that ultimately decides failure or success. Pramod made his choices. He could have chosen to wait for life to get better or to bemoan his ill fortune, but instead he chose to become a teacher. His courage to choose created a new world of possibility for himself and others.

Today, for the first time in world history, more people are governed by democracy than by a form of dictatorship. Today, we can choose our governments. Similarly, we can work for organisations that are less autocratic and more inspired. Anita Roddick, founder of The Body Shop and a business innovator, said, 'My vision, my hope, is simply this: that many business leaders will come to see a primary role of business as incubators of the human spirit, rather than factories for the production of more material goods and services.'[2]

Today we can choose our lifestyles. The era of one-stop careers is over. Many of us now choose to have three or four careers in one lifetime. We can choose to run with the rat race, to downshift, to simplify our lives, or to create our own enterprises. We can choose to work full-time, flexi-time, or part-time, according to our values and wishes. We can also choose our faith and our spirituality. We are world citizens now, and we can learn from all the great wisdom traditions of the world. Choices are everywhere, and our task it to choose intelligently.

The Renaissance Stage: Renaissance is the Creation Song of the human consciousness. It opens us up to our true being and identity. A formula for this stage is: me + the world = my life. In the Adaptation Stage we learn how to respond to the world; but in the Renaissance Stage we learn that the world also responds to us. The world changes because we do. Pramod lived in a village with little hope for any education. He adapted positively by choosing to become a teacher. Moreover, he has since become an embodiment of hope. 'My aim is to represent hope,' he says. His example, i.e., *his being,* is his teaching.

Success Intelligence teaches that we create the world on three levels: our actions, our thoughts, and our *being*. First, if we act differently, we create new outcomes. One new action can rearrange the world around us. A compliment, a smile, an apology, an act of forgiveness, for example, changes things. Second, if we think differently, we create new possibilities. We learn that by choosing our thoughts, we can choose our lives. For example, if I think happy thoughts, I feel happy, or if I think optimistic thoughts, I am more creative.

Third, on a level of being, we change the world by choosing *to be what we want*. For example, our lives change when we stop searching for happiness and we decide to *be* happy. For example, our relationships change when we stop trying to find love and we become a more loving person. The world changes when a person not only marches for world peace but also embodies peace. A true leader is born when he puts his rhetoric to the test and leads by example. Mahatma Gandhi lived his life like this. 'Be the change you want to see,' he said. And the whole world responded to him.

The final part of this book focuses on the challenge to take your true place in the world. In the chapter entitled 'Be the Goal', I examine the psychology of leadership and the courage to 'take the lead' in your life. In 'The Big Fear', I reveal the most hidden block to success that often stops people from realising their true potential. In 'A Ph.D. in Happiness', I explain why success won't make you happy, but how the temptation to give up is often strongest just before the dawn of success. I also emphasise the miraculous power of commitment to your goals and values.

Be the
Goal

Six days after September 11 2001, I gave a public talk at St. James's
Church in Piccadilly, London. My talk was hosted by Alternatives,
a non-profit organisation that offers an inspirational programme
of events 'to inspire new visions for living.'[3] St. James's Church is a
beautiful venue designed 300 years ago by Christopher Wren. It is the
baptism place of William Blake, the visionary poet, and has always
been a centre of creative spirituality. The large stained-glass window
over the altar depicts an ascended Christ, which is truly inspiring.

I arrived at St. James's Church at 6 P.M., an hour before my talk
was to begin. Steve Nobel, the director of Alternatives, greeted me
and together we talked about the tragedy of 9/11 and the enormous shock that had brought the world to a stop. 'I have no idea
how many people will come tonight. Our numbers could be low,'
said Steve. By 6:45 P.M. only 70 people had arrived, but by 7 P.M.
the number had risen to nearly 400. Many people told me later
that it had felt important, symbolic even, to show up that night.

Steve Nobel began the evening with a prayer for the victims
of 9/11. He then invited 12 people to step forward to the altar
to participate in a special invocation. Steve asked each person to
light a candle, place it on the altar, and offer a one-word prayer of
invocation. One by one, each candle was lit, and each invocation
was spoken. The 12 invocations were:

1.	'Leadership'	7.	'Leadership'
2.	'Leadership'	8.	'Love'
3.	'Leadership'	9.	'Leadership'
4.	'Vision'	10.	'Leadership'
5.	'Leadership'	11.	'Healing'
6.	'Leadership'	12.	'Leadership"

Leadership is on everyone's mind today. Prayers for inspired leadership ring out in cities and villages all over the world. More than ever, nations need inspired politicians who win elections because of their vision and integrity. More than ever, business needs ethical leaders who teach us that the heart of business is service. More than ever, religions need spiritual leaders who are prepared to be Christ-like, Buddha-like, and Mohammed-like. Society and individuals evolve principally by the power of example and by people showing us a better way.

Leadership is on everyone's agenda today. Every day a new request arrives at our offices for me and my colleagues to give a leadership seminar. These requests come from businesses and charities, hospitals and schools, government bodies and religious groups. More people also read and study about leadership today. If you visit **Amazon.com** and type in 'leadership', you can choose from over 15,000 books and 15 magazines on leadership. The book titles include *Intelligent Leadership, Evolutionary Leadership,* and *Exemplary Leadership.*

Leadership is everyone's business today. The primary challenge any community faces is how to encourage a spirit of leadership in everyone. Leadership has to exist not just at the top, but also in the heart of our communities. Traditionally, leadership has been about what 'someone else' will or won't do for us. Today, leadership is about a shared responsibility and about each of us stepping forward. Hence, the old prayer was 'God, send us a leader'; the new prayer is 'God, help me to be a leader.'

What is leadership? I meditate on this question each time I prepare for a leadership seminar. I believe that leadership is not a position you ascend towards; rather, it is an attitude that creates the life you lead. I believe that leadership is not a technique; it is about being authentic and courageous enough to tell the truth. I believe that leadership is not about status; it is about service. I believe that leadership is not about being better than anyone; it is about giving your personal best.

In my Success Intelligence seminars, I teach that the real challenge of leadership is to 'be the goal'. This means that leadership is about *bringing into being* what you most value. Thus, if you want honesty, you have to be honest. And if you want trust, you have to be trusting. Similarly, if you want true friendship, you have to be a true friend. And if you want love, you have to be loving. A person won't find love until he starts to love. Ultimately, if you want any change to happen, you have to think about how you can 'be the change' you want.

'Here to Be Seen'

At my seminars I often ask people to join in a greeting shared by the Zulu people of South Africa. The greeting is an invocation spoken in two parts. One part is *Sikhona,* which means 'I am here to be seen'; and the other part is *Sawubona,* which means 'I see you.' I usually demonstrate the greeting onstage with a volunteer. We stand facing each other, look deep into each other's eyes, and then I say, 'I am here to be seen,' and the volunteer replies, 'I see you.' Next, the volunteer says, 'I am here to be seen,' and I reply, 'I see you.'

I invite my audiences to greet at least ten people with 'I am here to be seen' and 'I see you.' I encourage them to use no other words during the greeting. I also recommend that they say the words slowly and that they notice their internal response to the words. In particular, I want them to feel the intention behind the words they say. Imagine greeting your family, your colleagues, and your friends with the conscious intention to see each other. Can you feel the power of this greeting? Think what effect it would have to greet everyone you know with this conscious intention.

After the group has finished greeting each other with 'I am here to be seen' and 'I see you', they return to their seats and we then take time for feedback and discussion. To appreciate the power of this Zulu invocation, it is helpful to look at it in four parts. First, it begins with two people looking deep into each other's eyes. This is powerful by itself. An uncommon depth of connection is established without any words. Eye contact is akin to soul contact. This sense of oneness always inspires better communication.

Second, the Zulu people believe that when a person says 'I am here to be seen', it invokes the person's spirit to be present. Saying 'I am here' is a declaration of intent to fully inhabit this moment. It signals a willingness to engage with integrity. Saying 'to be seen' emphasises 'no masks', 'no editing', and 'no defences'. It means 'This is the real me' and 'I will speak my truth.' It means 'I will be honest with you', and there will be no deception.

Third, 'I see you' is a powerful experience both for the person who says it and for the person who hears it. According to the Zulu tradition, to say 'I see you' offers an intention to release any preconceptions and judgments so that 'I can see you as God created you.' To hear 'I see you' is an affirmation that you do exist, that you are both equal, and that you have a person's respect. Many people say this is the most moving part of the greeting. Some say it strengthens their resolve to be more authentic and visible in their life.

Fourth, this greeting represents the Zulu philosophy of *ubuntu,* which translates roughly as 'humanity towards all'. *Ubuntu* is a spiritual ethic that advocates mutual support for 'bringing each other into existence'. To practise *ubuntu* is to help your brothers and sisters remember their true identity, recognise their true value, and participate fully. *Ubuntu* teaches that our purpose is to be a true friend to one another. Through *ubuntu* we bring out the best in ourselves and others – it is a training in true leadership.

I have taught this Zulu greeting at conferences with presidents, ambassadors, and heads of state saying to each other 'I am here to be seen' and 'I see you.' The dialogue that follows is more open and more powerful. I have taught this greeting to actors, singers, musicians, and dancers to help them be less performers and more true artists. I have shared this greeting with cancer patients, at AA meetings, in prisons, at churches, and so on. I have also used it in family therapy, with husbands and wives, fathers and daughters, and brothers and sisters.

To be successful in life, work, and relationships, you have to do one thing first – you have to show up. In other words, you have to be willing to show the world who you are and what you believe in. And you have to keep showing up in spite of the setbacks and the heartbreaks. The temptation to edit yourself and to hide will only leave you feeling dead inside. 'One's real life is so often the life one does not lead,' said Oscar Wilde. Yet the more authentic you are, the more true success you will enjoy and the more alive you will feel.

Success Intelligence is about finding the authenticity of each moment. The value of authenticity is that it encourages true authority, i.e., wisdom and inspiration. I recommend, therefore, that in every situation you ask yourself, 'What is my true goal here?' and listen. Also, in every conflict you are in, ask yourself, 'How can I be more honest?' and listen. And in every relationship, ask yourself, 'How can I be a true friend?' and listen. More authenticity enables greater effectiveness.

Where there is a lack of authenticity, a person will always feel that something is missing. When my clients complain that something is missing in a relationship or at work, I ask them to contemplate these three questions: (1) 'What am I not being?' (more honest, more present, more open, etc.); (2) 'What am I not giving?' (more attention, more commitment, more of 'me', etc.); and (3) 'What am I not receiving?' (includes patterns of sacrifice, independence, and closed-mindedness). In the middle of success, you are the answer.

'Be a Light'

I began my talk at St. James's Church on September 17 2001, by quoting a famous passage from the Bible: 'You are the light of the world' (Matthew 5:14). This is a categorical statement that appears in the exact same way in every Bible translation I have read. Nowhere does it translate as 'Some of you are the light of the world.' There are also no qualifying statements after 'You are the light of the world', such as 'if you had a happy childhood', 'if you haven't made any mistakes', or 'if you had an immaculate conception'.

It is common to dismiss spiritual aphorisms like 'You are the light of the world' as a nice metaphor or a poetic device. Yet the world's major wisdom traditions have all taught that the Unconditioned Self is an 'inner light', a 'divine radiance', or an 'eternal flame'. And they mean it literally. For example, your vision can illuminate any project or cause to which you give yourself; your wisdom can enlighten people and help them to see things differently; and your inspiration can transform perceptions and help people to shine.

To be the light of the world is to take spiritual ownership of your life. It challenges us not only to 'ask for light' or 'pray for light' but also to 'be a light'. Maybe, then, success lies in the answer to this simple question: 'Are you the sort of person who lights up a room when you walk in or when you walk out?' I like this question because everyone understands what it means. Some people enter a room and wait for 'the light' to happen; other people enter a room with 'the light'. Some people wish things could be different; other people decide to be the difference.

Spiritual ownership is the willingness to take your place in life. It is the ability 'to own' your wisdom, 'to own' your talent, and 'to own' who you really are. Here, 'to own' means to be honest and to stop dismissing what you are capable of being and doing. It means 'to acknowledge' and thereby 'to bring into being' what is possible. Thus, spiritual ownership is about connecting to your Unconditioned Self and invoking what is needed to be the goal and to be a light in any situation.

Spiritual ownership is also the challenge to 'be a light' now, not later. It is about giving your personal best now; it is about letting your light shine now; and it is about living the life you want now. Spiritual ownership is not about 'becoming', it is about 'being'. Thus, it is about invoking the person you aim to be now, and it is about being the leader you want to become now. A person can hope all he likes to become a light, but at some point he has to step forward and be a light.

SUCCESS INTELLIGENCE TIP 27 – *INTENTION*

Being the goal is about setting your intention for the day. Your intention is your personal power. It brings into focus your vision, your purpose, and your wisdom. Your intention is also what influences people and shapes outcomes. Therefore, it is wise to begin each day by meditating on 'How shall I be today?' – 'I will be relaxed', 'I will be wise,' 'I will be loving', etc.

Also, practice consciously setting your intention when you are in a meeting, communicating with someone, or working on something. Intention helps you *to be* successful.

The Big
Fear

You can't shrink your way to success.
- **Arthur Martinez**, CEO of Sears, Roebuck & Co.

I introduce now an idea that concludes a powerful trilogy of techniques for coaching success. In Part II, I wrote about the 'Success Contract', which represents a person's philosophy and beliefs about success; in Part V, I wrote about the 'Failure Policy', which outlines a person's attitude and approach to failures; and here I will explore 'The Fear Interview', a method that helps people to identify and better manage their fears.

People often hold themselves back in life because they will not face their fears. They will do anything to avoid fear, including keeping busy, working harder, playing small, and generally increasing the noise of their lives. Their fear of fear prevents them from following their passion, realising their talent, and finding their voice. Fear can be frightening, but as Rainer Maria Rilke, the Austrian poet, observed, sometimes our worst fears are like dragons guarding our deepest treasure.[4] In other words, by facing up to our fears we can clear the way for greater success.

I created The Fear Interview to help people have a more conscious dialogue with internal interferences, such as self-doubt and anxiety. The primary goal is to teach people how to stop resisting their fears and thereby release them faster. It is our resistance to fear, and not the fear itself, that holds us back. I always conduct The Fear Interview in a safe setting to ensure the best results. The structure of The Fear Interview is designed specifically to support the goal of each session. The first task of The Fear Interview is to establish a topic to explore, such as fear in relationship, fear of leadership, or fear about money.

Part I of The Fear Interview is about raising awareness – for example, 'What is my real fear?' I help people to listen with open attention to their real fears. In particular, I encourage people to learn about their fears by asking questions like 'What is the history of this fear?' Many fears stem from past failures and old wounds that we have not fully let go of. Another intelligent question to ask is 'What is the purpose of this fear?' Some fears are our egos' best attempts at self-preservation – 'if you give this public talk you will die onstage.'

Part II of The Fear Interview is about helping people to discern between fear and wisdom. The fears that 'speak' inside your head can often sound very authoritative. For example, I recently coached a politician who told me that he couldn't possibly voice his opposition to the American invasion of Iraq.

'What is the fear?' I asked.

'I fear not enough people share my views,' he said.

'Is that the truth, or is that just a fear?' I asked.

Two weeks later over a million people attended a peace march in London. Some of our fears are true, but most of our fears are just fears.

Part III of The Fear Interview is about seeing through your fears. I once coached a woman who had a dream to start a Montessori school in her town. She had nurtured this dream for over 15 years.

'If you had no fear, when would you start your school?' I asked.

'Today,' she said.

'So you can either wait for the fears to go away or face your fears now,' I said.

In that moment she began to dismantle her resistance to her fears. Quickly her fears gave way and she began to act. We explored intelligent questions like 'What would help me to let go of this fear?' and 'What extra support do I need to go beyond my fears?' Fear is often a call for extra help.

One of the most significant discoveries I made working with The Fear Interview is that fear is at the root of every block to success. At the deepest level of the mind there are no problems, only fear. There are also no conflicts, only fear; there is no lack, only fear; there is no devil, only fear; and there is no hell, only fear. It is literally true that the only thing to fear is fear itself. And yet, when people have the courage to face their fears and to talk honestly about them, their lives can move forward in the direction of their dreams.

Copyright 2001 by Randy Glasbergen.
www.glasbergen.com

**"Of course I'm afraid of success.
Handling a lot of money greatly increases
my chance of getting a painful paper cut!"**

Essentially put, I have identified two main groups of fears that can block success. The first group is the 'fears of failure'. These fears are about 'What if I fail?' Resistance to facing these fears can halt a person before he or she even begins. These unresolved fears can kill so many dreams and possibilities. They include the fear of not being good enough and the fear of making a mistake. They also include the fear of making a full commitment and the fear of possible rejection. Again, these fears need to be faced, listened to, and learned from. A dialogue is needed. Some fears are true, and most fears are a call for extra help.

The second group is the 'fears of success'. These fears are about 'What if I succeed?' They dwell on the potential negative consequences of success. It seems insane to be afraid of something you want, but these fears of success are much more common than I first realised. I find that people are mostly unconscious of their fears of success, yet when they resolve these fears it can create a tremendous surge of inspiration and success. These fears of success can include the fear of shining, the fear of happiness, the fear of playing big, and the fear of 'having it all'.

Fears of Success

I have conducted a lot of field research on the fears of success in recent years. These fears are usually the most unconscious blocks in a person's psychology of success. This is because they hide behind other fears, such as the fear of failure. Although few people talk openly about their fears of success, I think everyone experiences them to some degree. I also think that the fears of success are what ultimately prevent people from realising their true potential. Thus, in this chapter I will focus specifically on the fears of success.

In 2000, I created FOSI, a 'Fears of Success Indicator', which identifies some of the more common fears of success. I use FOSI in both my one-on-one coaching and my Success Intelligence seminars. Before I introduce people to FOSI, I first get them to explore four primer questions that are designed to raise awareness about the fears of success. These questions are as follows:

1. Is it safe to be successful in your workplace?
Many workplace cultures are anti-success. The vision for success is poorly defined and gets lost in busyness. The focus on success is slight compared to the full-time failure analysis. The criteria for success refer only to 'minimum standards' and 'core competencies', not to peak performance. The rewards for success are pitiful – some truly inspired work wins you a bottle of champagne at the next conference. The rules of the Annual Performance Review state that only 3 per cent of staff can achieve top recognition. Being too proactive, too talented, or too successful is likely to threaten the boss and annoy colleagues.

2. Is it safe to be successful in your family?

Many children receive mixed messages about success from their parents. They win praise for being at the top of the class, for their artistic talent, and for excelling at sports, but they are also warned not to have ideas above their station. They learn that success is good but that to talk about success is rude. They are encouraged to shine but not to attract attention. They are taught to think big but not to be too big for their britches. They notice that Dad or Mum is not always comfortable with their achievements. They learn to play things down so as to keep the peace.

3. Is it safe to be successful in your relationships?

Is this relationship big enough for both of us to grow and be successful? Can we both be talented, and can we both shine; or is that too threatening? In unhealthy relationships, one person usually plays small so as to preserve the balance of power. They find that when they attract attention, their spouses/friends feel insecure. Small successes are okay, but too much success can cause jealousy, competition, and power struggles. In a healthy relationship, both parties learn to be supportive and be inspired by each other's success. A win for one is a win for both.

4. Is it safe to be successful in the world?

People decide from an early age how safe it is to be in the world. Their family, their schooling, and their experiences teach them whether or not it is okay to be beautiful, okay to be intelligent, okay to be different, and okay to be successful. They see how much admiration champions and leaders receive, but they also notice the constant criticism and rotten tomatoes that are thrown at them. Many societies ritually attack the 'beautiful people' for their successes. The media cynically build people up and then publicly assault them. Everyone's Success Contract states how much success is okay and how much success is unsafe.

Overleaf is FOSI – the 'Fears of Success Indicator'. FOSI is made up of 15 statements, each of which highlights a common fear of success. I recommend that you read each statement three times so that it has your full attention. Then score each statement from 1 to 4, according to how much you identify with it. Add up your scores and check it against the 'fear gauge'. In the section that follows FOSI, I explore the 15 fears of success in some more detail.

FOSI – FEARS OF SUCCESS INDICATOR

How much can you identify with the following statements?

4–Completely   3–Very   2–Quite   1–Not at all

1. I am not always comfortable with the attention success attracts.

2. I worry that any major success I enjoy will attract envy or jealousy.

3. I believe that greater success leaves me more vulnerable to criticism and attack.

4. I think that any big success must inevitably require some sacrifice or loss.

5. I am uneasy about the high expectations that come with success.

6. I do not always believe I deserve all the success I experience.

7. When things are going really well for me, I often feel uneasy.

8. I believe that every major success has a high price or a hidden cost.

9. I wouldn't like the person that I'd need to become to achieve big success.

10. I think that success can ruin people and that it can create unhappiness.

11. I don't like the idea of success that comes too fast or is too big.

12. I think that success can lead to complacency and a loss of motivation.

13. I worry that success will leave me feeling empty and with nowhere to go.

14. I am not confident enough to see how successful I could really be.

15. I believe that success always leads to a fall in the end.

Fear Gauge

15–24 points: This score indicates that you have very few unresolved fears of success. This score is typical of people who face their fears and who are less afraid to shine. When they do feel fear, they call upon extra help and inspiration.

25–39 points: This score indicates an average level of unresolved fears of success. These fears may cause you to shy away from opportunities for greater success and happiness. You are probably playing small in your life.

40–50 points: This score indicates a high level of

unresolved fears of success. These fears may well conspire against your best efforts to succeed and will cause unnecessary struggle, setbacks, and failures.

51–60 points: This score indicates an extreme level of unresolved fears of success. This score is typical of people who suffer from dysfunctional independence, that is, who believe they have to 'do' success by themselves.

Beyond Your Fears

Success Intelligence recognises that if you want to be your best self and to contribute fully to life, you have to reach beyond your fears. These fears sometimes include the fears of success. Briefly, now, I will examine the fear of success that corresponds to each of the 15 statements in FOSI. These are:

1. Fear of being seen.　　　John was 22 years old when he was given his first management position. His team achieved a 900 per cent increase in profits in the first six months. John's boss was so surprised that he employed a team of accountants to check for financial irregularities and criminal deception. 'It almost put me off success for good,' said John.

Eileen had been overweight for many years. She decided to lose weight to restore her confidence. After she lost 42 pounds, she got lots of attention from men. 'And it terrified me,' she said. Success attracts all sorts of attention. The challenge is to trust in yourself and be true to yourself. Remember, extra help is also allowed.

2. Fear of envy and jealousy.　　Claire had been single for two years when she met and fell in love with Tom, her future husband. She was completely happy, almost. Claire's best friend, Louise, was in an unhappy marriage, and she seemed less than pleased for Claire.

'I never talk about Tom when I am with Louise, because her envy is too difficult to face,' said Claire. Any success can test the ego in us and others. True friends learn to be happy for each other. As a general rule, you will attract less envy and jealousy when you do the inner work and heal any envy and jealousy in yourself.

3. Fear of criticism and attack.   What are your motives for wanting to be successful? Is your success a gift to others or do you want to prove yourself, to compete against someone, to be superior, or to win revenge? Any of these 'attack motives' can unconsciously attract attacks against you. What are your private thoughts about people who are very successful? What is your attitude toward rich people? What do you think about people who are always happy? How critical are you of people you read about in the press? Anyone who attacks people for being successful will not feel entirely comfortable about his or her own success.

4. Fear of sacrifice and loss.   This fear corresponds to 'The Sacrifice Demand' in the Success Contract (see page 71). Anyone raised in a family with a strong martyr ethic will have internalised some beliefs about how 'success demands sacrifice' and 'love demands sacrifice' and 'talent demands sacrifice' and so on. They may also believe that they must choose between success and happiness, career and love, or money and purpose. This is just a fear, not the truth. True success does not ask you to sacrifice your true values – if it does, it is not true success. True success only asks you to sacrifice what is not important for what is.

5. Fear of expectations.   'The toughest thing about success is that you've got to keep on being a success,' wrote composer Irving Berlin. Some people practise 'learned averageness' in order to avoid expectations of success. They set low targets and do only moderately well to escape special attention. Kevin was crowned

Head Boy in his class when he was 11. 'I hated it,' he said, 'because after that everyone expected me to come first at everything.' Success can raise other people's expectations of us, and our lives can become a performance to please. Success can also raise our own expectations of ourselves, and we can attack ourselves mercilessly if we ever fall short.

6. Fear of deserving.   This fear corresponds to 'The Deserving Law' in the Success Contract (see page 69). Several dynamics may be at work:

- *Imposter Syndrome:* A person's self-criticism may be so blinding that he cannot own the positive qualities others see in him.

- *Fraud Guilt:* A person cannot update his self-image so as to identify with his new success.

- *Suffering Ethic:* A person believes he doesn't deserve such good fortune because there is so much suffering in the world. One answer is to make sure you use your good fortune – be it happiness, success, wealth – to help others.

7. Fear of abundance.   This fear corresponds to 'The Work Ethic' in the Success Contract (see page 69). After Hilary won a lottery jackpot she was wealthy but miserable. Hilary had grown up in a family that subscribed to the 'struggle ethic'. Hilary's father had taught her that an 'honest wage' is honourable, but that extreme wealth is not. The struggle ethic permits people to enter the lottery, but it is blasphemy to win it. Any fortune must be worked for, paid for, and earned because there is 'no free lunch'. Hilary felt guilty. 'It doesn't feel right,' she said. Hilary learned to enjoy her wealth once she realised what a gift it could be for everyone.

8. Fear of hidden costs. This fear relates to 'The Hidden Cost' in the Success Contract (see page 71). Two dynamics are at work here:

- *Fear of guilt:* Years ago, I ran a popular workshop called 'How to Be So Happy You Almost Feel Guilty, But Not Quite.' A major block to happiness is the 'learned guilt' that teaches people that they cannot afford too much happiness. This fear states that 'everything has a price', especially what you value most.

- *Fear of God:* For some people guilt is not an emotion, it is a way of life. Their religious conditioning has scared them into believing their personal success will be taxed by the Divine Auditor. Surely this sort of guilt is a mistake.

9. Fear of the shadow. Some people are afraid of success because they believe 'nice guys can't finish first.' They have learned to believe that people can only achieve great success if they sacrifice their values, bend the rules, lose their morals, and sell their souls. Clearly, anyone who believes this will think of success as the devil. It is highly likely you will encounter your shadow along the road of success. You will also meet your ego and you will be tempted to lie, cheat, and steal. You will have to choose between greed and purpose and between ambition and integrity. You will have to decide what true success is.

10. Fear of ruin. Some people are afraid of success because they fear it might ruin 'my character', 'my relationships', 'my health', 'my spirituality', and 'my happiness'. The media offer endless stories of people 'ruined by success', like corrupt politicians, criminal CEOs, insider trading, celebrity divorcés, showbiz scandals, game-fixing in professional sports, and rock stars in rehab. However, success does not ruin people. What ruins people is too much ego and selfishness and not enough vision and purpose. The world is full of examples of people who live successful and happy lives. Collect examples to inspire you.

11. Fear of chaos.   I have coached many people who have blocked success because of their fear of chaos. Several dynamics are at work:

- *Control:* People who want to be in control full-time limit their success. The really big successes often happen only when we let go of control.

- *Independence:* People who are dysfunctionally independent experience overwhelmingness and terror in the face of major success. They are ineffective because they believe they have to be entirely responsible for all the success.

- *Perfectionism:* Major successes are usually a humble learning curve full of mistakes, lessons, and opportunities to apologise.

12. Fear of complacency.   Graham was a manager notorious for being unfriendly, impersonal, and always critical of his team. He also had a policy of never giving praise.

'Praise leads to complacency,' Graham told me.

'Does your boss ever praise you?' I asked.

'Yes,' he replied.

'Does it make you complacent?' I asked.

'No, I give more,' he replied.

Many managers fear praise will cause performance to drop; many parents fear praise will give children a 'big head'; and many people dismiss their successes because they don't want to lose their edge. Yet genuine celebration of success is affirmative and can boost your ability to succeed further.

13. Fear of emptiness. This fear often causes people to procrastinate over unfinished projects and big successes. Two major fears are at work:

- *Fear of disillusionment:* The fear that a person's goals and dreams will fail to materialise in any deep joy. It is the fear of being successful and unhappy. It is about the 'failure of success' to bring satisfaction and peace of mind.

- *Fear of death:* The fear that after this current project you will have nothing left to give. You are afraid that your soul is now empty and that you have no more value to offer. This fear will cause you to procrastinate so as to put off retirement, golf, and death.

14. Fear of surrender. It is my experience that people with a great talent or great purpose are able to surrender their plans and their ego, in order to make way for inspiration and success. My friend Robert Norton is one of the most gifted musicians I know. Robert provides most of the live music at my public seminars. He has a stunning musical range, is a brilliant improviser, and he knows how to surrender to the goal. Robert once told me, 'To be truly creative you have to keep surrendering so as to see how far you can go.' When people are willing to surrender they can achieve more success than their egos ever dreamed of.

15. Fear of the fall. This is the fear that success is a prelude to a fall. It is the fear that love ends in heartbreak, that happiness ends in tears, and that power leads to a tragic end. It is the fear of heights – 'the higher they climb, the harder they fall.' As a client once told me, 'The trouble with being at the top is you can't fall up.' On an archetypal level, this fear is the reenactment of the 'fall from grace', when a person's success (the Garden of Eden) ends with a fall to Earth again. On a psychological level, this fear arises when people reach their own success threshold, as written by them in their Success Contract. A rewrite is now necessary.

My experience of teaching Success Intelligence and FOSI (Fear of Success Indicator) has proved consistently that when people resolve their fears of success they experience a personal renaissance that births greater creativity and success. By facing up to your fears of success and moving beyond them, you discover new ways to participate more fully in life. Thereby, the world enjoys the talents and gifts of your Unconditioned Self, and your successes can hopefully serve and inspire us all.

SUCCESS INTELLIGENCE TIP 28 – *COURAGE*

When you next review your major goals, uncover any unresolved fears of success. Think deeply about each goal and ask yourself, 'What are my fears of success here?' Check thoroughly.

Disowned fears of success can be found hiding in permanent busyness, constant struggle, and persistent bad fortune. They also work undercover in chronic shyness, personal dramas, and playing small.

Hidden fears (i.e., the fears you hide from) will interfere with your best efforts to succeed. Fears are a call for help. Call on God and your friends for inspiration and help.

A Ph.D. in
Happiness

*Joy is the holy fire that keeps our purpose warm and our
intelligence aglow. Resolve to keep happy, and your joy
and you shall form an invincible host against difficulty.*
– **Helen Keller**

In September 2003 I attended a graduation ceremony in Helsinki
to receive the award of Doctor of Philosophy (Ph.D.) for my work
on the Psychology of Happiness.[5] The whole occasion, complete
with academic cap and gown, marked another significant moment
in my own education and life journey. I have studied happiness
for over 20 years now, and I am convinced of the immeasurable
value of happiness in helping people be truly successful. I believe
real happiness is the 'holy fire' that inspires great success.

Surprisingly few psychologists have studied happiness. Only
in recent times has there been a significant increase in interest.
That said, for every 100 published articles on mental illness, there
is still only one article on happiness.[6] For my doctoral thesis
I summarised happiness research into three main groups, which
correspond to the three stages of consciousness I presented earlier.
These three groups – Determination, Adaptation, and Renaissance
– define happiness differently and raise important considerations
for how we also relate to success.

Subjective wellbeing: Warner Wilson led the first major
scientific review of subjective wellbeing (SWB for short) in 1967.[7]
The question Wilson asked was 'What really determines happiness?' His research, based on a *Determinism* theory, aimed to identify key circumstances that make people happy. Wilson's approach

defined happiness mainly as a response to an external stimulus, without which happiness does not exist. In other words, it is life events that primarily govern happiness. Presumably then, it is life events that ultimately determine if someone will be successful or not.

Wilson's orientation also corresponds with the 'having mode' about which Erich Fromm writes. His research identified a list of 'must haves' that determine happiness, such as 'I have a good income', 'I have a good job', and 'I have a good marriage.' Initially, researchers assumed that it must be 'having a good marriage', for example, that makes people happy. However, researchers now ask the question: *Is it that happy marriages make people happy or is it that happy people make happy marriages?* In other words, what really determines the success?

Positive psychology: The rise of positive psychology,[8] led by noted psychologists like Martin Seligman, former president of the American Psychological Association, is very welcome. While SWB research focuses mostly on external life circumstances that may or may not determine happiness, the field of positive psychology focuses much more on internal personality traits. Positive psychology corresponds with the *Adaptation* theory, which states that circumstances are important to happiness, but attitude is even more important. The same is true for success.

Positive psychology includes many modern schools of psychology that research positive traits, such as optimism, resilience, forgiveness, humour, and altruism. It also draws upon classical literature that supports the theory that happiness and success are a state of mind. 'The mind is the master over every kind of fortune; itself acts in both ways, being the cause of its own happiness and misery,' wrote Seneca, the Roman philosopher. Furthermore, when people learn how to be happy and how to choose their attitude, they increase their chances of success.

Joyful holism: The term *Joyful Holism* refers to the body of work by scientists and philosophers who have identified an innate happiness that abides in each person. This innate happiness is not a response to anything – it has nothing to do with a Mercedes, a Mont Blanc pen, or Manolo Blahnik shoes. This innate happiness is more than just positive thinking – it exists whether or not you are in a positive frame of mind. Teachers, ancient and modern, have described this innate happiness as 'inner gold', 'original joy', and 'pure being'. It is the 'holy fire' of which Helen Keller spoke.

This innate happiness – which I refer to simply as 'joy' – corresponds to the *Renaissance* theory of being. This joy is not dependent on circumstances or psychology; it is more real than that. It is impossible to quantify this joy, and any writer who writes about it has to hope the reader already has some *knowing*. This joy is inside you, always. This joy is your essence, minus your neurosis, minus your doubts, minus your busyness, etc. This joy is the signature of your Unconditioned Self. It is your original voice and it is your innate intelligence.

Success requires a good measure of these three types of happiness:

1. **Life satisfaction is enjoyable and rewarding.** To experience positive life events, like a happy marriage, a good income, and excellent health, makes life satisfying.

2. **Positive psychology is necessary and advantageous.** A positive mind-set promotes an 'I can' attitude, helps build resilience, and enables talent to express itself.

3. **Innate joy is the permanent touchstone that allows for grace and inspiration.** To work with joy, to serve with joy, to live with joy is what creates great success.

The Purpose of Happiness

Scientists have traditionally overlooked happiness because, in terms of evolution, it was judged to have only 'entertainment value' compared with the 'survival value' of emotions like fear or anger. Recently, however, thanks to psychologists like Barbara Fredrickson, there is growing evidence that happiness plays a big part in our growth and development. Happiness is not now dismissed as just a pleasurable emotion; it is valued more as a creative power that can help you to evolve and thrive.

Fredrickson's research is summarised using a broaden-and-build model of positive emotion. Fredrickson concluded that happiness broadens a person's thought-action repertoire, making him or her more creative, and builds a person's inner-directed reserves, making him or her more resilient.[9] In short, Fredrickson found that people who know how to be happy are strikingly confident, able, flexible, optimistic, sociable, energetic, and successful. Their joy helps them to perform well at work, makes them attractive to others, and gives them a positive advantage in life.

Happiness is a liberator of talent.   The conclusion of all my work with Success Intelligence is that *we do not become happy because we are successful; we become successful because we are happy.* I believe that if people keep asking themselves, 'What is true happiness?' and 'How can I be happier?' they will learn to live a life that is full of true value and success. As director of The Happiness Project I am often asked to comment on occupational research reports that conclude that happy people not only perform better but also get paid better.[10] Today, leaders are learning that happiness, talent, and success work together.

True happiness brings out the best in people. There has been much research in recent decades on the relationship between happiness and self. People who learn self-acceptance are particularly good at lessening self-attack and at liberating their talent. They know how to face their self-doubts and still choose a positive outlook in life. Their self-acceptance builds an inner confidence that increases their capacity for success. Research also shows there is a high correlation between inner happiness and positive relationships. Happy people tend to be good at relationships, unlike people with low self-acceptance, who often report they find relationships difficult.

Happiness is a compass for direction. What is the sense of building a business empire that takes ulcers and divorces to run it? What is the point of any career that does not ultimately increase the wellbeing of ourselves and others? What is the wisdom of working all hours to make huge mortgage payments on a home you have no time to enjoy? What is the sense of a relationship in which two people are not wholly committed to each other's happiness? What is the purpose of a lifestyle that is so busy there is no time for family, friendship, and happiness?

There is a world of difference between the pursuit of happiness and following your joy. The pursuit of happiness turns life into a race, it dismisses inner joy, encourages Destination Addiction, and confuses success with sacrifice. Following your joy lets your innate happiness teach you what you really value and what your true purpose is. People who follow their joy discover a depth of creativity and talent that inspires the world. They are assisted by grace and inspiration to contribute to the collective wealth of mankind. Their joy is their compass that navigates them through tough times.

Happiness is proof of authenticity. Chuck Spezzano, Ph.D., writes: 'Happiness must be our goal if we are to avoid losing ourselves, and what is true, in the midst of our busy lives.'[11] It is not possible to be inauthentic and feel successful, nor to be inauthentic and feel joy. My work is about helping people to listen to their inner joy more so that they can learn more about their authentic selves, their true strengths, and their real purpose. True happiness is a great teacher that can help you to realise your true self in relationships, work, and life.

Both happiness and unhappiness are messages – internal memos – that have something to teach you. When you are happy it is usually a sign you are in harmony with yourself. 'Happiness is when what you think, what you say, and what you do are in harmony,' said Mahatma Gandhi. When you are unhappy it may be a sign you are off-track and not listening to your wisdom. Asking an intelligent question like 'What is the lesson here?' can be very liberating. Letting your innate joy guide you may take great courage, but it will help you to live your real life and not some safe, dull other existence.

The Gift of Happiness

Tom Carpenter once said, 'The world will not be saved by miserable people; the world will be saved by happy people.'[12] The gift of happiness frees us from our personal neurosis, makes us less self-obsessed, and inspires us to give our best to the world. Happiness research confirms that true happiness makes us naturally inclined to want to contribute to the welfare of others. It appears that there is some 'secret agent' in happiness that motivates us to be generous and to use our success to support other people's success as well.

Happy people are less selfish. Many people have been taught to believe that happiness is selfish, but this is not true. Psychologist Bernard Rimland found a strong correlation between happiness and unselfishness in a major study in 1982.[13] In a similar study to Rimland's, I asked subjects to judge people they know as either 'mostly happy' or 'mostly unhappy' and as 'selfish' or 'unselfish'. I defined 'selfish' as 'not interested in other people's happiness' and 'unselfish' as 'interested in other people's happiness'. The results were:

1. 85 per cent of 'mostly happy' people were
    perceived as 'unselfish'.

2. 92 per cent of 'mostly unhappy' people were perceived
    as 'selfish'.

In the same study, I asked the question 'Are people more self-ish when they are unhappy or when they are happy?' A stagger-ing 98 per cent of people circled 'unhappy'. According to what researchers call the 'Big Five' method of analysis, happy people score consistently low on 'neuroticism' and consistently high on 'sociability', 'extroversion', 'friendliness', and 'openness'.[14] By contrast, many major investigations have found that depressed people exhibit strong traits of loneliness, individualism, narcis-sism, indulgence, alienation, and uninterest in others.[15]

Happy people are more altruistic.   Many research studies have found that people with high happiness scores are consistently more altruistic. Martin Seligman, author of *Authentic Happiness*, has reviewed many of these studies. He concludes:

> Before I saw the data I thought that unhappy people –
> identifying with the suffering that they know so well –
> would be more altruistic. So I was taken aback when the
> findings on mood and helping others without exception
> revealed that happy people were more likely to dem-
> onstrate that trait. When we are happy, we are less self-
> focused, we like others more, and we want to share our
> good fortune, even with strangers. When we are down,
> though, we become distrustful, turn inward, and focus
> defensively on our own needs. Looking out for number
> one is more characteristic of sadness than of wellbeing.[16]

Why are happy people more altruistic? One possible explana-tion is that at the deepest level happiness helps us to feel a greater empathy and oneness with people. Philosophers and writers of classical literature have often used the word 'joy' to describe the exhilaration of feeling a oneness with life. 'I saw one life and felt that it was joy,' wrote the poet Wordsworth. Another possible explanation is that at the deepest level happiness is connected to love. Many teachers have said that true happiness – the 'holy fire' of inner joy – is felt most when a person opens his or her heart and chooses to love.

Happy people engage in service. Albert Schweitzer believed service is the highest religion and said, 'I don't know what your destiny will be, but one thing I do know: the only ones among you who will be really happy are those who have sought and found how to serve.' People who choose to serve a cause or a purpose greater than themselves often report a sense of deep joy and inner fulfilment. Service certainly can promote happiness, but it is also true that happiness can promote a desire to serve.

Michael Argyle's research at Oxford University consistently found that happy people engage in activities to make the world a better place. He wrote: 'It is sometimes thought that political activity is motivated by discontent, but happy people are not deficient in voting; they do not take part in violent protests, but they do join community organisations a lot.'[17] David Myers' research also identified what he called a 'feel-good, do-good phenomenon' among people who feel happy and successful.[18]

'Service is the practice of wholeness,' wrote Molly Young Brown, author of *Growing Whole*. Psychology research consistently shows that service is natural to people who follow their joy. Through their joy, they serve; through their joy, they create; and through their joy, they commit to making the world a better place. There is no sacrifice in this, for it is a joy to do so. This is what makes people who follow their joy so inspirational to others. People who follow their joy experience the fullness of their being. They are the renaissance workers who evolve the consciousness of humanity.

Success Intelligence respects that when people commit to true happiness it helps them to listen to their wisdom, grow their talent, and live with courage. It takes them beyond narcissism, and it helps them to work with imagination, serve with love, and be more successful in every area of their lives. Their happiness is a gift to their families, their colleagues, and everyone they serve. Happiness really is a gift. At The Happiness Project, we recognize this great truth in our 'Vision Statement', which I include here to close this chapter. It reads:

> *It is because the world is so full of suffering,*
> *that your happiness is a gift.*
> *It is because the world is so full of poverty,*
> *that your wealth is a gift.*
> *It is because the world is so unfriendly,*
> *that your smile is a gift.*
> *It is because the world is so full of war,*
> *that your peace of mind is a gift.*
> *It is because the world is in such despair,*
> *that your hope and optimism is a gift.*
> *It is because the world is so afraid,*
> *that your love is a gift.*

SUCCESS INTELLIGENCE TIP 29 – *SERVICE*

Take time to reflect on the importance of service. Begin by asking yourself, 'What do I serve?' Identify the cause(s) you believe in and give yourself to. Name the heart of your work and what purpose it serves. Reflect also on the value of service.

Some people fear service because they believe it can cause unhealthy sacrifice and loss. Truthfully, service helps you to transcend your ego, evolve your gifts, and realise your potential. When you dedicate your success to the good of others, it activates all manner of inspiration and help.

Saying
Yes

I began this book by telling you the story of my dad, so it seems fitting that I should finish by sharing more of the story.

Nine years after my dad had left home, I finally got the call I had been dreading. My brother David said softly, 'Dad's in hospital. It doesn't look good. Get here as soon as you can.' I left my meeting at once. I drove over 200 miles, on a dark, starless night, with horizontal rain hitting the windshield of my car. I arrived just before midnight at the Hampshire County Hospital, but it was too late. David was waiting for me. We held each other tight. It was finally over. We went home to Mum.

For nine years I had watched my dad's epic struggle with life and death. His descent into alcoholism was like watching a knight being slain repeatedly by some invisible dragon. Some days he looked well, and you could tell that the life force in his body was strong, but on other days he looked like hell, and you could see he was fighting with his urge to die. Many times the light in his eyes would go out, only to come back on again. The doctors warned him repeatedly that he was killing himself with his drinking and yet somehow he kept on living.

Sometimes I thought my dad was fighting valiantly for life and love; other times he looked like he was hell-bent on a slow suicide. Right up to his death he was full of love and fear, hope and despair. In that way he was no different to the rest of us. Why he kept on living was obvious. He lived for his sons, and he wanted to see us grow up. He died on April 19, ten days after my 25th birthday and, most significantly, three days after David's 21st birthday. We were both grown men now. The coroner's report said the cause of death was 'non-specific.' Apparently, every major organ in Dad's body collapsed at once. I believe he chose his time to die.

It took me several years to put my dad's life and death into perspective. I grew up idolising him; he was a big-hearted man who was popular and kind and very loving. I wanted to be just like him. After his illness, my dreams died. At first, upon his death, I felt relief that the slow torture of his demise was over. Slowly, though, the full extent of my grief began to surface. While I tried to build new dreams for myself, I also became very dispirited. At times I sank into an abyss of meaninglessness and disillusionment. Some days I felt an irrepressible urge to die, and I wondered if this was the same pain my dad had felt.

The pain I experienced felt like death. Psychologists refer to this pain as a 'death drive' or 'death temptation'. Symptoms of death temptation vary from person to person, but common symptoms include a loss of hope, a sense of defeat, and feeling dead inside. Your vision is shattered, and your perception betrays you. All you can see is a dead end. You fear you can't go on and you just want to die. Sometimes a death temptation can lead to suicide, or it can contribute to illnesses like depression, alcoholism, or anorexia. Mostly it causes you to be cynical, to withdraw, and to resign. You don't die physically, but something inside you dies.

Death temptation is, in essence, about the choice to give up or go on. It is the last major block to success I will address in this book. Although people rarely speak about death temptation, everyone has experienced it at some time or another. No one alive has not thought privately, at least once, 'I want to die.' When a death temptation hits, it can take every bit of effort, faith, and grace to keep going. The philosopher Seneca said, 'Sometimes even to live is an act of courage.' Sometimes the ability to get through another day is a great success. We do well just to show up.

As I wrote this final chapter, I received an SOS call from a client who was in utter despair on the eve of a great success. For ten years she had worked on a manuscript for a TV drama and after countless rejections and disappointments she was finally about to meet a most influential commissioning editor. She told me, 'I should feel excited and be over the moon with joy, but instead

I feel sick, and all I want to do is lie down and die.'

She also said, 'One moment I'm dreaming about writing an acceptance speech for my award, and the next moment I'm dreaming about writing a suicide note.' When I asked her how many times she had been tempted to give up on her project, she said, 'A thousand times, at least.' All her past grief about her countless rejections had resurfaced and now, as part of the final act of success, she had to let her grief go. Together over the phone we prayed for healing and release. Her meeting the next day was a great success.

Which of us has not been tempted to give up on our most cherished dreams? The most successful people I have met have told me how they waved their fists at God and threatened to die many times before they won their victories. In history, the greatest leaders have walked through 'the valley of the shadow of death' in order to serve and inspire us. In art, the greatest artists have been tempted to throw away their talent. In business, the greatest entrepreneurs have often risen from the ashes. In sport, the greatest heroes have come back from the dead. In life, we all have to choose between love and death.

A death temptation is often the last block to a new level of creativity and success. Our despair is heightened because we fear we are so far from victory, and yet the truth is that we are closer than ever. At first I had no idea how to handle my own death temptation. I never actually tried to kill myself, but I was ready to give up on happiness, on people, and on God. For months I resisted vehemently the temptation to give up but it just grew stronger, so eventually I decided to stop fighting it. And in doing so I learned one of the most important secrets to success.

Here is the secret: whenever you are tempted to say 'I give up', notice that you are not being asked to give up on success, but that you are being asked to give up on everything that blocks success. In other words, use the feeling of 'I want to give up' as an opportunity to give up your grief, your wounds, and your heartbreaks. Surrender, and give up your independence, your control, and your plans. Pray and enquire, 'What am I being asked to give up?' Listen, and then give up your cynicism, your past, and your death temptation.

What looks like a 'dead end' to our egos is really an invitation to go higher than before. It is a lifting-off point where you are asked to give up your own efforts for more grace and to let go of your own plans for greater inspiration. Every dead end is a place in the road where you must let go of what does not really work for what really can. Hence, the death temptation is really a prelude to birth, recreation, and renaissance. Peter Kingsley, the author of *In the Dark Places of Wisdom,* explains this point so powerfully. He writes:

> If you're lucky, at some point in your life you'll come to a complete dead end.
>
> Or to put it another way: if you're lucky you'll come to a crossroads and see that the path to the left leads to hell, that the path to the right leads to hell, that the road straight ahead leads to hell, and that if you try to turn around you'll end up in complete and utter hell.
>
> Every way leads to hell and there's no way out, nothing left for you to do. Nothing can possibly satisfy you any more. Then, if you're ready, you'll start to discover inside yourself what you always longed for but were never able to find.
>
> And if you're not lucky?
>
> If you're not lucky you'll come to this point when you die. And that won't be a pretty sight because you'll still be wanting what you're no longer able to have.[19]

'The Yes Meditation'

My theory used to be that anyone who makes it to 30 years old has enough good reasons to give up on life for ever. I shared this theory recently at a workshop I gave in a prison in Kauai, Hawaii. The workshop was attended by 25 inmates, a few social workers, and the prison guards.

'You are full of shit!' shouted one inmate in a booming, aggressive tone. He was a big man, about 350 pounds, who looked like Barry White, except he wasn't about to sing a love song.

'How so?' I asked.

He rose to his feet and said, 'It ain't 30 years old, it's 18 years old. If you make it to 18 years old, you have enough reasons to give up. Trust me, man!'

As I looked around the room I noticed that all the fellow inmates, the social workers, and the prison guards were nodding in agreement with what this man said. Everyone knows what heartbreak feels like and what a death temptation feels like long before they make it to 18 years old. In the face of great loss and disappointment, it is so tempting to want to withdraw and resign from life. And yet, if we do so it greatly reduces our chances of success and happiness. Somehow, when we most want to close down and give up, we have to find a way to open up and keep growing.

After my father's death, I witnessed in myself a power struggle between wanting to close my heart to the world *and* also wanting to open my heart more fully than before. I reflected on three main questions, which were: 'What did Dad teach me?' 'What was his gift for me?' and 'How can I serve his memory?' In the end, all of my reflections settled on this one conclusion: *Even though life can be difficult, heartbreaking, and insane at times, the only way to really succeed is to keep saying 'Yes' to what moves your soul.* To keep saying 'Yes' marks your willingness to stay alive and to let life unfold for the best.

I usually close my Success Intelligence workshops with a meditation called 'The Yes Meditation'. This very moving meditation invokes the power of intention, i.e., 'What do I want to say "Yes" to?' It affirms what you most value and love. It strengthens your commitment and also your resilience during the dark times. In this meditation I invite everyone to imagine they are holding the world in their hands (sometimes I give them a miniature globe of the earth to hold). I ask them to close their eyes and to reflect upon their lives – the 'best of times' and 'worst of times'.

Next, I ask them to consider what – in spite of the difficulties, heartbreaks, and insanity in the world – they really do say 'Yes' to.

I then tell them to keep their eyes closed and to speak out loud everything they say 'Yes' to. There is usually some silence at first, and then the whole room fills with vows of purpose, declarations of intent, and messages of love. You can hear people affirm, 'I say "Yes" to love,' 'I say "Yes" to success,' and 'I say "Yes" to my family'. Words like 'inspiration', 'service', 'God', 'leadership', 'peace', and 'happiness' fill the air. In spite of all our wounds, we commit again to what is our true purpose.

Saying 'Yes' is the key to true assertiveness. To be successful and happy you have to know what it is you want to say 'Yes' to. Saying 'Yes' is not the same as 'hoping', 'trying', or 'maybe'. Saying 'Yes' is giving your 100 per cent commitment to what is really important in your life. A strong sense of 'Yes' helps to build a strong sense of 'No' to what is not important and not true. 'Yes' supports you in not letting wounds and disappointments distract you from your purpose. 'Yes' helps you to use everything as a spur and an encouragement to true success.

Success Intelligence is about knowing what you want to say 'Yes' to. This is simple to say, and incredibly powerful to do. Nothing moves the world more than the power of 'Yes'. To finish this book, then, I ask you to contemplate 'The Yes Meditation' a little more deeply. Below are seven focus points that correspond to the seven parts of this book. Consider each point carefully and decide what it is you really do say 'Yes' to. Your answers form a vow of success that will support you in your work, your relationships, and your life.

1. Say 'Yes' to life. I shall never forget my first meeting with Rabbi Joseph Gelberman. I had been invited to his apartment on the Upper West Side of Manhattan. The rabbi is over 80 years old and full of life. Over tea and biscuits he talked animatedly about interfaith worship, the Jewish Kabbalah, and Barbra Streisand.

Suddenly, the rabbi turned to me and asked, 'Are you alive, Robert?'

'Yes, Rabbi,' I replied.

'How do you know?' he asked.

I said, 'Because I feel my heart is open.'

'That is a good answer,' he replied.

My heart was also beating very fast at that moment.

I learned later that the rabbi likes to ask people 'Are you alive?' The rabbi grew up in Hungary, where he preached until the Holocaust forced him to seek asylum in America. Tragically, both his parents and all of his brothers and sisters were killed by the Nazis. The rabbi told me how he nearly died of a broken heart. In a talk he gave called 'Choose Life', he shared how he meditated deeply on the question 'Is life worthwhile or is it not?' In the end, he chose to say 'Yes' to life. 'Most of us die too soon in this life,' he says. The rabbi faced his pain, and he chose to live.[20]

What would you say if someone asked you, 'Are you alive?' Probe deeper and ask yourself 'From zero to 100 per cent, how alive am I?' Be honest about this. Assess how fully you are participating in your life. Is it 40 per cent, 60 per cent, or 80 per cent? What would happen if you decided to be 10 per cent more alive? Ask yourself, 'What is a successful life?' Stand still for a while, cease to be busy, and create a VISION for true success. Also, say 'Yes' to the possibility – even though you do not know how – that life can be both sweeter and richer.

2. Say 'Yes' to yourself.   In *The Sane Society,* Erich Fromm wrote: 'In the 19th century the problem was that God is dead; in the 20th century the problem is that man is dead.'[21] What signs of life are there in the 21st century? The mystics of old said that to live is to be slowly born. After physical birth, our task is to give birth to our divine potential for wisdom and creativity, skills and talent, love and service. Unfortunately, many of us have so little self-knowledge that we too readily dismiss our unlimited potential for success and inspiration.

'The ultimate import of our human birth is to discover or realise the truth of life. To do so, however, we are required to observe, understand, and transcend ourselves,' wrote John White, editor of *What is Enlightenment?*[22] Sometimes the major block to our success is our own psychology and our own self-image. Our task, therefore, is to enquire honestly, 'Who am I?' We have to give up our Learned Self in favour of our true Unconditioned Self. We can also increase our chances for success if we are prepared to rewrite our Success Contracts and to change our beliefs about ourselves.

'The tragedy of life is what dies inside a man while he lives,' said Albert Schweitzer. No one ever comes to the end of his or her potential for success. Your goal, therefore, is to keep saying 'Yes' to birthing your capacity for inspiration. The most powerful thing you can do is to place your hand over your heart and say 'Yes' to who you are and all that you can be. True self-acceptance is the key to liberating talent, to growing your strengths, and to contributing fully to the world. Unfortunately, most of us are too busy attacking ourselves to get anywhere in life.

3. Say 'Yes' to your wisdom. Sigmund Freud once observed, 'What a distressing contrast there is between the radiant intelligence of a child and the feeble mentality of the average adult.'[23] What a shocking and powerful statement this is. And yet isn't it true that most of us dismiss and neglect our own wisdom from a very early age? My work with Success Intelligence is about encouraging people to listen to their wisdom and to let themselves be guided by God's universal intelligence. You are a wise person, and when you honour your wisdom, your life works better for you.

In society today the temptation is to dumb down and to pretend not to care. We kid ourselves that 'ignorance is bliss', but there is absolutely no truth in this. It seems that we are afraid to say 'Yes' to our wisdom and to explore anything deep and meaningful. We are living in what Danah Zohar calls a 'spiritually dumb culture'. We keep everything superficial, and hence we fail to surrender to what would save us. Saying 'Yes' to wisdom is about connecting more to God, exploring your highest purpose on Earth, and being pulled along by what you most love.

4. Say 'Yes' to relationships. Dr. Chuck Spezzano identifies independence as a major block to success in our work and our relationships. He writes:

> In our culture we have been taught that the final stage of growth is independence – but, in truth, independence is just a stage along the way to interdependence or partnership. The final stage of independence is not success, but deadness, or what I affectionately call the dead zone. In the dead zone, you feel like a failure, no matter how much of a success you are to other people. You are also tempted to die because you feel such exhaustion and such a deep weariness.[24]

In 'The Yes Meditation', I invite participants to name out loud the relationships they most want to say 'Yes' to. By saying 'Yes' to our most precious relationships, we access new levels of creativity and success. By committing more to our partners and to our colleagues, we discover the joy of partnership and synergy. Whenever you feel blocked, exhausted, or at a dead end it is a sign that you are being too independent. On some level, the answer to every problem is a deeper level of connection and oneness. Every single success is a co-creative act.

5. Say 'Yes' to a purpose. While I was working for BT, I heard a remarkable story about an employee whom I will call Ken. Ken joined BT as an apprentice the day after his 16th birthday. He was a BT man who worked for the company for 33 years before he was killed in a car crash. In his will, Ken had left a most unusual request: he asked that the BT company logo be put on his gravestone. When I spoke to Ken's wife, she told me, 'Ken was a man who loved God first, who loved his family always, and who loved his work.'

The story of Ken's request soon appeared in the national press. Many reports launched mocking and derisory attacks on Ken and his family for making a 'baffling' and 'bizarre' request. Sadly, many of Ken's colleagues responded with the same cynicism and ridicule. I was left wondering what Ken had done to deserve such attack. His request was certainly unusual, but was it wrong? What is your response to Ken's story? More importantly, could you give yourself so completely to a purpose (or a company, etc.) that you would have it recorded on your tombstone?

6. Say 'Yes' to commitment. What is it that you stand for? What do you believe in? What do you give your heart to? The whole point of Success Intelligence is first to work out what it is you are committed to, and then to give yourself fully to that commitment. Once you do that, you will discover the extraordinary power of grace and inspiration. True commitment takes us far beyond what our individual egos are capable of, and we find ourselves connecting to the divine circuits of life. We become part of the universal dance of creation – and we are co-creators with God and all life.

The German philosopher Johann von Goethe famously wrote:

> Until one is committed, there is hesitancy, the chance to draw back, always ineffectiveness. Concerning all acts of initiative and creation there is one elementary truth, the ignorance of which kills countless ideas and splendid plans; that the moment one definitely commits oneself, then Providence moves too. All sorts of things occur to help one that would never otherwise have occurred. A whole stream of events issues from the decision raising in one's favour all manner of unforeseen incidents and meetings and material assistance which no one could have dreamed would have come his way.

Saying 'Yes' to commitment inspires collective assistance.

7. Say 'Yes' to love. During his illness with cancer, actor Michael Landon said, 'Somebody ought to tell us, right at the start of our lives, that we are dying. Then we might live life to the limit every minute of every day. Do it, I say, whatever you want to do, do it now.' We will all die – even if most of us do persist in saying 'if I die' instead of 'when I die'. The great Sufi teacher Mulla Nasrudin once said, 'If I do not die I shall be extremely surprised.' At some point we all have to leave our bodies behind as we go on to the next adventure.

Success Intelligence has to take into account that our adventure on earth is both transient and temporary. Therefore, an intelligent question to ask is, 'Knowing I will die, how shall I live?' I stayed up all night on the evening my dad died. I just couldn't sleep. In my mind I surveyed the world for something real and everlasting that does not die. Over and over again, like a mantra, I kept asking, 'What's real?' Eventually the answer came back to me: 'Love is real.' There have been many times since that night when I have forgotten to remember that 'love is real.' That said, I do believe I have found my answer to success. What is your answer?

SUCCESS INTELLIGENCE TIP 30 – *YES*

Success is not about driving yourself harder; it is about letting go of what blocks your heart. Think deeply about what you most want to say 'Yes' to. Be willing to let go of old heartbreaks and wounds to which you still cling. You didn't come into this world to shrink and play small. Nor are you here to play dead. You have gifts to share and a contribution to make. Each time you say 'Yes' to the possibility of success and happiness, you make it easier for God and everyone else to help you.

Acknowledgments

Success Intelligence is a project that began nearly ten years ago. Thank you to everyone who has ever organised or participated in one of my Success Intelligence seminars. Thank you to all the teachers I have met along the way. Thank you to my friend and mentor, Tom Carpenter, for your constant inspiration. Thank you, Miranda MacPherson, once again, for your boundless support and expert editing. Thank you also to my family, Alex Holden, Sally Holden, and David Holden, for all your love.

Thank you, Ben Renshaw, and everyone at The Happiness Project who has contributed to the work. Thank you, Anna Pasternak and Danah Zohar, for your generous editorial support. Thank you, Andrew Lownie, my agent, for believing in my work. Thank you, Helen Coyle and the team at Hodder & Stoughton. Thank you to Robert Norton for your music, which I listen to while I write. Thank you also to *A Course in Miracles* for teaching me so much and for inspiring me every day.

Notes

PROLOGUE

1. See *This Longing,* translated by Coleman Barks and John Moyne, page 36, Shambala Publications (2000).
2. This prayer comes from an ancient Hindu text called the *Brihad-Aranyaka Upanishad.* The full prayer is 'From the unreal lead me to the real! From darkness lead me to light! From death lead me to immortality!' *The Upanishads,* translated by Juan Mascaro, Penguin (1965).
3. William James coined this term in a letter he wrote to H.G. Wells on September 11, 1906. See *The Selected Letters of William James,* Anchor Books (1993).

PART I: VISION

1. James Gleick has written a well-researched book on the speeding up of business, technology, transport, and society. It is entitled *Faster,* Abacus (2000).
2. For some excellent research on our speeded-up world see *The 24-Hour Society* by Leon Kreitzman, Profile Books (1999).
3. See *The Penguin Dictionary of Psychology,* edited by Arthur Reber, page 416, Penguin (1985).
4. This hard-driving, aggressive personality type is a derivative of the 'Type A' personality type. For further information see *Treating Type A Behavior – and Your Heart* by Meyer Friedman, Random House (1974).
5. Hodder & Stoughton (1997). Also, for more information on Wayne Muller's work on success and neighborhood philanthropy visit the Website: **www.breadforthejourney.org**.
6. See 'The Busyness Survey' in Issue 97 of *Discipleship Journal.* For more information visit the Website: **www.navpress.com**. I also recommend the article 'How I Handle Busyness' by Susan Maycinik, which summarises 'The Busyness Survey.'
7. The first case of *karoshi* was reported in 1969 when a 29-year-old man died of a stroke when working in the shipping department of Japan's largest newspaper company. Dr. Katsuo Nishiyama and Jeffrey V. Johnson have written an excellent overview article on *karoshi* available online at: **www.workhealth.org/whatsnew/lpkarosh**.
8. 'The Quality of Working Life: 1999 Survey of Managers' Changing Experience', Les Worrall and Cary Cooper, Institute of Management (1999).
9. From an American survey entitled 'Job Satisfaction' by The Conference Board, Executive Action Report No. 68 (September 2003). The Conference Board is a nonprofit organisation specialising in business research. For more information visit the Website: **www.conference-board.org**.
10. Sourced from a Gallup Organization Poll entitled 'Corporate Corruption' (2002). For more information visit online at: **www.gallup.com/poll**.
11. Publishing in *American Medical News* on June 3, 2002. Visit online at: **www.amednews.com**

12. Copies of this documentary are available at The Happiness Project. Reference: 'How to be Happy', BBC Productions (1996). Also available is a QED book that accompanies the documentary entitled *QED How to be Happy* by Brian Edwards and Wendy Sturgess, BBC Education (1996).

13. Joe Kita has written an interesting article on the new depression, available online at: **www.menshealth.com/health/newdepression.**

14. This global study has given rise to more than 300 publications in 16 languages. For more information visit the Website: **www.wvs.sr.umich.edu.** Also see *Modernization and Postmodernization* by Ronald Inglehart, Princeton University Press (1997).

15. See *The Pursuit of Happiness* by David Myers, Avon Books (1993).

16. See *The American Paradox* by David Myers, page 374, Yale Nota Bene (2000).

17. Gerald Klerman has done as much as anyone to chart increases in depression in recent decades. Two major references: (1) 'Increasing Rates of Depression' by G. Klerman, et al, *Journal of the American Medical Association* (JAMA), Volume 261, pp 2229–2235 (1989); (2) 'The Changing Rate of Major Depression' by G. Klerman. *JAMA*. Vol. 268, pp 3098–3105 (1992). Another interesting reference is *Prozac Nation* by Elizabeth Wurtzel, Riverhead Books (1994).

18. Researcher T. Davies suggests that 20 per cent of adults suffer from psychiatric problems at any one time. See 'ABC of Mental Health' by T. Davies, *British Medical Journal*, Vol. 314, pp 1536–9 (1997).

19. A useful reference is *Juvenile Violence in a Winner-Loser Culture* by Oliver James, Free Association Books (1994).

20. A useful reference is 'Heroin Epidemics Revisited' by P. Hughes, in *Epidemiologic Reviews*, Vol. 17, pp 66–73 (1995). Also, for an excellent bibliography of research papers on substance abuse visit the Website for SAMHDA at: **www.icpsr.umich.edu/SAMHDA/SERIES/dawn-ibl.**

21. Suicide among young men in England and Wales increased dramatically from 1980–1990, by 33 per cent between 25–44 years and 85 per cent between 15–24 years. See 'Suicide' by E. Paykel and R. Jenkins, in *Prevention in Psychiatry*, Gaskell (1994).

22. Another excellent reference is *Britain on the Couch* by Oliver James, Century Books (1997).

23. See *The Joyless Economy* by Tibor Scitovsky, pp 4–5, Oxford University Press (1976).

24. For an excellent overview article that includes many research references, I recommend "If We Are So Rich, Why Aren't We Happy?" by Mihaly Csikszentmihalyi, in *American Psychologist*, Vol. 54, No. 10 (October 1999).

PART II: POTENTIAL

1. This is an unpublished manuscript. It formed the basis for several published articles including "Stress: The Ultimate Challenge?" in *Caduceus*, pp 6–8 (Spring 1990).

2. For an excellent overview of Carl Jung's work see *The Essential Jung*, edited by A. Storr, Princeton University Press (1999).

3. For further reading on my thoughts about The Unconditioned Self see my books *Happiness NOW!* and *Shift Happens!*

4. For an excellent read on Heisenberg's work I recommend *The Eyes of Heisenberg* by Frank Herbert, Tor Books (2002).

5. See *Social Foundations of Thought and Action* by Albert Bandura, page 395, Prentice-Hall (1986).

6. See *Psycho-Cybernetics* by Maxwell Maltz, page 2, Prentice Hall (1960). For more information on Maxwell Maltz's work on self-image visit the Website: **www.psycho-cybernetics.com/maltz**.

7. See *Now, Discover Your Strengths* by Marcus Buckingham and Donald Clifton, Simon & Schuster (2001). For more information on discovering your strengths, visit the Website: **www.strengthsfinder.com**.

8. See *Oprah* magazine, February 2003. For more information on the inspirational work of Oprah Winfrey visit the Website: **www.oprah.com**.

9. For further information on Fraud Guilt and the Imposter Syndrome see *If I'm So Successful Why Do I Feel Like a Fake? The Imposter Syndrome* by Joan Harvey with Cynthia Katz, St. Martin's Press (1985).

10. Dr. Chuck Spezzano and his wife, Lency Spezzano, have developed a problem-solving model of psychology called the 'Psychology of Vision.' A good reference book is *If It Hurts, It Isn't Love* by Dr. Chuck Spezzano, Hodder & Stoughton (1999). For further information on their excellent work visit the Website: **www.psychologyofvision.com**.

11. See *Physics and Philosophy* by James Jeans, RA, Kessinger Publishing Co. (January 2003).

12. This quotation comes from the Buddhist text called *The Dhammapada*, translated by Juan Mascaro, Penguin Books (1973).

13. See *Milton, Poet of Duality* by R.A. Shoaf, Yale University Press (1985).

14. Tom Carpenter is author of *Dialogue on Awakening*, Carpenter Press (1992). He has been a mentor to me in my life and work. His quote comes from a discussion we had together – one of many that have been published and distributed on audio cassette by Carpenter Press and The Happiness Project.

15. Graham founded Europe's largest coaching and leadership company, Alexander. He created the GROW Model, the world's best-known coaching framework. Graham and I have co-presented many coaching seminars. Graham's publications include *Super Coaching*, co-authored with Ben Renshaw, Random House (2005). Contact Graham at **graham@grahamalexander.com**.

PART III: WISDOM

1. I often feature the poetry of Hafiz in my seminars and workshops. I like the translations by Daniel Ladinsky in particular. This extract comes from a poem called 'Cast All Your Votes For Dancing,' in *I Heard God Laughing*, translated by D. Ladinsky, Sufism Reoriented (1996).

2. There are two famous studies which conclude that happiness and meaning are both rated higher than anything else, including money. See "What Makes a Life Good?" by L.A. King and C.K. Napa, *Journal of Personality and Social Psychology*, Issue 75, pp 156–165 (1998).

3. I first saw this prayer quoted in a column for the *Daily Express*, April 28, 1998. The author of the column is musician Boy George, but I don't know who wrote the prayer.

4. See *The Essential Fromm* by Erich Fromm, edited by Rainer Funk, page 68, Constable and Robinson (1995).

5. I recommend all of Staffan Linder's work. See 'The Acceleration of

Consumption' in *The Harried Leisure Class* by Staffan Linder, pp 77–93, Columbia University Press (1969).

6. See 'How to Lead a Rich Life' by Polly LaBarre, in *Fast Company* magazine, Issue 68, page 72 (March 2003).

7. See 'Well-Being and the Workplace' by P. Warr, published in *Well-Being*, edited by D. Kahneman, E. Diener, and N. Schwarz, Sage Publications (1999). Also, Michael Argyle presents a good summary of the healthy benefits of enjoyable employment in *The Psychology of Happiness*, pp 89–109, Routledge, 2nd Edition (2001).

8. See *50 Ways to Let Go and Be Happy* by Dr. Chuck Spezzano, pp 12–14, Hodder & Stoughton (2001).

9. See 'Love is the Killer App' by Tim Sanders, in *Fast Company* magazine, Issue 55, page 64 (2002).

10. There is so much evidence that people need more than money to enjoy their work and that job dissatisfaction can cause dissatisfaction with life. See 'Job Satisfaction and Life Satisfaction' by M. Tait, M. Padgett, and T. Baldwin in the *Journal of Applied Psychology*, Volume 74, pp 502–507 (1989).

11. This Internet survey was conducted by *Fast Company* magazine, Issue 26, page 108 (1999).

12. Anita Roddick offers an inspiring vision for work in *Business as Unusual*, page 37, Thorsons (2000).

13. See 'The Biology of Business: Love Expands Intelligence', a paper written by H. Maturana and P. Bunnel for the Society of Organizational Learning Member's Meeting, Amherst, MA (June 1998).

14. See reference 13. To read this article online visit the Website: **www.mit-press.mit.edu/journals/SQLJ/Maturana.pdf.**

15. See *A Return to Love* by Marianne Williamson, page 179, Harper Collins (1992). Also, visit the Website: **www.marianne.com** to learn more about Marianne's excellent work on spiritual renaissance.

PART IV: RELATIONSHIPS

1. See *Spiritual Intelligence* by Danah Zohar and Ian Marshall, pp 3–4, Bloomsbury (1999). Also, for more information on their work, visit the Website: **www.dzohar.com.**

2. See *Rewiring the Corporate Brain* by Danah Zohar, page 136, Berrett-Koehler Publishers (1997).

3. See *Physics and Philosophy* by W. Heisenberg, Harper, New York (1958).

4. See *Rewiring the Corporate Brain* by Danah Zohar, page 45, Berrett-Koehler Publishers (1997).

5. Quoted in *The Medium, the Mystic, and the Physicist* by Lawrence LeShan, page 61, Ballantine Books (1975).

6. English mathematician and philosopher, Alfred North Whitehead, said, 'Nature is a theatre for the interrelations of activities.' See *Process and Reality, an Essay in Cosmology* by A.N. Whitehead, et al, Macmillan USA (1985).

7. A David Bohm statement quoted in *Synchronicity* by Joseph Jaworski, page 79, Berrett-Koehler Publishers (1996).

8. David Bohm has written books which are acclaimed as masterpieces of the new physics. I recommend *Wholeness and the Implicate Order* by David Bohm, Routledge Classics (2002). Also, visit the Website: **www.muc.**

de/~heuvel/bohm.

9. This quotation is from an article in the *New York Post*, November 28, 1972.

10. The 2001 UK Population Census published by the Office of National Statistics, found that, 'In 2001, the number of divorces granted in the UK increased by 1.4 per cent, from 155,000 in 2000 to 157,000. This is the first time that the number of divorces has increased since 1996. In 1961 there were 27,000 divorces in Great Britain, which had doubled by 1969 to 56,000.
It then doubled again by 1972 to 125,000 in both Great Britain and the United Kingdom.' For more information, visit the Website: **www.statistics.gov.uk.**

11. There are 21,660,475 households in England and Wales according to Census 2001, and 30 per cent of these (6.5 million) are one-person households – up from 26.3 per cent in 1991. Nearly half of the one-person households (3.1 million) are one-pensioner-only households and three-quarters of these (2,366,000) are occupied by a woman living on her own. For more information, visit the Website: **www.statistics.gov.uk.**

12. From a 2003 survey by the Department of Trade and Industry's (DTI) Work-Life Balance Campaign and *Management Today* magazine. For more information visit the Website: **www.worklifebalance.com.**

13. I am indebted to social psychologist David Myers, who expertly collates such rich data. Quoted in *The American Paradox* by David Myers, page 197, Yale Nota Bene (2000).

14. See *The Popcorn Report* by Faith Popcorn, pp 27–28, Arrow Books, London (1992).

15. See *The Spirit of Community* by Amitai Etzioni, HarperCollins, London (1995). For more information on the philosophy and practice of Communitarianism read the quarterly journal *The Responsive Community*. Also I recommend the work of the Communitarian Network, which describes itself as 'a coalition of individuals and organisations who have come together to shore up the moral, social, and political environment. We are a nonsectarian, nonpartisan, transnational association.' Visit the Website: **www.gwu.edu/~ccps.**

16. For an excellent summary of many international surveys, see *Britain on the Couch* by Oliver James, Century Books (1997).

17. See *The Spirit of Community* by Amitai Etzioni, page 63, HarperCollins, London (1995).

18. See *The Corporate Eunuch* by O.W. Battalia and J.J. Tarrant, page 71, Crowell, New York (1973).

19. See *Love and Survival* by Dean Ornish, pp 12–13, HarperPerennial, New York (1998).

20. See 'Social Support Versus Companionship: Effects on Life Stress, Loneliness, and Evaluations by Others' by Karen S. Rook, *Journal of Personality and Social Psychology*, Vol. 52, pp 1132–47 (1987).

21. *Michelangelo* by William E. Wallace, Hugh Lauter Levin Associates (1998).

22. *How to Think like Leonardo da Vinci* by Michael J. Gelb, page 226, Dell Trade Paperback (Random House), New York (1998).

23. For an excellent account of Edison and his 'invention factory' see *Working at Inventing*, edited by William S. Pretzer, Johns Hopkins University Press (2002).

24. Reprinted in *The Times*, sports section, May 17, 2003, page 30.
25. Ibid, pp 29–30
26. See *The World As I See It* by Albert Einstein, edited by Alan Harris, page 1, Citadel Press (1979).
27. See 'Coming to Terms with Failure: Private Self-Enhancement and Public Self-Effacement' by J.D. Brown and F.M. Gallagher, *Journal of Experimental Social Psychology*, Vol. 28, pp 3–22 (1992).
28. For more on Social Comparison theory I recommend *Handbook of Social Comparison*, edited by Jerry Suls and Ladd Wheeler, Kluwer Academic/ Plenum Publishers (2000).
29. All these quotations are found in *The Wiley Book of Business Quotations*, edited by Henry Ehrlich, pp 73–75, John Wiley & Sons, Canada (1998).
30. From *She Who Dares Wins* by Eileen Gillibrand and Jenny Mosley, Thorsons, London (1995), quoted in: *The Penguin Book of Business Wisdom* by Stephen Dando-Collins, page 308, Penguin Books, Australia (1998).
31. See *Children First* by Penelope Leach, Michael Joseph, London (1994).
32. See *Natural Selection and Social Theory* by R. Trivers, Oxford University Press, New York (2002).
33. BT is a founding member of the Per Cent Club, which donates a minimum of one half per cent of annual pre-tax profits to not-for-profit causes. BT also contributes to many community projects through BT Better World. Visit the Website: **www.btplc.com/betterworld.**
34. These opinions come from the BT Survey 'Listening to the Nation' published in 1997. For further information about this survey, write to the BT Forum, PP501, Holborn Centre, 120 High Holborn, London.
35. Quoted in a special edition BT Forum newsletter entitled 'Forum: Listening to the Nation Project Update' (Summer 1997).
36. Social psychologist David Myers has collated excellent data on this in his book *The American Paradox*, pp 199–200, Yale Nota Bene (2000).
37. See reference 34.
38. See *About Time* by Patricia Hewitt, page 61, IPPR/Rivers Oram Press (1993).
39. Quoted in an article that appeared in *Daily Mail* on June 2, 2003, page 4.
40. Quoted in the 'BT Forum Newsletter' (Autumn 1996).
41. Published on the Department of Trade and Industry (DTI) Website as a press release for August 30, 2002 entitled 'UK Workers Struggle to Balance Work and Quality of Life as Long Hours and Stress Take Hold.' Visit the Website at: **www.work lifebalance.com/press300802.**
42. Ibid.
43. Conducted by the recruitment Website: **www.reed.co.uk** and Department of Trade and Industry's Work-Life Balance Campaign. Visit the Website: **www.work-lifebalance.com/newsurvey.**
44. Quoted in 'Work-Life Strategies for the 21st Century', a report by The National Work-Life Forum, page 27 (2000).

PART V: COURAGE

1. For a comprehensive statistical analysis of our changing society visit the Website: **www.statistics.gov.uk.**
2. See *British Medical Journal* Vol. 11, page 11 (1999). For further information visit the Website: **www.bmj.bmjjournals.com.**
3. In the second quarter of 2003, 48 per cent of households in the UK (12

million) could access the Internet from home, compared with just 9 per cent (2.2 million) in the same quarter of 1998. For further information visit the National Statistics Website: **www.statistics.gov.uk.**

4. See *Managing in the Next Society,* Peter Drucker, page 68, St. Martin's Press (2002).

5. Ibid. pp 67–68.

6. Ibid. See 'Knowledge Is All', pp 237–239.

7. For more information read the National Statistics UK Census 2001. Available online at: **www.statistics.gov.uk.**

8. See *The Cost of Communication Breakdown.* Janet Walker, pp 9–10, BT Publications (January 1995).

9. See *The Heart Aroused* by David Whyte, The Industrial Society (1997). Also visit the Website: **www.davidwhyte.bigmindcatalyst.com.**

10. Beechy is author of several books, including *A Challenge to Change,* co-authored with Josephine Colclough, Thorsons (1999). And also *Get Up and Do It,* co-authored with Josephine Colclough, BBC Books (2004). For more information on Beechy's public work, contact The Happiness Project.

11. See *Man's Search for Meaning* by Viktor Frankl, Washington Square Press (1984). Also visit the official Website for the Viktor Frankl Institute in Vienna at: **logotherapy.univie.ac.at.**

12. See *Feel the Fear and Do It Anyway* by Susan Jeffers, Rider (1991). Also, *End the Struggle and Dance with Life* by Susan Jeffers, Hodder & Stoughton (1996). Visit her Website: **www.susanjeffers.com.**

PART VI: GRACE

1. See *Successful but Something Missing* by Ben Renshaw, pp 3–4, Rider (2000).

2. See *Synchronicity* by C.G. Jung, page 10, Princeton University Press (1969).

3. Miranda MacPherson is founder and director of The Interfaith Seminary UK. Over 200 interfaith ministers have graduated from this training so far. For further information, contact The Interfaith Seminary at the Website: **www.interfaithseminary.co.uk.**

4. Found in *The Forbes Book of Business Quotations,* edited by Ted Goodman, page 453, Konemann (1997).

5. Found in *The Learning Paradox* by Jim Harris, page 1, Macmillan Canada (1998). See also *The Living Company* by Arie de Geus, Nicholas Brealey Publishing Ltd. (1999).

6. See *The Circle of Innovation* by Tom Peters, page 133, Hodder & Stoughton (1997). For more information about Tom Peters' work visit the Website: **www.tompeters.com.**

7. This remarkable book combines perennial wisdom and spiritual psychology principles about vision, truth, and love. For more information contact The Miracle Network, 12a Barness Court, 6/8 Westbourne Terrace, London W2 3UW. Their Website is: **www.miracles.org.uk.** And also, Foundation for A Course in Miracles, 1275 Tennanah Lake Road, Roscoe, New York, 12776-5905, Tel: (607) 498-4116. Book reference: *A Course in Miracles,* Foundation for Inner Peace, 2nd Edition (1975).

8. For more on the honkosecond and other temporal misadventures, see *A Geography of Time* by Robert Levine, pp 151–152, HarperCollins (1997).

9. See *Seeds of Hope* by Henri J.M. Nouwen, Darton, page 103, Longman &

Todd Ltd. (1989).

10. See *Evangeline and Selected Tales and Poems* by Henry Wadsworth Longfellow, New American Library Classics (1964).

11. Found in *Guide for the Advanced Soul* by Susan Hayward, In-Tune Books (2000).

12. Found in a report called 'Real Time: Exploring our Attitudes to Time' *Observer Magazine* (March 2003). For more information visit the Website: **www.observer.co.uk/time.**

13. See 'Happiness of the Very Wealthy' by E. Dineer, et al, *Social Indicators Research*, Vol. 16, pp 263–74 (1985).

14. See 'Lottery Winners and Accident Victims: Is Happiness Relative?' by Philip Brickman, Dan Coates, and Ronnie J. Janoff-Bulman, *Journal of Personality and Social Psychology*, Vol. 36, pp 917–927 (1978).

15. See 'Lee Atwater's Last Campaign' by Todd Brewster, *Life* magazine, page 67 (February 1991).

16. Most of these statistics were found in the 'Real Time' report in *Observer Magazine*. See reference 12.

17. See 'The Dubious Rewards of Consumption', by Alan Thein Durning, *New Renaissance* magazine, Vol. 3, No. 3, 1992. For more information visit the Website: **www.ru.org.**

18. From a report by the Cambridge Consumer Credit Index, issued on July 8, 2003.

19. See *Successful but Something Missing* by Ben Renshaw, page 196, Rider (2000). For further information on Ben's work, visit the Website: **www. happiness.co.uk.**

20. Tom is author of *Dialogue on Awakening*, Carpenter Press (1992). We have recorded many dialogues over the years. This quote comes from *Returning to Awareness: Hearing the Song of Self*, Carpenter Press (1998).

21. See *Something More* by Sarah Ban Breathnach, page 323, Time Warner International (2000).

22. See *Spiritual Intelligence* by Danah Zohar and Ian Marshall, page 8, Bloomsbury (2000).

23. See *Unconditional Success* by Nick Williams, Bantam Press, pp199–200 (2002). For more information on Nick's other books and his seminars visit the Website: **www.unconditionalsuccess.com.**

24. See *Boundless Love* by Miranda Holden, page 75, Rider (2002). For more information on Miranda's publications and her public workshops visit the Website: **www.happiness.co.uk.**

25. See *A Course in Miracles*, Workbook page 79, Foundation for Inner Peace, 2nd Edition (1985).

26. See *The Hidden Connections* by Fritjof Capra, page 220, HarperCollins (2002). For more information on the Center for Ecoliteracy visit the Website: **www.fritjofcapra.net.**

27. See NIDA Research Report 'Methamphetamine Abuse and Addiction', NIH Publication No. 02–4210, Printed April 1998, Reprinted January 2002. For more information visit the Website of the National Institute for Drug Abuse at: **www.drugabuse.gov.**

28. See 'Modern Cardiology: The Biopsychosocial Approach to Heart Disease,' *Caduceus*, interview by Robert Holden, pp 6–9, (Summer 1998).

29. See *Love Always Answers* by Diane Berke, Crossroads (1994). For more information on Diane's excellent work visit the Website: **www.onespiri-**

tonefaith.org.
30. See *The People's Religion* by George Gallup Jr., Macmillan (1990).

PART VII: RENAISSANCE
1. See *The Alchemist* by Paulo Coelho, page 18, HarperCollins (1995).
2. See *Business as Unusual* by Anita Roddick, page 26, Thorsons (2000).
3. For more information about the current programme of events visit the Website: **www.alternatives.org.uk.**
   An excellent back catalogue of audio recordings of previous talks is also available.
4. The quote is 'Our deepest fears are like dragons guarding our deepest treasure.' Rilke also wrote: 'Perhaps all the dragons in our lives are princesses who are only waiting to see us act, just once, with beauty and courage. Perhaps everything that frightens us is, in its deepest essence, something helpless that wants our love.' These quotes are in *Letters to a Young Poet*, edited by Stephen Mitchell, Random House (2001).
5. You can obtain an e-copy of my doctoral dissertation through The Happiness Project. Contact: **hello@happiness.co.uk** for more information.
6. There are many approximations of the ratio between research papers on happiness and illness. Martin Seligman, ex-president of the APA, writes: 'For every one hundred articles on sadness, there is just one on happiness', in *Authentic Happiness* by Martin Seligman, page 6, The Free Press (2002).
7. See 'Correlates of Avowed Happiness' by Warner Wilson, *Psychological Bulletin*, Vol. 125, pp 276–302 (1999).
8. See 'Positive Psychology, Positive Prevention, and Positive Therapy' by Martin Seligman, *Handbook of Positive Psychology*, edited by C. R. Snyder and S. J. Lopez, page 3, Oxford University Press (2002).
9. See 'What Good Are Positive Emotions?' by Barbara Fredrickson, *Review of General Psychology*, Vol. 2, pp 300–319 (1998).
10. See 'Employee Positive Emotion and Favorable Outcomes at the Workplace' by B. Staw, et al, *Organizational Science*, Vol. 5, pp 51–71 (1994).
11. See *50 Ways to Let Go and Be Happy* by Dr. Chuck Spezzano, page 11, Hodder & Stoughton (2001).
12 . In discussion in Kauai, Hawaii, in 1998. For more information on Tom's books and talks, contact The Happiness Project.
13. See 'The Altruism Paradox' by Bernard Rimland, *Psychological Reports*, Vol. 51, pp 521–522 (1982).
14. See 'The Happy Personality: A Meta-Analysis of 137 Personality Traits and Subjective Well-Being' by K. DeNeve and H. Cooper, *Psychological Bulletin*, Vol. 124. pp 197–229 (1998).
15. Reis and Franks studied 846 individuals who were 33 years old and over and found that anxiety, depression, illness, and a higher number of doctor visits corresponded with low intimacy and social support ratings. Reference: 'The Role of Intimacy and Social Support in Health Outcomes: Two Processes or One?' by H. Reis and P. Franks, *Personal Relationships*, Vol. 1, pp 185–197 (1994).
16. See *Authentic Happiness* by Martin Seligman, page 43, The Free Press (2002). For more information on Seligman's work visit the Website: **www.authentichappiness.org.**
17. See *The Psychology of Happiness*, 2nd Edition by Michael Argyle, page 216,

Routledge (2001).

18. There are several good references to the link between happiness and altruism in *The Pursuit of Happiness* by David Myers, Avon Books (1992).

19. See *In the Dark Places of Wisdom* by Peter Kingsley, page 5, Golden Sufi Publishing (1999).

20. See both Chapter 8 'Choose Life' and Chapter 14 'Are you Alive?' in *The Quest for Love* by Joseph Gelberman, Sabina Graphics (1985).

21. See *The Sane Society* by Erich Fromm, page 352, Routledge Classics (2002).

22. See *What Is Enlightenment?* by John White, Aquarian Press (1988).

23. See *Introductory Lectures on Psychoanalysis* by Sigmund Freud, Penguin Books (1991).

24. See *If It Hurts, It Isn't Love* by Dr. Chuck Spezzano, page 80, Hodder & Stoughton (1999).

Intelligent Goals System

The Intelligent Goals System is a very important part of my work with Success Intelligence. I have used this system in both one-on-one coaching and team coaching for many years now. It is a system that is divided into three essential stages, using the acronym AIM – in which the 'A' stands for 'Assessment', the 'I' stands for 'Implementation', and the 'M' stands for 'Measurement'.

Assessment

Stage One is about assessing your true goals in work, relationships, and life. Intelligent Goal assessment begins with identifying the goals that are most important to you. This involves the ability to discern between true goals and fleeting desires and between true purpose and vague busyness. In short, it is about the 'what' and the 'why' of goals, i.e., 'What are my true goals?' and 'Why are they my true goals?'

In the Intelligent Goals System, there are seven types of goals. The lines of distinction between these goal types are not hard and fast, and there is certainly room for overlap. For example, some of your Spiritual Goals could also be described as Achievement Goals, and so on. Creating different goal types is designed to help you begin by exploring your 'Spiritual Goals' first, followed by your 'Character Goals', and then other goals.

Spiritual Goals – Vision and Values
Your Spiritual Goals are the goals that matter most to you. They are about your vision, your values, and what you deem to be sacred. These are the goals to which you give your life. They are

the rock, the basis, for every other goal you set. A useful way to identify these goals is to ask questions like 'What is my true purpose?' 'What do I most value?' and 'What do I love?' Another good exercise is to complete the following sentence: 'If I could choose one purpose for my life it would be . . .'

Character Goals – Being

Your Character Goals are about being your true self. The key question here is 'Who am I?' Another good question to ask is 'Who is the real me?' These goals are about finding your voice and taking your place in the world. Your Character Goals are also about realising your true potential, i.e., discovering your spiritual DNA (Divine Natural Ability). This process includes owning your wisdom and discovering your strengths. It is also about being the sort of person, friend, and partner you most want to be.

Achievement Goals – Doing

Your Achievement Goals are about what you want to do with your life, your work, and your leisure. These goals include the job you want to do, the projects you want to accomplish, the education goals you have, your single-digit golf handicap, your targets for optimum health, your hobbies and leisure, and your aspirations for travel and adventure. There is so much to do in life, and your goal is to establish what is most worth doing. One way to identify these goals is to complete the following sentence: 'Before I die, I want to . . .'

Acquisition Goals – Having

Your Acquisition Goals include your financial goals and ownership goals. Think about how important money is to you. What are your financial goals? What income do you want or need? What about pensions, savings, etc.? How much money is enough? Think also about your ownership goals. This is your shopping list for home, car, clothes, televisions, etc. You may also include here other things you want to 'have', such as good health, good education, or good insurance. What are the real priorities on your shopping list?

Relationship Goals – Giving

Your Relationship Goals are about growing essential qualities for relationships, such as intimacy, communication, forgiveness, and love. I place great emphasis here on 'giving', especially giving your true self to relationships and also giving proper time, energy, and attention to relationships. A good exercise is to think of each person you know and ask, 'What is my gift for this person?' To give well, you also have to receive well. Therefore, think of each person you know and ask yourself, 'What is their true gift for me?'

Destination Goals – Going

Your Destination Goals are your horizon goals. For example: 'By 30, I want to . . .' 'By 40, I want to . . .' These goals are future-focused. They are about where you are heading and when you want to get there. They are about how far up the company ladder you want to go, how far you want to take a talent, where you want to be living in ten years' time, and what you will do after retirement. A powerful exercise is to write 'My Obituary', in which you describe the most valuable successes you hope to have enjoyed by the end of your life.

Present Time Goals – Now

Your Present Time Goals are about keeping your eye on the journey of your life, not just the destination. These goals are about making the most of each day. They are about happiness now, success today, precious moments, and living all of the days of your life. Your Present Time Goals are about being focused, congruent, and present. Good questions to ask include 'What is it that I most value about this day?' and 'How can I make the most of my life today?'

Implementation

Stage Two is about skilfulness in action. It is about deciding the best strategy, the best timing, and the best way to implement your goals. Intelligent implementation is about establishing what is correct effort (how to be most effective). It is essential to be able to distinguish between effort and effectiveness, adrenaline and inspiration, and busyness and grace. Intelligent implementation is also about recognising the need for appropriate support, i.e., who can help you to succeed with your goal? Every success in life is really a team effort.

Another very important aspect of implementation is identifying potential blocks to success. Broadly speaking, there are two types of blocks – external blocks and internal blocks. Every good strategy takes into consideration potential blocks to success. The external blocks are situation-specific. The internal blocks to success will inevitably feature a person's perceptions, beliefs, and thoughts. Other internal success-blockers may include inner doubts, old wounds, and personal fears. A useful exercise is to complete the following sentence: 'If I knew of an internal block to this goal, it would be . . .'

Potential blocks are a call for extra help.

Measurement

Stage Three is a regular process of review. The review is a good discipline for refocusing on the big picture of your life. It is an excellent tool for punctuating the busyness of your life and for remembering what is most important to you. It is a chance to be honest with yourself about what is working and what is not. It is also an opportunity to recommit yourself to what you most value. Stage Three is also about personal acknowledgment. It is about acknowledging how well you are doing, affirming your successes, and being grateful for what is.

Success Intelligence Library

I recommend the following list of books and talks for further inspiration on success.

A Course in Miracles. Penguin Arkana, 1975.

Annunzio, Susan. *Evolutionary Leadership*. Fireside, 2001.

Battalia, O.W. and Tarrant, J.J. *The Corporate Eunuch*. Crowell, 1973.

Berke, Diane. *Love Always Answers*. Crossroads, 1994.

Bohm, David. *Wholeness and the Implicate Order*. Routledge Classics, 2002.

Breathnach, Sarah Ban. *Something More*. Time Warner International, 2000.

Brown, Molly Young. *Growing Whole*. Simon & Schuster, 2001.

Buckingham, Marcus and Clifton, Donald. *Now, Discover Your Strengths*. Simon & Schuster, 2001.

Carpenter, Tom. *Dialogue on Awakening*. Carpenter Press, 1992.

Chopra, Deepak. *The Seven Spiritual Laws of Success*. New World Library, 1994.

Coelho, Paulo. *The Alchemist*. HarperCollins, 1995.

Cohen, Alan. *A Deep Breath of Life*. HarperCollins, 1995.

———. *Joy is My Compass*. Hay House, 1996.

Colclough, Beechy and Colclough, Josephine. *Get Up and Do It*. BBC Books, 2004.

Covey, Stephen. *The 7 Habits of Highly Successful People*. Simon & Schuster, 1989.

Einstein, Albert. *The World As I See It*, edited by Alan Harris. Citadel Press, 1979.

Etzioni, Amitai. *The Spirit of Community*. HarperCollins, 1995.

Frankl, Viktor. *Man's Search for Meaning*. Washington Square Press, 1984.

Fromm, Erich. *To Have or To Be?* Abacus, 1987.

———. *The Sane Society*. Routledge Classics, 2001.

———. *The Art of Being*. Constable & Robinson, 1993.

Gallup, George. *The People's Religion*. Macmillan, 1990.

Gibran, Kahlil. *The Prophet*. Arrow, 2000.

Gelb, Michael. *How to Think like Leonardo da Vinci*. HarperCollins, 1998.

Geus, Arie de. *The Living Company*. Nicholas Brealey Publishing Ltd., 1999.

Gillibrand, Eileen and Mosley, Jenny. *She Who Dares Wins*. Thorsons, 1995.

Goleman, Daniel. *Emotional Intelligence*. Bantam, 1995.

Gleick, James. *Faster*. Abacus, 2000.

Harvey, Joan and Katz, Cynthia. *If I'm so Successful, Why Do I Feel Like a Fake? The Imposter Syndrome*. St. Martin's Press, 1985.

Holden, Miranda. *Boundless Love*. Rider, 2002.

———. *Relationships and Enlightenment*. THP, 1997.

————. *Accepting Joy.* Audio. THP, 1998.

————. *Being Good Enough.* Audio. THP, 1998.

————. *Forgiveness: Transforming Difficult Relationships.* Audio. THP, 1998.

————. *Letting Go of Struggle.* Audio. THP, 1998.

————. *Choosing Peace.* Audio. THP, 1998.

Holden, Robert. *Happiness NOW!* Hay House, 2007.

————. *Hello Happiness.* Hodder & Stoughton, 1999.

————. *Stress Busters.* HarperCollins, 1992.

————. *Laughter, The Best Medicine.* HarperCollins, 1993.

————. *PhD in Joy.* Audio. THP, 1999.

————. *Success Intelligence.* Audio & video. THP, 2001.

————. *Making a Success of Your Life.* Audio. THP, 1999.

———— and Ben Renshaw. *Balancing Work & Life.* Dorling Kindersley, 2002.

Hooper, Alan and Potter, John. *Intelligent Leadership.* Random House, 2000.

James, Oliver. *Britain on the Couch.* Century Books, 1997.

Jaworski, Joseph. *Synchronicity.* Berrett-Koehler, 1996.

Jeffers, Susan. *Feel the Fear and Do It Anyway.* Rider, 1991.

————. *End the Struggle and Dance with Life.* Hodder & Stoughton, 1996.

Jung, Carl. *Synchronicity.* Princeton University Press, 1969.

Lasch, Christopher. *The Culture of Narcissism.* W.W. Norton & Co, 1979.

Lazear, Jonathon. *Meditations for Men Who Do Too Much.* Thorsons, 1992.

Linder, Staffan. *The Harried Leisure Class.* Columbia University Press, 1969.

Lynch, James. *The Broken Heart.* Basic Books, 1977.

Maltz, Maxwell. *Psycho-Cybernetics.* Prentice Hall, 1960.

Mandino, Og. *Secrets for Success and Happiness.* Ballantine Books, 1995.

Muller, Wayne. *Legacy of the Heart.* Hodder & Stoughton, 1997.

Myers, David. *The Pursuit of Happiness.* Avon Books, 1993.

————. *The American Paradox.* Yale University Press, 2000.

O'Neil, John R. *The Paradox of Success.* J.P. Tarcher, 1994.

Ornish, Dean. *Love and Survival.* HarperPerennial, 1998.

Panzer, Richard. *Relationship Intelligence.* Center for Educational Media, 1999.

Pearsall, Paul. *Toxic Success.* Inner Ocean Publishing, 2002..

Popcorn, Faith. *The Popcorn Report.* Arrow Books, 1992.

Renshaw, Ben. *Successful but Something Missing.* Rider, 2000.

————. *Together but Something Missing.* Rider, 2001.

———— and Graham Alexander. *Super Coaching.* Dorling Kindersley, 2005.

Riesman, David. *The Lonely Crowd.* Revised edition. Yale Nota Bene, 2001.

Roddick, Anita. *Business as Unusual.* Thorsons, 2000.

Scitovsky, Tibor. *The Joyless Economy.* Oxford University Press, 1976.

Seligman, Martin. *Authentic Happiness.* The Free Press, 2002.

Shiller, Robert J. *Irrational Exuberance.* Princeton University Press, 2001.

Spezzano, Chuck. *If It Hurts, It Isn't Love.* Hodder & Stoughton, 2001.

————. *50 Ways to Let Go and Be Happy.* Hodder & Stoughton, 2001.

Tawney, R.H. *The Acquisitive Society.* Fontana, 1961.

Trine, Ralph Waldo. *In Tune with the Infinite.* HarperCollins, 2001.

Vasari, Giorgio. *The Lives of the Artists.* Oxford University Press, 1998.

White, John. *What is Enlightenment?* Aquarian Press, 1998.

Whyte, David. *The Heart Aroused.* The Industrial Society,1997.

Williams, Nick. *The Work We Were Born To Do.* Element, 2000.

———. *Unconditional Success*. Bantam Press, 2002.
———. *Powerful Beyond Measure*. Bantam Press, 2003.
Williamson, Marianne. *A Return to Love*. Thorsons, 1992.
Zohar, Danah. *The Quantum Society*. Bloomsbury, 2004.
———. *The Quantum Self*. Bloomsbury, 1990.
———. *Rewiring the Corporate Brain*. Berrett-Koehler, 1997.
——— and Ian Marshall. *Spiritual Intelligence*. Bloomsbury, 2000.

More Success Intelligence Information

Masterclasses — Classes— Products — Workshops

Robert Holden, Ph.D., is the Director of Success Intelligence and The Happiness Project – two pioneering projects that work closely with leaders in business, health care, education, and politics. His innovative work on success and happiness has been featured on *The Oprah Winfrey Show* and on two major BBC TV documentaries – *The Happiness Formula* and the award-winning *How to be Happy* – which were shown in 16 countries to more than 30 million television viewers.

Robert is a consultant and coach to leading brands and organisations such as Dove, Virgin, The Body Shop, and Unilever. He gives public lectures worldwide and has shared the stage with Deepak Chopra, Wayne Dyer, Patch Adams, and Paul McKenna. He is the author of ten best-selling books including *Happiness NOW!* and *Shift Happens!*

For further information on the work of Robert Holden, Success Intelligence, and The Happiness Project, please contact the head office at (0 11 44) (0) 845 430 9236. Also, visit the Web links below. Both Websites are updated daily and include free daily coaching tips, weekly articles, an events calendar, and a product store.

Websites: **www.successintelligence.com,**
www.robertholden.org and **www.happiness.co.uk**